Research Methods
A Qualitative Reader

Research Methods

A QUALITATIVE READER

J. MITCHELL MILLER
University of South Carolina

RICHARD TEWKSBURY
University of Louisville

PEARSON
Prentice
Hall

Upper Saddle River, New Jersey 07458

Library of Congress Cataloging-in-Publication Data

Miller, J. Mitchell.
   Research methods : a qualitative reader / Richard Tewksbury.—1st ed.
      p. cm.
   ISBN 0-13-169025-6
   1. Criminal anthropology—Research. 2. Criminal anthropology—Field work. 3. Criminal
behavior—Research. 4. Deviant behavior—Research. I. Tewksbury, Richard A. II. Title.
   HV6035.T49 2005
   364.2'072—dc22

2005008362

Executive Editor: Frank Mortimer, Jr.
Assistant Editor: Mayda Bosco
Editorial Assistant: Kelly Krug
Executive Marketing Manager: Tim Peyton
Managing Editor: Mary Carnis
Director of Manufacturing and Production:
   Bruce Johnson
Production Liaison: Brian Hyland
Manufacturing Buyer: Cathleen Petersen

Design Director: Cheryl Asherman
Senior Design Coordinator: Miguel Ortiz
Cover Design: Michael Ginsberg
Cover/Photo: Mitchell Funk, Getty Images/
   Photographer's Choice
Composition/Full-Service Project Management:
   Jan Pushard/Pine Tree Composition, Inc.
Printer/Binder: The Courier Companies

Credits and acknowledgments borrowed from other sources and reproduced, with permission, in this textbook appear on the appropriate page within text.

Pearson Education LTD.
Pearson Education Singapore, Pte. Ltd
Pearson Education, Canada, Ltd
Pearson Education—Japan
Pearson Education Australia PTY, Limited
Pearson Education North Asia Ltd
Pearson Educación de Mexico, S.A. de C.V.
Pearson Education Malaysia, Pte. Ltd

10 9 8 7 6 5 4 3 2 1
ISBN: 0-13-169025-6

Contents

Preface

Research Methods: A Qualitative Reader promotes the "criminological ethnographic enterprise," which is the use of both traditional and alternative qualitative research methods to study crime and deviance. Fieldwork, or *ethnography*, is vital to our understanding of crime and deviance and has a rich tradition in the history of social science dating to the 1920s and the Chicago school of fieldwork. Often discredited or dismissed, fieldwork has been forced into a secondary or supplemental role deemed inferior to positivistic, variable analytic approaches. This book contains selections that argue and demonstrate otherwise—that qualitative approaches are vital to our understanding of social—especially crime and deviance-related—phenomena and feature considerable potential for discovering new knowledge. To better understand the readings (i.e., the research strategies advocated), we offer the following comments.

It is ironic that fieldwork on crime and deviance is infrequent and even discouraged. The methodological tradition of sociology in the United States associated with the Chicago school in the interwar years featured firsthand observation, participation, and interaction with subjects in their natural environments. Many of the pioneering social science works were conducted within this tradition and fieldwork was the leading paradigm (model) of research.

The rise of positivism during the 1950s as the leading philosophy of science, coupled with the popularity of functionalist theorizing, marked the dawn of a dark period that witnessed the demise of ethnography as standard science. Positivism advocates identifying causality through a hypothetic-deductive research process that entails statistical analysis of relationships between variables thought to represent social realities. Emulation of this natural science approach fostered widespread use of quasi-experimental designs and theory tests that were discrepant with ethnography in terms of research questions and goals. The philosophy of positivism and the strategy of variable analysis have held dominion since its rise, rendering qualitative research as (in the minds of many researchers) a second-tier alternative.

The paradigmatic shift to positivism as the preferred research model has been supported because of (partially false) attacks on competing approaches. Fieldwork on crime and deviance, for example, has often been suppressed on grounds of ethical impropriety and danger rather than more substantial scientific grounds. As some of the following selections relate, beliefs over the misuse of human subjects, unnecessary exposure to harm, and the controversies associated with secrecy and illegality discourage criminological ethnography. These ethical and legal objections have raised awareness within our universities that restrict crime ethnography through institutional review boards toward the practice of "proper science" and minimizing legal liability. Some qualitative research is approved, however, and other projects are conducted outside the realm of university control.

Unfortunately, the result has been the widespread observation that fieldwork on criminals is not rewarded and best avoided, in turn generating a strong methodological training bias wherein new generations of researchers never seriously consider qualitative options. There is something odd and ironic that social science is not very socially involved any more—that is, it has forsaken fieldwork for a quasi-laboratory approach. Our subject matter is in society, however, and that is where we should engage it—to balance the sterility of social science research conducted through surveys and statistical analyzes that can be detached altogether from first-hand human and social interaction. In the case of crime and deviance this is particularly problematic.

A long-standing issue in criminology centers on the fact that much of the knowledge base is derived from known criminals and identified crime. This information is pieced together after the fact in a variety of ways, both quantitatively and qualitatively. Studying crime that has already occurred relies on accuracy of memory, honesty, and the absence of selection biases. Such reliance is likely problematic when the subject group is comprised of criminals and deviants who naturally resist inspection from outsiders and often make no distinction between criminal justice system representatives and researchers. In short, it is almost always in the best interests of criminals to hide and minimize their behavior, while the goal of research is to expose it. So, in order to understand the realities of crime and the behaviors of criminals, fieldworkers study criminals in their natural settings to observe crime as it occurs—a form of inquiry known as *edge ethnography*. The term makes sense when you think about it. Why do people walk over to the edge of scenic overlooks in national parks, for example? The answer is obvious—to have an unobstructed view and to see more. The analogy is true for qualitative crime research, too. You can see more from the edge; a basic belief that is reflected in the selections that follow.

Richard Tewksbury
J. Mitchell Miller

Research Methods

A Qualitative Reader

Part 1: Crime and Deviance Fieldwork

Studying crime and responses to crime through qualitative methods presents challenges that, if met, can produce a great wealth of new knowledge. Sometimes, we study things simply because we want to know with no particular plan or scheme in mind, a pursuit referred to as *basic research*. Other research strategies facilitate *applied research* goals of determining if criminal justice system initiatives work or how they might be improved. Qualitative methods are central to each of these research orientations and offer many advantages that cannot be realized through quantitative methods. Qualitative research goals are usually reduced to the exploration and description of some issue, problem, or group. While qualitative methods are concerned with exploration and description, it would be a false assumption to believe that exploration and description are always the end goals of the qualitative process. Perhaps a juvenile delinquency program intended to alleviate truancy is found to be ineffective per the statistically significant findings of a traditional quasi-experimental design. The findings do not necessarily tell us whether the lack of success is attributable to theory failure (the program was based on faulty logic/bad ideas) or implementation failure (the program may be based on sound logic but was conducted in an unprofessional manner). A number of qualitative methods, including in-depth interviewing, focus group interviews, or participant observation, however, can reveal what exactly failed and inform possible solutions. Sometimes, there is a real need to look for social realities that have not been effectively captured through measurement. Of course, it is much easier to interview professional staff or youth in a program than criminals in the real world where a number of research issues emerge.

This first section addresses some of the leading issues faced by qualitative researchers, particularly gaining access to the hidden, dangerous, and sometimes removed world of criminal and deviant subcultures. Notice that the authors simultaneously voice both advocacy of qualitative methodology and justification of it. Notice also that the qualitative approaches are vested in the philosophy of science, logic, and theory. Collectively, these selections demonstrate the utility of qualitative research strategies for a range of crime-related research questions that likely would not, and in some cases could not, be addressed through traditional approaches.

In the first two articles, Tewksbury and Miller discuss ways in which researchers can study highly secretive communities that usually have strict barriers that prohibit outsiders from knowing about their members, their activities, and how their social life is structured. Both of these articles advocate observational research techniques that allow researchers to get inside a community and see people and their activities as they are actually experienced—a condition known as *immediacy*. In the first article by Tewksbury consideration is given to how researcher presentation affects acceptance by study populations. By presenting oneself as someone who may potentially engage in all the activities within a setting, the researcher can see and experience the full range of behaviors therein. Building on the first article's suggestions, Miller advocates the use of covert participant observation and outlines the long-standing debate in the social sciences about whether it is ethical to conduct research from a disguised vantage point.

The third article by Ferrell situates qualitative crime research, especially edge ethnography, in social science theory and also calls for firsthand observation of research foci in order to best understand social realities without the distortion effects that can accompany mainstream, overt methods. The Tunnell selection combines an unusual level of candidness and masterful wordsmithing to demonstrate what criminological fieldwork entails, ethical consideration, and advantages of conducting research on the edge.

Questions to Consider

1. What does it mean to act like an insider? What are the possible advantages and disadvantages of this approach?
2. How is covert participant observation ethically defended in response to allegations of bringing harm to human subjects, the field of science, and to the researcher?
3. What does "immediacy" mean and why is it important to the study of crime and deviance?
4. Would the researcher in the Tunnell article likely have collected the same data that was obtained through a more traditional research approach? How is the research strategy described in this selection edge ethnography? Is it ethical? What are the trade-offs involved?

1. Acting Like an Insider:
Studying Hidden Environments as a Potential Participant

Richard Tewksbury

Studies of hidden environments traditionally draw on some form of observational or participant observation research but have been hampered by researchers' methods of gaining access to such settings. This paper outlines an alternative approach to covert participant observation: the potential participant role. This approach emphasizes data collection through observation in an apparently complete membership role but with self-imposed limitations on participation so as to maintain ethical standards. Such an approach to qualitative research emphasizes observational and experiential data. Issues of implementation and ethical considerations for such practices are discussed.

Research of behaviors and interactional processes in sexualized settings is a uniquely challenging form of social science. Such research, in seeking descriptive and analytic insights, typically relies on qualitative research methodologies, as these provide greater opportunities to access depth and breadth of understandings. However, the specific methodologies employed in studying "hidden" or "marginalized" sexual environments may require unique modifications and may present potential ethical dilemmas. This paper presents one methodological approach that can be successfully employed in studies of sexual environments: the observational role of the *potential participant*.

The potential participant is a distinct role available to participant observation researchers that is especially suited for the study of interactants in sexual environments. Whereas others have differentiated between membership roles that are peripheral, active, or complete (Adler and Adler, 1987) or complete participant, participant as observer, observer as participant, and complete observer (Gold, 1969), these characterizations can be restrictive and can guide researchers into mistakenly believing that some forms of understanding can be accessed, which in fact may not be possible with such approaches. The potential participant can and does access otherwise inaccessible aspects of the experience and can provide first-hand understandings of the culture and persons under study.

As a clear outgrowth of the legacy of the Chicago school of sociology, potential participation is a way for researchers to gain a depth of understanding not otherwise accessible. However, the break from the Chicago school is most obviously seen in the fact that the majority of research produced by these pioneers relied on overt observational roles (Adler and Adler, 1987; Lofland and Lofland, 1995). The Chicago school believed that, with the researcher himself as the primary instrument, an intense involvement with those being studied would distort the observations and research. Although as the Chicago sociologists clearly demonstrated, and is continued herein, researcher roles in observational work are fluid and ever changing.

3

The potential participant is a covert (or unknown) observational role and offers researchers all of the opportunities and advantages of covert observation, but it establishes limits on participation. In some ways, this is a call for entrance to sexualized worlds similar to Freilich's (1970) "marginal native." However, even here, the original idea called for being able to "observe the essence of ongoing activity while inconspicuously fading into the background" (Adler and Adler, 1987:19). A potential participant does not "fade into the background" but, rather, is a recognized member of the community being studied.

The potential participant approach also draws on the existential approach of experiencing a setting as a true participant and feeling as true participants feel. However, limits are recognized here on *what* is fully experienced. While recognized as, in some ways, a contradiction to the Chicago school's concern with the dilemmas of "going native," the existential approach nonetheless emphasizes depth and insider involvement in gaining understandings (Adler and Adler, 1987). In this way, the presently proposed role bridges the gaps between these apparently divergent approaches to investigation.

In addition, a potential participant role draws on ethnomethodological approaches in which researchers become members of their communities of study. Here the Chicago school's dilemma of going native is actually established as a goal. Only through becoming what one studies, or "mak[ing] a total commitment to becoming the phenomenon in order to study it" (Adler and Adler, 1987:32) can one know the world from the perspective of those being researched. However, the ethical difficulties in such an approach to the study of sexuality are clear.

A major obstacle to qualitative research in sexuality research is found in the opportunities for violating ethical standards and intruding upon the rights of the participants. Qualitative social science, especially sexuality research, is often stigmatized as unethical, due mostly to attacks upon a few unique works (Humphreys, 1975; Horowitz, 1967; Styles, 1979). However, not only can qualitative methodologies yield a vast amount of rich data, but they can do so while remaining within the parameters of ethical considerations. The discussion below outlines both the parameters and utilization of the potential participant role and the ethical considerations in using such an approach.

This paper draws on applications of a potential participant role in two sexualized, subcultural, homosocial environments: an adult bookstore video peep-show and a public park frequented by men seeking sexual liaisons with other men. As such, it focuses on the utilization and inherent obstacles to such work, efforts at overcoming obstacles, and questions of maintaining professional, scientific ethics in such research.

The Research Settings

The adult bookstore and accompanying video peep-show area presents some unique challenges and obstacles to conducting research. The most important of these is the complete maintenance of anonymity and secrecy among location participants. Whereas one purpose for visiting such locales may be to participate in

impersonal and anonymous sex, patrons exhibit a high degree of wariness of in-
quisitive others. Hence, any attempts to discover and elaborate on participants
and their activities are presented with a variety of obstacles (see Sundholm, 1973;
Tewksbury, 1990, 1993; Weatherford, 1986).

Public parks known for "cruising" have rarely been studied (Ponte, 1974;
Tewksbury, 1995, 1996), as have similar meeting places (Corzine and Kirby, 1977;
Delph, 1978; Donnelly, 1981; Gray, 1988; Humphreys, 1970). In part, this lack of
scholarly investigation can be attributed to the difficulties social scientists encounter. Whereas public park cruising is not an entirely silent behavior, the level
of anonymity among participants is high, and the "public" nature of the setting
presents both special challenges and opportunities for observational research.

The Potential Participant Role

The potential participant role combines aspects of complete observation, complete participation, and covert observational research designs. Whereas the researcher adopting a potential participant role seeks to appear to those being
researched as a "real" setting member, the "science" activities are conducted in
covert manners. To anyone noticing the potential participant, the researcher is a
real member of the setting being studied. To the scientific community, the potential participant is a complete observer, acting in a covert manner *inside* the research environment. By maintaining such a scientific distance, the potential
participant actively avoids "going native," and losing an analytical perspective
(Adler and Adler, 1987; Hammersley and Atkinson, 1983). In sexualized settings
this means that there is a side-stepping of the potential ethical dilemmas involved
in becoming sexually involved with research subjects.

However, this is not to say that some who have researched sexual environments have not used the ethnomethodological approach. Especially in sexual environments, the temptation for some to "learn by doing" can be quite great. As
explained by one researcher of gay bathhouses,

> For a month or so I continued to separate my research and my sexual activity by con-
> ducting them in different bathhouses. Gradually, however, the asexual observation be-
> came more and more tiresome, more tedious, and more frustrating until I simply gave
> up observing without sexual intent and plunged fully into the sex life of the baths.
> (Styles, 1979:142)

As a result of his complete immersion in the activities of the bathhouse, not only
does Styles (1979) report that "my important objects of inquiry changed dramatically" (p. 142), but also "my sexual participation allowed me to move closer to an
ideal typical insider researcher strategy" (p. 152). Importantly, there is an acknowledgment that "there are many issues that can be raised about my research.
There are ethical and moral issues", including whether or how protection of
human subjects was achieved, the political rights of gay men, issues regarding
the effect of such disclosures on an academic career and "substantive issues concerning my research findings" (p. 147).

Covert research designs are not without their dilemmas, however (see Miller, 1995). In large part because of the difficulties posed to the actual conduct of covert participant observation and the personal stresses such methodologies may induce, this is an approach that has been often described as our least-used method of research.

> It is unfortunate that covert research is so rarely conducted because a veiled identity can enable the examination of certain remote and closed spheres of social life, particularly criminal and deviant ones, that simply cannot be inspected in an overt fashion. . . . Clearly, complicated ethical issues inherent to secret investigations have created a methodological training bias that has suppressed their application. (Miller, 1995:97).

What is it, then, about a potential participant role that can overcome these biases? Clearly, the more weighty advantage offered by a form of covert observational investigation is the insight and depth of data that can be uncovered, especially when incorporating experiential aspects of sexualized setting investigations with straightforward observational data. Covert research, though, "means full participation in various group and individual activities, many of which contain risks" (Miller, 1995:99).

Typically, covert research is conducted by investigators who are true ("complete") members of the settings in which they work (Adler and Adler, 1987). However, when membership in a subculture precedes investigative undertakings, the likelihood of biases and skewed interpretations of derived data are great (despite the ethnomethodologists' belief that this is the "only" way to get valid data). The possibilities of skewed interpretations may be especially true when the subculture being investigated is a stigmatized, or hidden, population and/or a population that is built around "deviant" (i.e., sexual) activities.

Whereas much of the specifics of using the potential participant method is patterned (at least in part) on Humphreys' (1970) classic work in tearooms, many specifics of his approach must be modified. Humphreys' oft' criticized approach to securing interviews subsequent to observation is not replicated. Rather than using Humphreys' method of covertly recording license plate numbers of vehicles at tearooms and later tracing these so as to identify the participants and, at a later date, in disguise, conducting "public health surveys," the interviews that have been used to supplement public park observations are openly solicited from setting participants. However, the focus in this discussion is on the observational data collection methods.

Both Humphreys and Delph (1978) conducted observations while inside tearooms, functioning as either a lookout during sexual encounters or as a naïve intruder. My modification of the functional role is to present myself as a potential participant, in setting activities, not as a lookout, accidental intruder, or sexually active setting member. This role is both created and reinforced by the structure and organization of men's homosocial, sexual environments. To be present, and to present oneself as an individual others may define and respond to as a sexually motivated individual, is facilitated by the number of men present in such settings.

By being present, emulating the activities (waiting behaviors, eye contact, gestures, silence, and slow circulation throughout the setting), an observer has access to the full range of behaviors men enact in public sex environments. This includes being identified and propositioned for anonymous sexual encounters. Such a role presentation provides first-hand experiences of the processes involved, not merely observation. However, perhaps the primary distinction between the potential participant role and one of a complete member is the limitation the potential participant role imposes: data can be gleaned only on the experiential components up to the point of sexual propositions. To further experience setting activities would invite serious ethical questions. However, because many sexual encounters are truly public in these settings, pure observational data on sexual activities, to some degree, is accessible (see Styles, 1979 and Weinberg and Williams, 1975).

In both adult bookstores and public parks, the majority of men initiate sexual approaches to other men only when no third parties are present. It is in this regard that presenting oneself as potentially interested in sexual activities is critical to data access. If a researcher were to adopt a role suggesting he was merely observing, or accidentally happening by, his presence may in fact impede and inhibit the very behaviors and interactions he is seeking to observe and understand. Furthermore, the accidental passerby is limited in the number of times he can realistically happen by the setting; more than one or two short visits to the research setting are likely to raise suspicions, as some sexually involved men spend lengthy periods, and visit repeatedly, such environments.

Perhaps the greatest advantage offered by the potential participant role is the experiential insight provided to the researcher, while balancing against personal and professional ethical positions. Whereas a complete participant role certainly provides the greatest depth of experiential data, in sexualized environments and with studies of "marginal" sexual populations and activities, stresses will undoubtedly arise. The ways in which a complete participant responds to and manages such stresses can easily make or break a research project, as well as (perhaps) the researcher's career.

How better to understand sexual propositions than to receive them? As a potential participant in adult bookstores and public parks, receiving sexual propositions is a key component to the research. Simply observing cannot and will not provide complete data. One important reason for this is that only the most aggressive (or least cautious) setting participants are likely to proposition others in a researcher's presence. A second reason full data are inaccessible with a strict reliance on observation is that the critical experiential components are not available. Clearly, the "real" activities of the setting would not be uncovered using a traditional observational approach.

Rites of Passage

By looking at perceived setting norms and rites of passage, it is clear that a potential participant role facilitates researchers' integration in sexual environments. Ethnographers access to valid data can be significantly enhanced through covert approaches in which the researcher successfully "passes" as a setting native. Access to settings may require special permission, knowledge, or skills (Lofland and Lofland, 1995). Studying highly stigmatized, secretive settings (such as an adult bookstore or a sexualized public park) may present researchers with initially seeming, anomalous encounters: but, upon closer inspection these events can be seen as heavily veiled rites-of-passage ceremonies. These seemingly minor, or to some perhaps, indistinguishable occurrences are gatekeeping procedures known as such only by knowledgable, true setting participants.

In order to most effectively present oneself as a potential participant, it is necessary to be able to act (and when necessary interact) as one who knows "how the game is played." However, when seeking entrance and acceptance in hidden populations some researchers may find themselves having only rudimentary knowledge (or more often, expectations) about how setting participants "really act." After all, if we knew very much about what goes on, the research might not be necessary.

When entering a hidden, sexual setting it may be necessary to enter and find your way as opportunities present themselves. This trial-and-error approach can be highly stressful, and, if not successfully navigated, it can set the investigator up for embarrassment, ostracization, and, in extreme cases, deal a fatal blow to the research. These situations are not unique to researchers, however. Filters and gatekeeping procedures are established for the explicit purposes of insulating the setting and its participants from unwanted intruders and prying "outsiders." The researcher is an outsider, striving for acceptance and endorsement for his presence. In short, rites-of-passage rituals confront all newcomers to the setting.

The rites of passage encountered in hidden, sexual environments illustrate Arnold van Gennep's (1960) three-stage conceptualization of rites of passage. When entering a new cultural environment, three stages of tests (actually composing one larger, all-encompassing rite of passage) are encountered. These separate rites can be distinguished as stages of separation, transition, and incorporation.

In hidden, sexual environments these stages are operationalized respectively by the entrance behaviors, acknowledgment of others present, and methods of receiving sexual approaches. All three stages present apparently normless situations that differentiate between those who do and those who do not know setting norms. A truly astute and quick-thinking researcher may be able to successfully navigate the separation and transition rites phases, however, only the truly knowledgable will pass the third rite of passage stage.

The researcher who successfully navigates all three rites of passage by maintaining normative behaviors will have access to the environment that true participants enjoy. At this point the researcher is on equal footing with true-setting participants and can present himself as a potential sexual partner.

An obvious hazard in the potential participant role is the risk some may face of going native, and losing objectivity (per the Chicago school) or violating professional ethical standards. It remains of utmost importance to carefully delineate one's role as researcher and observer. The researcher needs to project an image as a potential participant but at all times maintain a focus on the primary mission: observation.

This raises an obvious limitation regarding participant observation research. Regardless of how carefully planned and implemented a research methodology may be, it still falls short (to some degree) of actual participation. Observational researchers must continuously assess their abilities to pass in reference to the available benchmarks (re: rites of passage examinations).

Ethical Considerations

Ethical standards also necessitate a distinction between a researcher who successfully completes rites-of-passage examinations and a researcher who deliberately misrepresents either 1. his/her identity, or 2. his/her purpose for being present in the research setting. Discussing the ethical demands of observational research, Erikson (1967:373) defines two rules regarding misrepresentations:

1. It is unethical . . . to deliberately misrepresent his identity for the purpose of entering a private domain to which he is not otherwise eligible.

2. It is unethical . . . to deliberately misrepresent the character of the research in which he is engaged.

Although simple and straightforward, such requirements are somewhat contrary to the inherent demands of any form of covert observation. A potential participant does not violate these standards. Careful definition, design, and execution of the role provides the means for ethical conduct. Hidden, sexual environments acknowledge and, by default, legitimize observations of others. In this way, one's identity is not misrepresented, but, rather, identities and purposes are presented. Second, whereas the research is conducted covertly, no definition of the research need be presented to setting participants. Hence, the adoption of a potential participant role requires neither the researcher's identity nor his purpose to be misrepresented.

A corresponding ethics issue centers on informed consent. When observing and recording the interactions of others, ideally, all should be informed and should consent to being observed. As discussed earlier, the hidden nature of such a setting and behaviors prohibit the utilization of informed consent. In a setting of anonymous individuals engaging in highly stigmatized behavior the likelihood of any setting participants positively responding to invitations for participation is highly unlikely. If consent were sought, knowledge of the research focus would likely spread among the participants, thereby stigmatizing the researcher and impeding any further research efforts. Certainly the degree of privacy that needs to be accorded to setting participants may be debated. Hidden, sexual environments are, by definition, open environments. It is clear, nevertheless, that an attempt to protect observed subjects from any possible negative consequences necessitates absolute confidentiality and anonymity. This is easily maintained by careful attention to the actual definition and implementation of the researcher role.

The point here is that some, if not many, critics may criticize researchers (such as myself) for purportedly being true participants in sexual activity. I have never engaged in sexual encounters in these settings, nor have I made contacts for off-site sexual activity. This, however, is not to say that such activities could not be beneficial to the research effort (see Styles, 1979). However, the violation of ethical standards is obvious. Not only would the researcher directly influence setting activities, but the very nature of engaging in sexual activities with those one studies is a violation of ethical canons.

The consequence of such a personal decision regarding "complete" data collection is that experiential data can be gathered only up to a certain point in the sequence of behavior. The processes involved in these latter stages of interactions, though, do pose numerous questions for subsequent research. Although perhaps controversial, covert research designs can be an effective and ethical method of obtaining valid, in-depth data on interactional processes of hidden, sexual settings.

The completion of such research is possible while remaining within the parameters of ethical standards. Ethical considerations do impose some limitations on data collection. However, with careful and continuous attention to the definition and implementation of the researcher's role, data collection in sexualized settings is possible while also ensuring protection of setting participants' rights.

Although far from an easy task, research in hidden sexual environments is a valuable endeavor and can be conducted in an ethical manner. The key to successful research in such settings appears to be the actual conduct of the researcher. Covert participant-observers in sexualized settings are bound by professional ethics (as well as personal morals) to provide absolute anonymity and confidentiality, minimal influence and intrusion on the setting, and no risk of physical, psychological, or social harm to each and every setting participant. Such settings certainly present obstacles for researchers to overcome, but none so great as to deter the committed, professional, social scientist.

References

Adler, P.A. & Adler, P. (1987). *Membership Roles in Field Research*. Newbury Park, CA: Sage Qualitative Research Methods Series, No. 6.

Corzine, J. & Kirby, R. (1977). Cruising the Truckers: Sexual Encounters in a Highway Rest Area. *Urban Life, 6*, 171–192.

Delph, E. (1978). *The Silent Community: Public Homosexual Encounters*. Beverly Hills, CA: Sage.

Donnelly, P. (1981). Running the Gauntlet: The Moral Order of Pornographic Movie Theaters. *Urban Life, 10*, 239–264.

Erikson, K. (1967). Disguised Observation in Sociology. *Social Problems, 1*, (4), 368.

Freilich, M. (1970). *Marginal Natives*. New York: Harper & Row.

Gennep, A. (1960). *The Rites of Passage*. Chicago: University of Chicago Press.

Gold, R. L. (1969). Roles in Sociological Field Observation, in G. J. McCall & J. L. Simmons (eds.) *Issues in Participant Observation*, Reading, MA: Addison-Wesley.

Gray, J. (1988). *The Tearoom Revisited: A Study of Impersonal Homosexual Encounters in Public Settings*. Unpublished PhD dissertation, The Ohio State University, Columbus.

Hammersley, M. & Atkinson, P. (1983). *Ethnography: Principles in Practice*. New York: Tavistock.

Horowitz, I.L. (1967). *The Rise and Fall of Project Camelot*. Cambridge, Mass.: MIT Press.

Humphreys, L. (1970). *Tearoom Trade*. Chicago, IL: Aldine.

Lofland, J. & Lofland, L. H. (1995). *Analyzing Social Settings (3rd ed)*. Belmont, CA: Wadsworth Publishing.

Miller, J. M. (1995). Covert Participant Observation: Reconsidering the Least Used Method. *Journal of Contemporary Criminal Justice, II*, (2), 97–105.

Ponte, M (1974). Life in a Parking Lot: An Ethnography of a Homosexual Drive-In. *Deviance: Field Studies and Self-Disclosures*, edited by J. Jacobs. Palo Alto, CA: National Press Books.

Styles, J. (1979). Outsider/Insider: Researching Gay Baths. *Urban Life*, 8:135–152.

Sundholm, Charles A. 1973. The Pornographic Arcade: Ethnographic Notes on Moral Men in Immoral Places. *Urban Life and Culture*, 2, (1), 85–104.

Tewksbury, R. (1995). Adventures in the Erotic Oasis: Sex and Danger in Men's Same-Sex, Public Sexual Encounters. *Journal of Men's Studies*, 4, (1):9–24.

Tewksbury, R. (1996). Cruising for Sex In Public Places: The Structure and Language of Men's Hidden, Erotic Worlds. *Deviant Behavior*, 17, (1): 1–19.

Tewksbury, Richard. 1990. "Patrons of Porn: Research Notes on the Clientele of Adult Bookstores." *Deviant Behavior*, 11, (3):259–271.

Tewksbury, Richard. 1993. "Peepshows and 'Perverts': Men and Masculinity in an Adult Bookstore." *Journal of Men's Studies*, 2, (1):53–67.

Weatherford, Jack. 1986. Porn Row. New York: Arbor House.

2. Covert Participant Observation:

Reconsidering the Least Used Method

J. Mitchell Miller

The goal of any science is not willful harm to subjects, but the advancement of knowledge and explanation. Any method that moves us toward that goal is justifiable (Denzin 1968).

Social scientists have virtually ignored the qualitative technique covert participant observation. This variation of participant observation is either not mentioned or described in less than a page's length in social science research methods texts. The majority of qualitative methods books provide a few illustrative examples, but scarcely more in terms of detailed instruction. Manifested in the selection of alternative field strategies, this disregard has made covert observation the truly least used of all the qualitative methods.

It is unfortunate that covert research is so rarely conducted because a veiled identity can enable the examination of certain remote and closed spheres of social life, particularly criminal and deviant ones, that simply cannot be inspected in an overt fashion. Consequently, covert research is well-suited for much subject material of concern to criminology and the criminal justice sciences. Also applicable in some situations where overt designs appear the appropriate or only option, covert schemes are infrequently considered.

• • •

This brief commentary reintroduces covert participant observation and presents the principal advantages of using the technique. Theoretical, methodological, and pragmatic grounds are offered for exercising covert research. Ethical matters long associated with the stifling of its use are also reconsidered in the context of criminal justice. The ethicality of secret research, relative to other qualitative methods, is upheld for some research problems with certain stipulations.

Defining Covert Participant Observation

Covert participant observation is a term that has been used rather interchangeably with other labels: "secret observation" (Roth 1962), "investigative social research" (Douglas 1976), "sociological snooping" (Von Hoffman 1970), and most frequently "disguised observation" (Erickson 1967;1968; Denzin 1968). Disguised observation has recently been defined as "research in which the researcher hides his or her presence or purpose for interacting with group" (Hagan 1993:234). The

J. Mitchell Miller. "Covert Participant Observation: Reconsidering the Least Used Method." *Journal of Contemporary Criminal Justice. Vol. 11. No. 2. May 1995.* Copyright 1995. Reprinted by permission of Sage Publications.

distinguishing feature is that the research occurrence is not made known to subjects within the field setting.

Disguised observation is too inclusive a term often used in reference to those who simply hide in disguise or secret to observe, such as Stein's (1974) observation via a hidden two-way mirror of prostitutes servicing customers. Covert participant observation likewise involves disguise, however, the researcher is always immersed in the field setting. Additional elements—intentional misrepresentation, interpersonal deception, and maintenance of a false identity over usually prolonged periods of time are entailed. "Covert participant observation" is therefore a more technically correct term than "disguised observation" because it better indicates the active nature of the fieldwork essential to the technique (Jorgensen 1989).

Covert participant observation is essentially "opportunistic research" (Ronai and Ellis 1989) conducted by "complete-member researchers" (Adler and Adler 1987) who study phenomena in settings where they participate as full members. Admission to otherwise inaccessible settings is gained by undertaking a natural position and then secretly conducting observational research. Examples of the methods include Steffensmeier and Terry's (1973) study of the relationship between personal appearance and suspicion of shoplifting involving students dressed either conventionally or as hippies, Stewart and Cannon's (1977) masquerade as thieves, Tewksbury's (1990) description of adult bookstore patrons, and most recently Miller and Selva's (1994) assumption of the police informant role to infiltrate drug enforcement operations.

The most pronounced example of covert research, however, is Laud Humphreys' infamous Tearoom Trade (1970). Shrouding his academic interest in sexual deviance, Humphreys pretended to be a "watchqueen" (i.e., a lookout) for others so that he might observe homosexual acts in public bathrooms. He also used this role to record his subjects' license plate numbers to obtain their names and addresses in order to interview them by means of another disguise—survey researcher interested in sexual behaviors and lifestyles.

There are other versions of disguised or covert participant observation wherein certain confederates are made aware of the researcher's true identity, purpose and objectives (Asch 1951; Formby and Smykla 1981). The reasons for working with cooperatives are plain: to facilitate entry and interaction in the research site, to become familiar with nomenclature and standards of conduct, to expedite the happening of that which the researcher hopes to observe, and to avoid or at least minimize potential danger. Such reliance may be counterproductive, though, in that observations and consequent analysis of the social setting may be tainted by confederates' values, perceptions, and positions within the research environment.

If only a few individuals within a research site are aware of the researcher's true identity, it is possible, indeed likely, that interaction will be affected and spread to others within the setting. Hence, data distortion can become a potential validity and reliability problem with the use of confederates. The researcher must be completely undercover to avoid this problem and utilize the covert role so as to optimally exploit a social setting.

The goals of covert participant observation are no different than the standard objectives of overt participant observation: exploration, description, and, occasionally, evaluation (Berg 1989).

• • •

Most aspects of the methodological process, such as defining a problem, observing and gathering information, analyzing notes and records, and communicating results, are nearly identical to conventional participant observation as well. The covert approach may thus be considered a type of participant observation rather than a distinctive method.

There are aspects of the covert participant observation research cycle, however, that are unconventional. One controversial point is gaining entry to a setting through misrepresentation. It is the closed nature of backstage settings and the politics of deviant groups that negates announcement of the researcher's objectives and requires deception via role assumption if certain topics are to be examined.

The character of the participation is also much different and more demanding on the researcher. Covert role assumption means full participation in various group and individual activities, many of which contain risks. The direct study of crime by means of an undercover role can be doubly enigmatic to both the researcher's well-being and the inquiry. Assuming a role either as a criminal or in close proximity to crime for the purpose of research does not absolve the researcher from real or perceived culpability; thus moral decisions and the possibility of arrest and legal sanction must be considered prior to the onset of fieldwork.

The recording of notes from a clandestine position would divulge the researcher's cover and is obviously inadvisable. Extended periods of time in the field often yield rich and rare insight, but, without a chance to withdraw and log events, recollection of temporal/causal sequence can become muddled due to information overload and understandable fatigue. Resolves to this concern have been the use of mnemonics—a process of memorizing through abbreviation and association (Hagan 1993;195), taking photographs when possible, and the use of hidden mini-tape recorders and even body wires (Miller and Selva 1994).

The Ethics of Covert Observation

The ethicality of disguised or covert observational techniques has long been controversial as evidenced by the "deception debate" (Bulmer 1980; Galliher 1973; Humphreys 1970; Roth 1962;). Participants in this debate have tended to assume one of two polarized positions: moralistic condemnation or responsive justification. Deception is explicitly equated with immorality and is so unconscionable for some they would have covert observation banned from social science research altogether (Erikson 1967). The major objection is that deceptive techniques often violate basic ethical principles including informed consent, invasion of privacy, and the obligation to avoid bringing harm to subjects.

Critics further contend that misrepresentation not only causes irreparable damage to subjects, but also to the researcher, and to science by evoking negative public scrutiny and making subject populations wary of future researchers (Polsky 1967). Risk to the researcher, however, is a matter of individual decision.

• • •

The argument of isolating future research populations is seemingly unsound as well. Many settings of interest to criminal justice are essentially restricted and typically occupied with subjects already suspicious of strangers due to the threat of legal penalty associated with disclosure. Because researchers as outsiders will usually be distrusted and excluded from such settings, it is logical to assume that its occupants are already ostracized from researchers. The more substantial points that remain and must be confronted are interrelated: the use of deceit and the harm subjects may encounter as a result of the research process.

The topic of dishonesty in covert research is not as clear as opponents of the method suggest and nebulous in comparison to the frequent disregard for ethical standards demonstrated in other qualitative deviance research. Klockars' award winning "The Professional Fence," for example, describes research conduct far more offensive than the duplicity intrinsic to covert participant observation. This case history of a thirty year career of dealing in stolen goods was enabled by an intentionally misrepresentative letter in which the researcher admittedly lied about: 1. his academic credentials, 2. his familiarity and experience with the subject of fencing, 3. the number of other thieves he had interviewed, and most seriously 4. the possible legal risks associated with participating in the project (Klockars 1974:215). Klockars deception is reasoned in near blind pursuit of his research objective:

> "I thought the claim would strengthen the impression of my seriousness" and "the description of what I wanted to write about as well as the whole tone of the letter is slanted . . . and did not warn Vincet (the research subject) of his rights" (Ibid).

Surprisingly, Klockars book and projects have not produced controversy on par with covert strategies. The terms "case history" and "personal interview" simply do not provoke the interest and suspicion generated by the labels "covert" and "disguise." Covert methods can be considered, relative to the exercise of some techniques, forthright in that the level of deception is predetermined and calculated into the research design (Stricker 1967). The decision of whether or not to use deception to gain entry and thus enable a study can be made on the ends versus the means formula described below.

A Basis for Covert Research?

Justifications for the use of covert techniques have been presented on various levels. The most common practical argument is that those engaged in illegal or unconventional behavior, such as drug dealers and users, simply will not submit to or participate in a study by overt methods. Likewise, those in powerful and authoritative positions have been considered secretive and difficult to openly observe (Shils 1975). Police chiefs, white-collar criminals, prison wardens, and drug enforcement agents benefit from the existing power structure which inhibits study of their behavior in these official roles. A covert design is often the only way to conduct qualitative evaluation research of certain enforcement and intervention programs closed to principal participants.

Beyond a "last-resort" rationale, there are other reasons, methodological and theoretical, for employing the covert technique. An evident reason is that of qualitative methodology in general—the desirability of capturing social reality. By concealing identity and objective, researchers can avoid inducing a qualitative Hawthorne effect (i.e., a covert approach can minimize data distortion). Covert participant observation is justified theoretically by dramaturgical and conflict perspectives. If Goffman (1959) is to be taken seriously, then all researchers should be viewed as wearing masks and the appropriateness of any inquiry viewed in its context. Following Goffman, Denzin has also argued that ethical propriety depends upon the situation:

> "the sociologist has the right to make observations on anyone in any setting to the extent that he does so with scientific intents and purposes in mind" (1968:50).

Dramaturgy also provides a theoretical framework from which to assess topics of concern to the covert observer. The duplicity of roles already present in criminal settings under analysis (eg., undercover police, fence, snitch, racketeer) are only multiplied when such a role is assumed with the additional post of social scientist.

Consideration of the well known consensus-conflict dialectic also provides logic supportive of covert research. Conventional field methods, such as in-depth interviewing and overt observation, are based on a consensus view of society wherein most people are considered cooperative and willing to share their points of view and experiences with others (Patton 1990). This assumption is highly suspect however, in stratified and culturally diverse societies. To the extent that acute conflicts of interests, values, and actions saturate social life to the advantage of some and not others, covert methods should be regarded proper options in the pursuit of truth.

• • •

Perhaps the most compelling basis for the use of disguise in some research, however, is "the end and the means" position first stated by Roth (1962), then Douglas (1976) and Homan (1980), and most recently Miller and Selva (1994). Employing this reasoning in defense of covert observation, Douglas (1972:8–9) notes:

> "Exceptions to important social rules, such as those concerning privacy and intimacy, must be made only when the research need is clear and the potential contributions of the findings to general human welfare are believed to be great enough to counterbalance the risks."

That the purpose may absolve the process has also been acknowledged by the British Sociological Association, which condones the covert approach "where it is not possible to use other methods to obtain essential data" (1973:3); such is the case in many criminal justice research situations. The benefits of investigating and reporting on expensive, suspicious, and dysfunctional facets of the criminal justice system, then, may outweigh its potential costs. Failure to study how various initiatives and strategies are actually implemented on the street could condemn other citizens to misfortune and abuse should the behavior of the system be inconsistent with stated legitimate objectives.

To rule out study of covert behavior, whether engaged in by the powerful or the powerless, simply because it cannot be studied openly places artificial boundaries on science and prevents study of what potentially may be very important and consequential activities in society. The propriety and importance of research activities must always be judged on a case by case basis. Drug enforcement's use of asset forfeiture, for example, has been questioned by the press and media with such frequency and intensity that scholarly evaluation is warranted. The very nature of the allegations, however, have prompted the police fraternity to close ranks, thus compelling covert analysis. Abandoning such a study because it can not be out overtly would mean that potential misconduct and betrayal of public trust by government officials would remain unexposed.

The means and end rule, of course, requires the subjective interpretation of plausible harm to subjects, what exactly constitutes benefit, and who will be beneficiaries. To assess the balance between these elements it is necessary that they be highly specified, a requirement that is not easily met. The means and end formula is thus ambiguous and the choice to use a covert technique must be carefully deliberated. Certainly, deceptive observation carries ethical baggage less common to other qualitative methods, yet its ethicality is negotiable through detailed purpose and design.

Conclusion

The study of crime invites and sometimes requires the covert method as does examination of the clandestine nature of many facets of the formal social control apparatus. How other than through covert participant observation can topics such as undercover policing and inmate-correctional officer interaction be fully understood and evaluated? Those in the criminal justice system, as well as criminals, have vested interests in maintaining high levels of autonomy which require degrees of secrecy. This is evident in various labels such as "police fraternity", "gang", and "confidential informant."

The very things that make a criminal justice or criminological topic worthy of investigation and suitable for publication in a social science forum can preclude overtly exploring it. Methodologically sustained by the theoretical foundations of qualitative inquiry, covert designs tender opportunities to reach relatively unstudied topics.

• • •

This comment has briefly surveyed the methodological, theoretical, and practical reasons to utilize covert participant observation in criminal justice research. The most difficult facet of using this method will undoubtedly remain ethical factors that must be dealt with on a case by case basis. But these too can be overcome with caution, conviction, and adherence to established scientific guidelines for qualitative research (Glaser and Strauss 1967). The spirit of selecting methods on technical merit and relevance to research objectives rather than ethical pretense is an outlook consistent with the goals of social science. To the extent that this perspective thrives, covert participant observation may well become more commonplace; perhaps to the point of no longer being the least used method.

References

Adler, P.A. and P. Adler. (1987) "The Past and Future of Ethnography." *Journal of Contemporary Ethnography* 16:4–24.

Asch, Solomon E. (1951) "Effects of Group Pressure upon the Modification and Distortion of Judgement." in H. Guetzkow (Ed.) *Groups, Leadership and Men.* Pittsburgh. PA: Carnegie Press.

Berg, Bruce L. (1989) *Qualitative Research Methods for the Social Sciences.* Boston, MA: Allyn and Bacon.

British Sociological Association. (1973) Statement of Ethical Principles and their Application to Sociological Practice.

Bulmer, Martin. (1980) "Comment on the Ethics of Covert Methods." *British Journal of Sociology* 31:59–65.

Denzin, Norman. (1968) "On the Ethics of Disguised Observation." *Social Problems* 115:502–504.

Douglas, Jack D. (1976) *Investigative and Social Research: Individual and Team Field Research.* Beverly Hills, CA: Sage.

Erickson, Kai T. (1967) "Disguised Observation in Sociology." *Social Problems* 14:366–372.

Formby, William A. and John Smykia. (1981) "Citizen awareness in Crime Prevention: Do They Really Get Involved?" *Journal of Police Science and Administration* 9:398–403.

Galliher, John F. (1973) "The Protection of Human Subjects: A Reexamination of the Professional Code of Ethics." *The American Sociologist* 8:93–100.

Glaser, Barney G. and Anselm Strauss. (1967) *The Discovery of Grounded Theory.* Chicago, IL: Aldine.

Goffman, Erving. (1959) *The Presentation of Self in Everyday Life.* New York: Doubleday.

Hagan, Frank E. (1993) *Research Methods in Criminal Justice and Criminology.* 3rd ed. New York: Macmillian Publishing Co.

Homan, Roger. (1980) "The ethics of covert methods." *British Journal of Sociology* 31:46–59.

Humphreys, Laud. (1970) *Tearoom Trade: Impersonal Sex in Public Places.* New York: Aldine Publishing Co.

Jorgensen, Danny L. (1989) *Participant Observation: A Methodology for Human Studies.* Newburry Park, CA: Sage.

Klockars, Carl B. (1974) *The Professional Fence.* New York: The Free Press.

Miller, J. Mitchell and Lance Selva. (1994) "Drug Enforcement's Double-Edged Sword: An Assessment of Asset Forfeiture Programs." *Justice Quarterly* 11:313–335.

Patton, M. Q. (1990) *Qualitative Evaluation and Research Methods.* 2nd ed. Newbury Park, CA: Sage.

Polsky, Ned. (1967) *Hustlers, Beats, and Others.* New York: Anchor Books.

Ronai, C. R. and C. Ellis. (1989) "Turn-ons for money: Interactional strategies of the table dancer." *Journal of Contemporary Ethnography* 18:271–298.

Roth, Julius A. (1962) "Comments on Secret Observation." *Social Problems* 9:283–284.

Shils, Edward A. (1975) "Privacy and Power" in *Center and Periphery: Essays in Macrosociology.* Chicago. IL: University of Chicago Press.

Steffensmeier, Darrell J., and Robert M. Terry. "Deviance and respectability: An observational study of reactions to shoplifting." *Social Forces,* 51, 4, 417–426.

Stein, Martha L. (1974) *Lovers, Friends, Slaves . . .: The Nine Male Sexual Types,* Berkeley, CA: Berkeley Publishing Corp.

Stewart, John E. and Daniel Cannon. (1977) "Effects of Perpetrator Status and Bystander Commitment on Response to a Simulated Crime." *Journal of Police Science and Administration* 5:318–323.

Stricker, L. J. (1967) "The True Deceiver." *Psychological Bulletin* 68:13–20.

Tewksbury, Richard. (1990) "Patrons of Porn: Research Notes on the Clientele of Adult Book-stores." *Deviant Behavior* 11:259–271.

Von Hoffman, N. (1970) *"Sociological Snoopers."* Washington Post (Jan. 30).

3. Criminological *Verstehen:*

Inside the Immediacy of Crime

Jeff Ferrell

Many past and present studies in criminology have developed out of engaged and often il-legal field research—that is, field research in which the researcher of necessity crosses over into the world of criminality. Contemporary reevaluations of methodology, and specifi-cally the role of the researcher in the research process, provide a framework for exploring anew the implications of such field research. In addition, a variety of contemporary crimi-nological studies highlight the importance of the meanings and emotions that emerge in-side criminal events, and thus confirm the need for methodologies that can situate researchers to some degree inside illegality. Drawing on Weber's notion of verstehen, *this essay proposes one such situated methodology: criminological* verstehen. *It con-cludes by suggesting broader applications of this methodology in present and future crim-inal and criminal justice research situations.*

Among the many methodological approaches that enrich criminology and crimi-nal justice, one approach—direct field research inside the worlds of criminal life and criminal action—offers a particularly potent mix of problems and potential. In this essay I explore the vivid and often dangerous dynamics of criminological field research. I argue that the risky dynamics of field research offer criminolo-gists not only access to criminals and criminal groups, but also, and perhaps more important, an opportunity for partial immersion in the situated logic and emo-tion that define criminal experience. Moreover, although I focus on field research inside criminal worlds and in illegal settings, I suggest that such immersion can provide equally important insights into the experiences of crime victims, crime control agents, and others. Put simply, I propose that experiential immersion by field researchers can begin to unravel the lived meanings of both crime and crimi-nal justice.

Such a methodological orientation embodies a troubling tangle of ethical con-tradictions and legal ambiguities. Researchers who pursue a strategy of deep en-gagement with criminal (or even criminal justice) worlds must be prepared to face numerous personal and professional risks, to confront and acknowledge the human consequences of their research, and to make difficult decisions about per-sonal and professional responsibility. Recent reconsiderations of research and re-searchers' roles, however, emphasize that such difficulties need not disqualify this or other methods from use; instead they can provide important opportunities for investigating both the nature of scholarly inquiry and the nuances of the re-search subject. An excerpt from my own research can perhaps best introduce the

Justice Quarterly, Vol. 14 No. 1, March 1997 © 1997 Academy of Criminal Justice Sciences odd mix of ethics and inquiry that informs a field researcher's immersion in the experience of criminality.

A Report from Inside the Immediacy of Crime

On a late August night, I head out—as I have done many times before—for a night of wandering, drinking, and painting with members of the local hip hop graffiti underground. By this time I have engaged in almost two years of intensive participant observation inside the underground—that is, inside the world of nongang graffiti "writers" who, drawing on the hip hop graffiti conventions first developed in New York City in the 1970s, organize themselves and their activities around illicit public displays of alternative artistry and style. Though my research focuses on the subcultural dynamics that drive the underground, it also explores the increasing criminalization of these writers and their activities under a legal/political campaign against graffiti begun in this city some years before. Given both my acceptance into the underground and my awareness of the aggressive legal measures directed against it, I have decided long before this night that if I should encounter police officers, gang members, or others, I will try not to hide behind the cloak of researcher or scholar, but rather will participate as fully as possible in these risky social processes as well.

The night holds great promise in that I am going out with one the most acclaimed "kings" of the local scene—Eye Six, a talented artist known both in the graffiti underground for his brilliant murals and in the legitimate alternative art world for his innovative gallery shows. But the night holds great danger as well. Many of the more experienced members of Syndicate, the graffiti "crew" to which Eye Six belongs, cannot go along this night; among the missing is another "king," Rasta 68, who often functions on outings as an important organizer, guide, and lookout. In their place we are accompanied by Toon, Frost, and other "toy" writers—young writers whose artistic inexperience is matched, we fear, by an unbridled enthusiasm and a relatively undeveloped street sense that may well draw unwanted attention. Moreover, we have decided to paint in the old lower downtown railyards, a popular graffiti setting and a place of darkness, of inaccessibility to automobiles, and thus of relative safety. On our way, however, plans change (as they regularly do in the underground), and we land in an old warehouse district on the edge of the yards, a district with brighter lights, better roads, and a larger population of street gang members. By this time I have been in the underground long enough to know the informal rules and street-level safeguards, but also to know how often these are broken in the haphazard contingencies of late-night adventure.

Settling into a narrow, half-lit alley between rows of warehouses, Eye Six and I begin the lengthy process of "piecing"—that is, of painting a large, graffiti-style mural. Having brought along the usual supply of "forties" (40-ounce bottles of malt liquor), "shooters" (small bottles of Jack Daniels and Yukon Jack), cigarettes, and Krylon spray paint, we and the other writers anticipate a long night in the alley. As the hours pass, the other writers tire of making minor contributions to the mural or keeping watch. They begin to wander the alley, climb fences, "tag" (write their underground nicknames on walls and fences), and generally create a bit too much noise and movement. Eye Six and I remain busy with the piece; a vague commentary on a nearby nuclear weapons facility, or perhaps more broadly on the aesthetics of modern science, it features hooded laboratory workers and stenciled images of gaseous bubbles. In these hours of piecing, we share not only work on the mural but also an experience about which graffiti writers talk regularly: the tense excitement, the dangerous, almost intoxicating pleasure, of artistic production interwoven with illegality and adventure.

By three or four a.m., we are almost out of malt liquor, paint, and energy. Though the piece is not quite finished (Eye Six tags "6 B Back" on it to indicate its incompletion), we pack to leave. Suddenly two cars round the corner into the alley a block and a half away, and accelerate toward us at high speed. Having dealt with police officers, security guards, huffers (paint sniffers), and various street toughs on previous late-night graffiti excursions, I am overcome not only by a remarkably powerful rush of adrenaline and fear, but also by an awful uncertainty: Are these gangsters or police?

In any case, the other writers and I run for it. Eye Six and Frost stumble and fall, dive under a nearby loading dock, and thereby escape. I run out of the alley and down the street, intending to turn toward the dark salvation of the railyards, which lie only a couple of blocks to my left. A high fence blocks my way, though, and as I continue down the street, I hear a high-performance engine closing on me and decide that it must be the police behind me.

In the next instant, I am pinned against the fence by a policeman, whose partner has caught up with Toon nearby. There follow barrages of questions about my accomplices (which I decline to answer), a seemingly endless string of derogations about the sort of university professor who would vandalize private property, threats of jailing, photographs of me and Toon, and finally a summons and complaint ordering me to court on charges of "destruction of private property." The police report notes that "suspect had paint on hands matching colors on mural." It also includes (as I knew it would from my previous research) a special notation alerting the district attorney and judge that this is not a generic case of private property destruction, but rather the sort of "graffiti vandalism" case that the city now targets.

A month later, I appear in court. Engaging in the usual rituals of pretrial negotiation, my attorney meets with an assistant district attorney to work out a deal. He reports to me, however, that the assistant DA isn't willing to deal much on this case. The best he can get for me is a deferred judgment and sentence, dismissible on completion of one year's probation and payment of court costs. Though others in court that day seem to be negotiating less stringent resolutions to domestic violence cases and other criminal situations, I agree and enter the courtroom. But as the judge is reading the judgment, he pauses and threatens to reject the plea bargain unless arrangements have been made to remove this "graffiti vandalism."

"Your honor," replies my lawyer, "we have no evidence that the property owner *wants* the mural removed." And indeed, years later, the mural remains.

Some people surely could argue that this incident exposes the thoroughly unprofessional nature of my criminological research and the dangers, to use an unfortunate phrase, of "going native." Others might argue that it transforms my status irrevocably from criminologist to criminal, and certainly I could have been charged that night, along with destruction of private property, with resisting arrest, public drunkenness, and contributing to the delinquency of a minor. In another sense, however, the incident locates this sort of research alongside many of the fundamental works in criminology, precisely (and only) because of its odd interweaving of criminology and criminality.

For if we look again at Becker's (1963) field research among marijuana-smoking jazz musicians, Polsky's (1969) field experiences with hustlers and gangsters, Humphreys' (1975) work with the gay clientele of public bathrooms, Adler's (1985) participant observation with upper-level drug users and dealers, Padilla's (1992) field research with gangs and gang drug dealers, Wright and Decker's (1994) street-level work with residential burglars, and countless other cases of criminological field research, we realize that many of the respected figures in criminology could well be considered a rogues' gallery of common criminals. Whether through direct participation in illegal activities, witnessing criminal behavior, or simply the sort of "dirty knowledge" that constructs them as accomplices or accessories to crime, criminological field researchers regularly have crossed the lines of legality in developing important and influential accounts of crime and criminality. Put another way, criminology consistently has been enriched not only by case study method and qualitative field research, but also by case and field studies directly entangled in the experience of criminality and illegality (Adler 1985; Geis 1991; Polsky 1969). In this light, the many past and present cases of engaged and illegal field research raise for criminology the narrow issues of an individual's professionalism or propensity for illegality, as well as broader issues of methodology, morality, and criminological insight.

A Methodological Framework

By first engaging in illegal field research, and then openly "confessing" this research strategy and my role in it, I situate myself and my research within established traditions of criminological fieldwork, but also within newer reconceptualizations of research methodology and scholarship. My research, and this reporting, take shape within recent feminist, postmodernist, and existentialist reconsiderations of research, and of the researcher's role, in criminology and elsewhere (Adler and Adler 1987; Burawoy et al. 1991; Caulfield and Wonders 1994; Clifford and Marcus 1986; Clough 1992; Daly and Chesney-Lind 1988; Fine 1993; Fonow and Cook 1991; Gelsthorpe 1990; Sanders 1995). These perspectives emphasize the necessity of interpretive, ethnographic methods—methods that can help us "understand crime at close range" (Daly and Chesney-Lind 1988:517) and thus "reveal parts of the social world that remain hidden by more traditional techniques" (Caulfield and Wonders 1994:223).

Such perspectives further insist that these ethnographic methods are, and must remain, inherently personal, political, and partial endeavors. In doing so, they reintroduce the researcher's humanity into the research process and make a case for critical, reflexive, autobiographical accounts and understandings (Begley 1994)—for "profound self-disclosures" (Adler and Adler 1987:86) and openness to the "subjective experience of doing research" (Gelsthorpe 1990:93)—as part of the field research process. Thus they call for "true confessions"—that is, accounts of field research that in fact undermine absolutist notions of scholarly truth by incorporating situationally truthful representations of field researchers' lived and limiting experiences (Fine 1993).

These perspectives further emphasize that methodologies inevitably intertwine with theoretical stances, political choices, and the social situations in which they are practiced. Because of this intertwining, criminological (and other) field researchers cannot conveniently distance themselves from their subjects of study, or from the legally uncertain situations in which the subjects may reside, in order to construct safe and "objective" studies. Instead criminological field research unavoidably entangles those who practice it in complex and ambiguous relations to the subjects and situations of study, to issues of personal and social responsibility, and to law and legality. This approach to research methodology thus serves as both a report and a manifesto, as evidence and as argument that conventional canons of objectivity and validity are not and cannot be followed in the everyday practice of criminological field research (Becker 1967). It also points to a situated, reflexive sociology of criminological field research—an accounting of the collective experiences, social relations, and webs of politics and power in which criminological field research unfolds.

A research agenda of engagement with subjects of study, a methodology that moves beyond objectivity to immersion in the actualities of daily criminality, forces new understandings not only of research methods, but of research morality as well. From inside a tradition of objectivity and scientific detachment, the lines of legality and illegality, morality and immorality in research may seem straight and clean. But as many criminologists know, these lines quickly become tangled and uncertain in the field—inside the lives of graffiti writers, gang members, drug users, or professional thieves. These newer perspectives on criminological research are distinguished from older ones in part by a willingness to acknowledge this moral and legal uncertainty—a willingness to abandon the myth of objectivist detachment, and instead to "confess" the inherently ambiguous morality and shady legality of criminological field research (Sanders 1995).

As we step out from behind the facade of objectivity, we thus gain fresh insights into field research projects involving illegality and crime. Objectivist perspectives would characterize illegality in field research as an unfortunate methodological side effect at best, and a personal and professional failure at worst; here, however, illegality can be explored more openly for its methodological potential. In the same way, a researcher's strict conformity to legal codes can be reconceptualized less as a sign of professional success than as a possible por- tent of methodological failure. Close adherence to legality doubtless shuts the field researcher off from all kinds of field contacts and social situations, and per- haps relegates him or her to the role of "jailhouse or courthouse sociologist" (Pol- sky 1969:141; see Hagedorn 1990); a willingness to break the law may open up a variety of methodoligical possibilities. To put it bluntly, for the dedicated field re- searcher who seeks to explore criminal subcultures and criminal dynamics, obey- ing the law may present as much of a problem as breaking it.

If, however, these new perspectives on research are characterized by a more open and more honest stance, we should also be honest about their potentially negative consequences. In older scientific and objectivist models, the openly ille- gal approaches discussed here would likely have constituted professional suicide. They still may. A researcher who engages in illegal fieldwork may face jail time, court costs, betrayal of or by subcultural accomplices, and censure by colleagues. Moreover, any openly illegal research may generate negative public perceptions of the individual researcher and, more important, may produce the sort of nega- tive media coverage and public imagery that contribute to broader contemporary attacks on the credibility and legitimacy of academic scholarship. Criminologists who consider this methodological path must also consider carefully which kinds of criminality are appropriate or inappropriate for study. In addition, they must weigh carefully their responsibilities to the criminals, crime control agents, and crime victims affected by their research, and must anticipate for themselves a va- riety of personal, professional, and disciplinary consequences.

Criminological Field Research and Criminological *Verstehen*

Despite the potential costs, participatory criminological field research is worth considering as a methodological strategy not only for broad reasons of subcul- tural access or experience, but also because of a distinctive methodological and epistemic issue—an issue that returns us to the alley and the criminal event in which I was caught. This is the notion of *criminological verstehen* (Ferrell and Sanders 1995:312–13; Hamm and Ferrell 1994:29). As formulated by Max Weber (1949, 1978) and developed by later theorists (Adler and Adler 1987:85–87; Outh- waite 1976; Truzzi 1974), *verstehen* denotes a process of subjective interpretation on the part of the social researcher, a degree of sympathetic understanding be- tween researcher and subjects of study, whereby the researcher comes in part to share in the situated meanings and experiences of those under scrutiny. As Weber (1978:4–5) argued, in a sociology that "concern[s] itself with the interpretive un- derstanding of social action . . . empathic or appreciative accuracy is attained when, through sympathetic participation, we can adequately grasp the emotional context in which the action took place."

For Weber (1978:3–24), this empathic understanding was a component of a larger science of sociology, and was balanced with various rational understandings of social action and social meaning. In contemporary criminological field research, and within the emerging methodological orientations just considered, the concept of *verstehen* can be defined somewhat more narrowly and more modestly as a situated strategy in the always partial and imperfect process of research into criminality. As used here, then, criminological *verstehen* denotes a researcher's subjective understanding of crime's situational meanings and emotions—its moments of pleasure and pain, its emergent logic and excitement—within the larger process of research. It further implies that a researcher, through attentiveness and participation, at least can begin to apprehend and appreciate the specific roles and experiences of criminals, crime victims, crime control agents, and others caught up in the day-to-day reality of crime.

The methodological utility and theoretical importance of criminological *verstehen* in turn hinge on a particular etiology of crime—an etiology that locates the origins and meaning of crime largely inside the criminal event (Katz 1988). An understanding of crime and criminality as constructed from the immediate interactions of criminals, control agents, victims, and others, and therefore as emerging from a tangled experiential web of situated dangers and situated pleasures, certainly refocuses theories of criminal causality on the criminal moment. It produces a second, methodological understanding as well: that criminologists must situate themselves as close to the (inter)action as possible—perhaps even inside the interaction—if they are to catch the constructed reality of crime (Ferrell 1992, 1996).

This etiology thus implies that criminologists will need the sorts of grounded, ethnographic methods already discussed, a broad "methodology of attentiveness" (Ferrell 1995:87), in place of safely distanced survey research or statistical analysis. It suggests that criminologists must develop a certain intimacy with illegality, a criminological *verstehen* through which they can begin in part to feel and understand the situated logic and emotion of crime. It means that criminologists, as far as possible within the limits of personal responsibility and professional identity, must be there in the criminal moment—in the dark alley described earlier, and in many other situations as well—if they are to apprehend the terrors and pleasures of criminality. It means that criminologists must venture inside the immediacy of crime.

A variety of research findings and theoretical trajectories confirm the importance of situated criminal meanings and experiences, and thus the need for a criminological *verstehen* that can begin to explore them. Katz (1988) has considered broadly the "foreground" of criminality, the immediate, interactional interplay through which a criminal event takes shape, and specifically the "magical" excitement of shoplifting and other crimes. As implied by my adventure in the alley, and confirmed in many other research moments under bridges and down back alleys, my own work likewise has shown that graffiti writers piece and tag largely because of what they call the "adrenaline rush." Experienced and described by writers time and again, in graffiti undergrounds from Los Angeles to Berlin, this rush is an immediate, incandescent "high" that results from the execution of long-practiced art in dangerously illegal situations (Ferrell 1995, 1996). Lyng (1990; Lyng and Bracey 1995) has similarly documented the experience of "edgework"—the exhilarating, momentary integration of danger, risk, and skill—

that drives a variety of deviant, criminal, and noncriminal experiences. In a related view, Nehring (1993:7) has described the "outlaw emotions" that define both moments of cognitive insubordination and various deviant or insurgent subcultures.

Other researchers, especially those investigating the day-to-day dynamics of juvenile delinquency and delinquent subcultures, have uncovered similar patterns. Miller's (1958:9) influential work listed "excitement"—that is, "sought situations of great emotional stimulation . . . the search for excitement or 'thrill' . . . sought risk and desired danger"—among the "focal concerns of lower class culture" that could precipitate gang delinquency. In his study of British working-class delinquency, Willis (1977:16) found that delinquency and youthful resistance to adult authority were grounded in daily pleasure and experience; as one of his respondents reported in distancing himself from a less delinquent boy, "We've been through all life's pleasures and all its fucking displeasures . . . frustration, sex, fucking hatred, love and all this lark, yet he's known none of it. . . . He's not known so many of the emotions as we've had to experience. . . ." Hamm (1993) describes the "emotional capacity" that neo-Nazi skinheads collectively develop as part of "going berserk" episodes aimed at outsiders; Vigil (1988; Vigil and Long 1990) and others similarly note the collective emotion and experience developed by Latino gang members in "going crazy" *(loco, locura)* against rival gangs and other groups.

As Presdee (1994) reports, nongang delinquents also revel in the intense pleasure and excitement that accompanies their participation in seemingly mundane forms of criminality such as "stealing objects" and "stealing travel." Even some of the adult property criminals whom Tunnell (1992:45) studied, though they operate within a rationalized "criminal calculus," report that stealing is "a high . . . it's exhilarating. . . . I get off going through doors." Similarly, Wright and Decker (1994:117), in a reprise of Lofland's (1969) findings, report that many burglars are "committed to a lifestyle characterized by the quest for excitement and an openness to 'illicit action,'" and that some go so far as to burglarize occupied homes in order to make "the offense more exciting."

Taken together, these criminological findings address Riemer's (1981:39) concern about traditional conceptualizations of deviance: that deviance has "rarely . . . been considered a spontaneous, 'just for the hell of it' activity, in which the participants engage simply for the pleasure it provides." And as O'Malley and Mugford (1994:209) argue, even where pleasure has been considered, it "has appeared in traditional criminologies as a more or less 'obvious' explanatory variable . . . the category and experience of pleasure . . . appeared to need no investigation." Echoing Foucault's (1985, 1990) groundbreaking investigations of pleasure and its political frameworks, his demonstration that "power is in our bodies, not in our heads" (Fraser 1994:11), these findings in criminal and delinquent worlds demonstrate the importance of paying close attention to the situated sensuality, the definitive dangers and pleasures, of crime. Together these perspectives demonstrate that if we are to make sense of any number of deviant and criminal experiences, we must understand them to be "affectually determined" (Weber 1978:9), and therefore must find ways to partake in some of the immediate emotions and perceptions that define them. We must develop a criminological *verstehen* that can take us inside the many specific moments of illegality. This methodological position in turn implies not only that criminologists must be present in criminal (and criminalized) subcultures and situations, but also that they must be present *affectively*; that is, they must share to whatever extent possible in the dangers, pleasures, emotions, and experiences that constitute criminal activity as part of their understanding of that activity.

In this sense, the notion of criminological *verstehen* as employed here necessitates a grounded methodology that transcends objectivity and distance, as well as new epistemic frameworks that transcend the rationalist assumptions embedded in traditionally objectivist methods. Given the sense of sympathetic understanding incorporated in the notion of *verstehen*, making sense of immediate criminal experiences means not merely "understanding" them by locating them within exterior intellectual or analytic models, but appreciating the specific kinds of situated logic and emotion that emerge within them (Katz 1988; Weber 1978:7). Moreover, and perhaps most radically, criminological *verstehen* implies a certain emotional empathy, a notion that pleasure, excitement, and fear can teach us as much about criminality as can abstract analysis (Fonow and Cook 1991:9-11). It embodies a sense that adrenaline rushes and outlaw emotions matter to criminals and criminologists alike, that our understanding of criminal experiences may come to us, as researchers, as much in the pits of our stomachs, in cold sweats and frightened shivers, as in our heads.

Given this talk of shivers, sweats, and emotions, it is worth nothing that the subject of study remains social, and the method of criminological *verstehen* sociological. The edgework and the adrenaline rush that define joyriding, drug taking, shoplifting, graffiti writing, and gangbanging are largely constructed collectively, from the subcultural participants' common experiences and from the shared cultural codes of criminal groups (Becker 1963; Lyng and Snow 1986). Their meaning is likewise constructed linguistically, as graffiti writers or gangbangers give shape to their experiences by encasing them in the collectively meaningful argot of the subculture. Thus, following Mills (1940) and Cressey (1954), what might first appear as isolated, individual, or impulsive experiences reflect a shared "vocabulary of motive," a repertoire of meanings common to those involved in them. Because of this, the practice of criminological *verstehen* does not require that criminologists somehow mystically penetrate the criminal's heart or mind, but rather that they engage in sociological research—that they participate in the collective experiences, emotions, and meanings of those they study.

Yet even as the collective construction of criminal pleasure and excitement opens these experiences to a method such as criminological *verstehen*, it closes them to some degree as well. Different criminologists occupy different positions in structures of social class, gender, age, and ethnicity, and often hold distinctly different positions than those they seek to study. Because of these differences in identity, some criminologists who pursue membership and participation in a criminal subculture may not succeed; even those who do so can never succeed more than partially, no matter how attentively they go about the process. Therefore, insofar as membership in the subculture shapes the collective experience of criminal pleasure and excitement, the criminologist's ability to achieve criminological *verstehen* is limited at best, even where she or he encounters the same situations as others. And thus, given that the meaning and appeal of these criminal experiences reflect not only subcultural dynamics but also larger structures and one's location within those structures, a criminologist who partakes of criminal events may neither fully experience nor fully understand the seductions found there by others who lead different lives.

Moreover, the very nature of these collective experiences as dangerously illegal events further limits the criminologist's participation. Activities such as graffiti writing, illegal cruising, motorcycle gang "runs," and even drug and alcohol use may lend themselves to some degree of direct participation by certain criminologists, and thus to some degree of direct criminological *verstehen*. Other activities, which a criminological researcher judges to incorporate intolerable degrees of threat, violence, or moral danger—or which simply stay closed to the researcher because of differences in age, gender, ethnicity, or social class—may be accessible only through intensive interviewing and other techniques that perhaps can imaginatively reconstruct, to some degree, the experience of criminological *verstehen*. As stated above, the very strength of criminological *verstehen*—its volatile mix of insight and immersion—demands caution in its application.

Even as an inherently dangerous and imperfect method, however, criminological *verstehen* remains an important component of research. If we understand that many forms of criminality are grounded in the immediate experience of excitement, pleasure, and fear, we must also imagine methods that can explore this experience. In discussing his research on skydiving as edgework, Lyng states that "many edgework enthusiasts regard the experience as ineffable," and adds,

> . . . [T]he data collected in my study of the skydiving group were not easily acquired. In the early stages of the study, I was constantly frustrated in my attempt to get sky divers to talk about the jump experience. The typical response to my probing questions was, "If you want to know what it's like, then do it!" It was only after the respondents became convinced that I shared their commitment to edgework that they were willing to try to articulate their feelings about the experience. (1990:861, 862n)

My ethnographic research into urban graffiti writing followed a similar pattern. I gained entry into the graffiti writers' subculture through a series of informal tests of my willingness to participate in the dangerous pleasures and excitement of graffiti writing: all-night wandering, social drinking, illegal painting, and (mostly successful) strategies for avoiding legal authority. In turn my participation in these activities created a level of collective trust and experiential camaraderie essential to intensive interviewing and other aspects of long-term criminological fieldwork. Here, then, we see the necessity of criminological *verstehen* in particular research situations, and also the positive secondary effects of shared or sympathetic understanding in opening other avenues of grounded research into crime and criminality.

Finally, the concept of criminological *verstehen* as an essential component of criminological fieldwork returns us to the particular dangers faced not only by criminals (and their victims), but also by those who conduct this sort of research with them. Indeed, criminological *verstehen* in a sense constitutes the researcher's deepest sort of submersion in the dangers of criminality; this submersion takes the researcher both inside the setting and inside the emotions and experiences that animate it. Moreover, a field researcher immersed in adrenaline rushes or edgework may well be immersed at the same time in a net of police surveillance, or may be facing arrest by legal authorities for whom this type of research quite understandably constitutes a simple case of criminal misconduct, or worse, a clear case of sympathy for the devil. Even a criminological field researcher who attempts to stay somehow inside the boundaries of legality, or who chooses to conduct research not with criminals but with criminal justice practitioners, may risk later redefinition by crime control agents or others as a criminal accomplice or accessory (Leo 1995; Marquart 1986; Scarce 1995).

Here we encounter an essential issue in criminological field research and criminological *verstehen*: As all criminologists know, criminality is decided as much by legal and political authorities, and by their strategies of criminalization, enforcement, and control, as by criminals themselves. Thus the nature and limits of criminological field research and criminological *verstehen* are determined in part by the field researcher and those under study, but also in part by legal and political decision makers, shifting and selective legal enforcement and prosecution, and the broader political climate of crime control. To engage in (potentially) illegal field research, to pursue the insights afforded by criminological *verstehen*, is therefore to engage a larger set of moral issues and political dynamics, and to confront one's own theoretical and political responses to those dynamics.

In this sense, a field researcher's participation in illegal activities and criminological *verstehen* dramatically resurrects the question posed by Becker (1963, 1967) in the sociology and criminology of the 1960s: Whose side are we on? In the dynamics of criminological research, as Polsky (1969) and others have shown, neutrality is seldom an option. Where conflict between legal authorities and criminals not only predates the researcher's participation but also pervades the situations and decisions within which the researcher operates, there is little chance of having it both ways, of working honestly, openly, and empathically with both criminals and legal control agents. By the design of the fieldwork, the dynamics of its evolution, and the demands of its shared experiences and emotions, researchers must time and again align themselves more with one group than with the other, and must live out, at least temporarily, a decision as to whose side they are on.

Field research that stretches or breaks conventional boundaries of legality or morality thus calls into play, along with important methodological issues, the researcher's essential theoretical and political affiliations. Insofar as a criminological researcher understands the law to be a relatively fair and just representation of social concerns and shared values, violation of the law or empathic participation with criminals during research may constitute an inexcusable breach of professional ethics, and of the larger social contract to which the researcher is a party. Yet insofar as the researcher operates on the fundamental assumption of a more critical criminology—that the law in part reflects, incorporates, and perpetuates social privilege and social injustice—such field research still may pose professional problems, but will hardly present itself as a desecration of the social contract. Instead it may take on positive theoretical and political connotations that mirror its methodological possibilities, and which come to serve as a lived affirmation of the researcher's theoretical and political convictions. Whatever a researcher's affiliations, however, criminological field research and criminological *verstehen* constitute profound, if impermanent, processes of confrontation both with criminality and with a researcher's own criminological orientations. And whatever a researcher's affiliations, these methodologies appear to hold promise and danger both in the types of situations just described and in a variety of emerging contexts.

The Future of Criminological Field Research and Criminological *Verstehen*

The ever-changing contours of law, enforcement, and public debate regarding crime and justice continually reshape the methodological and political contours of criminological field research and criminological *verstehen*. As moral entrepreneurs (Becker 1963) and political leaders work to criminalize new areas of social and cultural life, as crime is portrayed as a pervasive problem and crime control is constructed as social salvation in the contemporary political climate, criminologists of all kinds face a double set of consequences. First, these changing circumstances guarantee an ever-expanding domain of criminological inquiry; each newly criminalized identity or situation, each new crime control controversy, offers fresh opportunities for research. Yet they also promise more and more research situations in which field researchers may find themselves crossing over into illegality, and perhaps also into public excoriation by concerned criminal justice officials, outraged moral entrepreneurs, or others.

Field researchers who run back alleys with graffiti writers, loiter with gay men in Humphrey's (1975) public tearooms, or hang with heroin users in backlot shooting galleries traditionally have been at risk. But as other social situations and cultural activities are criminalized, so, potentially, is field research in those areas. As young people's everyday (and every-night) activities come under the purview of expanded curfews (Ruefle and Reynolds 1995), anticruising laws, and other antidelinquency measures, for example, those who would conduct field research with young offenders increasingly risk charges or accusations of contributing to youthful delinquency. As new legal regulations of urban space and urban life increasingly criminalize the lives and actions of homeless people and dislocated urban populations (Barak 1991; Barak and Bohm 1989; Davis 1992; Kress 1994), field researchers engaged in participant observation with those persons increasingly face situations in which their own activities also may be construed as violating numerous new or newly enforced ordinances relating to vagrancy, loitering, curfew, trespass, panhandling, public lodging, and public nuisance. As anti-immigrant policies fuel harsher controls on undocumented workers at the U.S. border and elsewhere, those conducting research among them may increasingly face charges of harboring fugitives, abetting escape, or encouraging illegal immigration.

While these and other contemporary trends point to the increasing likelihood and necessity of illegal criminological field research, they also point to new efflorescences of criminal danger, excitement, and pleasure, and thus to new occasions for criminological *verstehen*. Lyng (1990:869, 871), for example, locates the drive toward the voluntary risk taking of legal and illegal edgework in a "social system associated with class conflict, alienation, and the consumption imperative," and in "conditions of trivialized, degraded labor." Under such general conditions, the development and application of precise survival skills in edgework situations generate for those involved the purposeful meanings and grounded identities unavailable in everyday life and work. Similarly, the adrenaline rush of graffiti writing results from the pleasures of practiced artistry, as amplified within the dangerous illegality of the act. For graffiti writers, as for other edgeworkers, the excitement of the act provides immediate gratification but also a frame-work for inventing an identity, a sense of crafted self, that resides to some degree outside the usual limits of youthful status degradation, low-end wage work, and enforced legality (Ferrell 1995, 1996).

Thus the combination of two contemporary trends—the growth of marginalized, low-status work, especially among the young, and the increasing push toward punitive crime control policies—suggests that the appeal of criminal pleasure and excitement can only increase. The spreading disintegration of the work process, the growing confinement of youths and adults in fractured and relatively meaningless work situations (when they can find work at all), surely will continue to heighten the seduction of edgework and adrenaline rush experiences as moments of cleansing terror and desperate rehumanization. The growing criminalization of social and cultural life, especially among young people, ethnic minorities, and the poor, will further close off avenues of legitimacy, construct more opportunities for criminal edgework and adrenaline, and in turn amplify and enhance the edgy pleasure and excitement that these experiences contain. As criminologists we can anticipate more situations of illegal field research, and more situations in which criminological *verstehen* will be needed as an avenue inside the dangers and pleasures that define them.

The changing and expanding dynamics of social, cultural, and criminal life thus demand that field researchers in all sorts of situations—even in those not traditionally viewed as criminal—remember Polsky's (1969:118, 127) cautionary maxim, that one had best consider the personal and professional limits of law, crime, and field method *before* beginning field research: "In field investigating, before you can tell a criminal who you are and make it stick, you have to know this yourself. . . . You need to decide beforehand, as much as possible, where you wish to draw the line. . . ."

More generally, the increased likelihood and necessity of conducting field research in criminalized contexts require that criminology as a discipline—as taught to students, discussed at conferences, and displayed to the public—incorporate an awareness and consideration of law, crime, and field research in its day-to-day operations. Most generally, these emerging issues suggest that we as criminologists now may want to consider other possible futures for criminological field research and criminological *verstehen.* What kind of field research, for example, would be appropriate if abortion again were made illegal? If gay and lesbian life in effect were outlawed, what would be the role of the field researcher immersed in the experiences and emotions of that life? If homeless and other inner-city populations continue to be marginalized and criminalized, where will we as criminologists draw the line between ethnography and activism, legality and illegality?

Illegal criminological field research and criminological *verstehen,* then, would seem to be important methodological strategies not only in a variety of current situations but also in research on various forms of criminality that may emerge from developing social and political arrangements. Yet however wide the applicability of these methodologies in the future, they would seem also to have a wider utility in the present than I have indicated so far. For an attentiveness to situated danger and excitement, in revealing something about contemporary criminality, also suggests insights into the broader relationships between crime, crime victimization, and criminal justice.

As a starting point, it seems likely that adrenaline and excitement, pleasure and fear animate not only the experiences of everyday criminals, but equally so the experiences of other everyday participants in crime, crime control, and criminal justice. Police officers involved in high-speed automobile pursuits, foot chases, or undercover/sting operations (Marx 1988) certainly experience—and, to some degree, savor—these situations as adrenaline-charged adventures, and in this sense may find in their day-to-day lives the same hyped pleasures as do those they seek to control. In the middle-of-the-night chase down a dark alley, a degree of tense excitement surely energized not only my experience and that of the scattering graffiti writers, but that of the pursuing police officers as well. The often anxious and aggressive excitement of police work, as played out in day-to-day operations and reproduced in the language and values of police subcultures, may help in turn to explain the close social and emotional bonds among police officers. It also may help to explain the ferocity of certain encounters between police and citizens (who may well be caught up in their own excitement and fear), and to account for the situated dynamics that sometimes transform these encounters into eruptions of violence and brutalization (Kappeler, Sluder, and Alpert 1994; Kraska and Kappeler 1995).

Similarly, victims of crime seem to regularly experience victimization not as a rationally calculable loss of property or safety, but as an overwhelming moment of terror and despair that haunts them long after property or safety is restored. Attention to the lived reality of crime victimization thus can lead us closer to a *verstehen*-oriented victimology, a sympathy and support grounded in interpretive understanding and shared experience. For the many criminologists who have been victimized by crime, an understanding of the costs of crime perhaps can emerge as much from an examination of their own emotional experiences, and from a contextualization of these experiences within those of others, as from an objective examination of crime victims or crime victimization rates. This understanding in turn may begin to explain the ease with which public hysteria about crime is constructed, and to reveal how political leaders and others are able to anchor crime control policies not in rational evaluation but in experiential anxiety. Thus adrenaline and excitement, terror and pleasure seem to flow not only through the experience of criminality but through the many capillaries connecting crime, crime victimization, and criminal justice. And as these terrors and pleasures circulate, they form an experiential and emotional current that illuminates the everyday meanings of crime and crime control.

Given this, the methodological utility of criminological *verstehen* may well extend beyond the field research described here, and into all kinds of criminological and criminal justice research. If the experiences of criminals, crime victims, crime control agents, and others are shaped by terror, pleasure, and excitement—and shaped differently according to their location in networks of crime and criminal justice, and in larger structures of social class, gender, age, and ethnicity—researchers must work toward particular forms of criminological *verstehen* attuned to these differences. As part of a larger methodology of attentiveness and engagement, criminological *verstehen* at its best can take criminologists at least partially inside the tangle of lived situations that constitute crime and crime control. It can perhaps also begin to take criminologists inside the many meanings and emotions that emerge there, and finally inside the immediacy of crime for all involved.

References

Adler, P. A. 1985. *Wheeling and Dealing*. New York: Columbia University Press.

Adler, P. A. and P. Adler. 1987. *Membership Roles in Field Research*. Newbury Park, CA: Sage.

Barak, G. 1991. *Gimme Shelter: A Social History of Homelessness in Contemporary America*. New York: Praeger.

Barak, G. and R. Bohm. 1989. "The Crimes of the Homeless or the Crime of Homelessness?" *Contemporary Crises* 13:275–88.

Becker, H. S. 1963. *Outsiders: Studies in the Sociology of Deviance*. New York: Free Press.

———. 1967. "Whose Side Are We On?" *Social Problems* 14:239–47.

Begley, A. 1994. "The I's Have It." *Lingua/Franca* 4:54–59.

Burawoy, M., A. Burton, A. A. Ferguson, K. Fox, J. Gamson, N. Gartrell, L. Hurst, C. Kurzman, L. Salzinger, J. Schiffman, and Shiori Ui. 1991. *Ethnography Unbound: Power and Resistance in the Modern Metropolis*. Berkeley: University of California Press.

Caulfield, S. and N. Wonders. 1994. "Gender and Justice: Feminist Contributions to Criminology." Pp. 213–29 in *Varieties of Criminology*, edited by G. Barak. Westport, CT: Praeger.

Clifford, J. and G. Marcus. 1986. *Writing Culture: The Poetics and Politics of Ethnography*. Berkeley: University of California Press.

Clough, P. 1992. *The End(s) of Ethnography: From Realism to Social Criticism*. Newbury Park, CA: Sage.

Cressey, D. 1954. "The Differential Association Theory and Compulsive Crime." *Journal of Criminal Law and Criminology* 45:49–64.

Daly, K. and M. Chesney-Lind. 1988. "Feminism and Criminology." *Justice Quarterly* 5:497–535.

Davis, M. 1992. *City of Quartz*. New York: Vintage.

Ferrell, J. 1992. "Making Sense of Crime." *Social Justice* 19:110–23.

———. 1995. "Urban Graffiti: Crime, Control, and Resistance." *Youth and Society* 27:73–92.

———. 1996. *Crimes of Style: Urban Graffiti and the Politics of Criminality*. Boston: Northeastern University Press.

Ferrell, J. and C. Sanders, eds. 1995. *Cultural Criminology*. Boston: Northeastern University Press.

Fine, G. 1993. "Ten Lies of Ethnography: Moral Dilemmas of Field Research." *Journal of Contemporary Ethnography* 22:267–94.

Fonow, M. and J. Cook, eds. 1991. *Beyond Methodology: Feminist Scholarship as Lived Research*. Bloomington: Indiana University Press.

Foucault, M. 1985. *The Use of Pleasure*. New York: Pantheon.

———. 1990. *The History of Sexuality: Volume 1: An Introduction*. New York: Vintage.

Fraser, N. 1994. "Foucault on Modern Power." Pp. 3–20 in *Social Control: Aspects of Non-State Justice*, edited by S. Henry. Aldershot, UK: Dartmouth.

Geis, G. 1991. "The Case Study Method in Sociological Criminology." Pp. 200–23 in *A Case for the Case Study*, edited by J. Feagin, A. Orum, and G. Sjoberg. Chapel Hill: University of North Carolina Press.

Gelsthorpe, L. 1990. "Feminist Methodologies in Criminology." Pp. 89–106 in *Feminist Perspectives in Criminology*, edited by L. Gelsthorpe and A. Morris. Milton Keynes, UK: Open University Press.

Hagedorn, J. 1990. "Back in the Field Again: Gang Research in the Nineties." Pp. 240–59 in *Gangs in America*, edited by C. Huff. Newbury Park, CA: Sage.

Hamm, M. 1993. *American Skinheads: The Criminology and Control of Hate Crime*. Westport, CT: Praeger.

Hamm, M. and J. Ferrell. 1994. "Rap, Cops, and Crime: Clarifying the 'Cop Killer' Controversy." *ACJS Today* 13:1,3,29.

Humphreys, L. 1975. *Tearoom Trade: Impersonal Sex in Public Places.* Enlarged ed. New York: Aldine.

Kappeler, V., R. Sluder, and G. Alpert. 1994. *Forces of Deviance.* Prospect Heights, IL: Waveland.

Katz, J. 1988. *Seductions of Crime: Moral and Sensual Attractions in Doing Evil.* New York: Basic Books.

Kraska, P. and V. Kappeler. 1995. "To Serve and Pursue: Exploring Police Sexual Violence against Women." *Justice Quarterly* 12:85–111.

Kress, J. 1994. "Homeless Fatigue Syndrome: The Backlash against the Crime of Homelessness in the 1990s." *Social Justice* 21:85–108.

Leo, R. 1995. "Trial and Tribulations: Courts, Ethnography, and the Need for an Evidentiary Privilege for Academic Researchers." *American Sociologist* 26:113–34.

Lofland, J. 1969. *Deviance and Identity.* Englewood Cliffs, NJ: Prentice-Hall.

Lyng, S. 1990. "Edgework: A Social Psychological Analysis of Voluntary Risk Taking." *American Journal of Sociology* 95:851–86.

Lyng, S. and M. Bracey Jr. 1995. "Squaring the One-Percent: Biker Style and the Selling of Cultural Resistance." Pp. 235–76 in *Cultural Criminology*, edited by J. Ferrell and C. Sanders. Boston: Northeastern University Press.

Lyng, S. and D. Snow. 1986. "Vocabularies of Motive and High-Risk Behavior: The Case of Skydiving." Pp. 157–79 in *Advances in Group Processes*, edited by E. Lawler. Greenwich, CT: JAI.

Marquart, J. 1986. "Doing Research in Prison: The Strengths and Weaknesses of Participation as a Guard." *Justice Quarterly* 3:15–32.

Marx, G. 1988. *Undercover: Police Surveillance in America.* Berkeley: University of California Press.

Miller, W. 1958. "Lower Class Culture as a Generating Milieu of Gang Delinquency." *Journal of Social Issues* 14:5–19.

Mills, C.W. 1940. "Situated Actions and Vocabularies of Motive." *American Sociological Review* 5:904–13.

Nehring, N. 1993. *Flowers in the Dustbin: Culture, Anarchy, and Postwar England.* Ann Arbor: University of Michigan Press.

O'Malley, P. and S. Mugford. 1994. "Crime, Excitement and Modernity." Pp. 189–211 in *Varieties of Criminology*, edited by G. Barak. Westport, CT: Praeger.

Outhwaite, W. 1976. *Understanding Social Life: The Method Called Verstehen.* New York: Holmes and Meier.

Padilla, F. 1992. *The Gang as an American Enterprise.* New Brunswick, NJ: Rutgers University Press.

Polsky, N. 1969. *Hustlers, Beats, and Others.* Garden City, NY: Anchor.

Presdee, M. 1994. "Young People, Culture, and the Construction of Crime: Doing Wrong versus Doing Crime." Pp. 179–87 in *Varieties of Criminology,* edited by G. Barak. Westport, CT: Praeger.

Riemer, J. 1981. "Deviance as Fun." *Adolescence* 16:39–43.

Ruefle, W. and K. Reynolds. 1995. "Curfews and Delinquency in Major American Cities." *Crime and Delinquency* 41:347–63.

Sanders, C. 1995. "Stranger Than Fiction: Insights and Pitfalls in Post-Modern Ethnography." *Studies in Symbolic Interaction* 17:89–104.

Scarce, R. 1995. "Scholarly Ethics and Courtroom Antics: Where Researchers Stand in the Eyes of the Law." *The American Sociologist* 26:87–112.

Truzzi, M. 1974. *Verstehen: Subjective Understanding in the Social Sciences.* Reading, MA: Addison-Wesley.

Tunnell, K. 1992. *Choosing Crime: The Criminal Calculus of Property Offenders.* Chicago: Nelson-Hall.

Vigil, J. 1988. *Barrio Gangs: Street Life and Identity in Southern California.* Austin: University of Texas Press.

Vigil, J. and J. Long. 1990. "Emic and Etic Perspectives on Gang Culture: The Chicano Case." Pp. 55–68 in *Gangs in America,* edited by C. Huff. Newbury Park, CA: Sage.

Weber, M. 1949. *The Methodology of the Social Sciences.* New York: Free Press.

———. 1978. *Economy and Society.* Berkeley: University of California Press.

Willis, P. 1977. *Learning to Labour.* New York: Columbia University Press.

Wright, R. and S. Decker. 1994. *Burglars on the Job: Streetlife and Residential Break-Ins.* Boston: Northeastern University Press.

4. Honesty, Secrecy, and Deception in the Sociology of Crime

Confessions and Reflections from the Backstage

Kenneth D. Tunnell

I'm driving down Highway 41 for a scheduled rendezvous in town with Robert, who then will lead me to his house in the country. I'm running late and pushing hard across the curvy, hilly roads of rural east Tennessee. Finally, I arrive and meet Robert at the appointed spot, his father's business, where he has worked since his release from prison just nine months prior. He looks different than when we first met, as he was nearing the end of his second stint in prison for burglary. On that late evening, we had spent two or three hours together in a small office normally used by prison counselors, but made available to us for my interview with him. Then, he seemed small, drawn, and pale with his hair slicked back; but today he seems different, in ways evidently characteristic of recent freedom—well fed, tanned, erect, with his hair stylishly cut.

I follow as he leads the way through town and across winding country roads. We arrive at a nearly new mobile home on a large, shaded lawn of maples and oaks, behind a clearly middle-class home—his father's, as I later discovered. Once inside we make small talk for a while and he offers me a beer, which I accept. "Where can you get beer around here on Sundays?" I query, for I had tried buying some for the drive back but learned it was not available. "Ah, you can git it, butcha gotta know the local bootlegger," he explains. We both sit on the couch and, after I've reminded him of his rights as a participant and assured him of confidentiality, I turn on the tape recorder and begin the interview. Just more than an hour into it, the beer necessitates a pause. I turn off the tape recorder, and Robert, pointing to it, says, "I don't know about you, but that thing makes me nervous as hell." "Why don't we keep it off and just talk a bit?" I suggest. "Great," he replies, then asks, "Wanna burn one?" I feel inclined, and we sit smoking and sharing stories of our childhoods in similar parts of the mountainous areas of rural east Tennessee. As we talk, he opens up and speaks of matters more central to the research. He describes his large number of marijuana plants growing in the nearby hills, the small select clientele to whom he sells, and his casual and ongoing operation of buying and selling stolen goods. Ironically, just shortly before turning off the tape recorder, he had assured me that he had been involved in no illegalities since his release from prison. But now there must be something about the intimacy, the real freedom to talk without words being captured on cassette, and the loosening effects of a couple of beers and a joint that provides a setting for some honest interaction, and some revelations of crime after prison and of his difficulty in doing straight time.

There I was, in the living room of a twice-convicted felon, an ex-con, surrounded by electronic and decorative items collected from previous burglaries, smoking dope, and being made privy to his recent crimes. There was something surreal about this, but also something deviant, for I was actively engaging in a crime of ceremony with him and hearing of his wrong-doings after prison. Perhaps turning off the tape recorder and turning on with him were necessities for establishing that level of trust, closeness, and rapport. After we returned to the recorded interviewing, he seemed more relaxed, up front, reflective, and, at the same time, less cautious than earlier. I felt that I came away with some excellent data made possible by a connection established through methods other than those promulgated by hard science, objectivity, and researcher neutrality—a connection lubricated by weed and drink. I had participated in human rather than stereotypical interviewer/participant exchange; he had willingly detailed activities that others had guarded. Departing from a science of distancing oneself from others allowed the human qualities, interactions, and rationales of doing crime to emerge.

This chapter is my confessional of participating in illegalities, intentionally taking sides, withholding information, deceiving, and lying to authorities, all while engaged in qualitative research into the decision making of property offenders and in a lengthy case study of a specific violent crime. I engaged in some of these actions as manifestations of siding with the underdog, and because I determined such actions would mostly benefit the research participants. Never were they intended to harm anyone, least of all the respondents, and I fully believe that no harm resulted from my decisions and actions. This essay reflects my "coming clean" by articulating these actions and the relationships between the participants and myself. Such actions are probably not that unusual, for the reflexive dynamics of human interaction within research settings often yield problems the solutions of which are not covered in the latest methodological treatises (and today are best confronted in feminist methodologies). The unusual quality is that such confessions rarely appear in print. Indeed, the methodologies of "muddy boots" and "grubby hands" implicitly mean taking sides, recognizing the politics of one's research, engaging in impression management, and hedging the truth. But actually writing about such things is, at some level, liberating, and it is indicative of political acts and decisions—a confessional, so to speak, as things are revealed that usually don't appear on the front stages of scholarly publications and that are tangential to other research strategies.

Deception and Lying

Whenever we as researchers gain entree into the world of deviants and personally learn the activities of hustlers, thieves, and drug peddlers, for example, we become privy to information normally accessible only to occupants of such

Kenneth D. Tunnell. "Honesty, Secrecy, and Deception in the Sociology of Crime: Confessions and Reflections from the Back Stage." *Ethnography at the Edge: Crime, Deviance, and Field Research.* Pp. 206–220, 1998. Reprinted by permissions of Northeastern University Press.

trades. A resultant problem, and one described by other ethnographers, is that legal authorities may learn of the research and exact damning information from researchers. During my interview research with property criminals, I was aware of the possibility that crime-control managers might demand access to the data. After all, I had information about crimes (and in several cases violent ones) that remained unsolved.

To ensure that such access was never gained and to maintain confidentiality, I initiated certain safeguards. For example, I never spoke participants' names during the recorded interviews, which were themselves quickly transcribed and the tapes erased. Although I kept an identifier list and assigned numbers to pertinent information obtained from individuals' case files, names were not connected to the information from the files or interviews. If, by chance, legal authorities learned of the project, realized that I had information about crimes that had not been cleared, decided to subpoena my records, and in the end actually gained access to them, they would have only nameless files. If ordered to court and directed to relate a particular transcript to an individual participant, I was prepared to lie by claiming that it was simply impossible to connect specifics to a single person from the dozens interviewed. This was a calculated strategy to minimize risks to the participants, to myself, and to the success of this research. I was prepared to deceive and lie to authorities if ever questioned about the particulars of my research, and, as the following reveals, I did just that.

During the property offender study, I interviewed an individual in prison who, I discovered afterwards, had assumed the identity of a man who actually had died in the mid-1960s (I will refer to him as Jimmy Morini). Everyone believed he was Morini. His case files used that name, prison administrators called him Morini, and, in the end, his false identity played a significant part in his early release from prison and placement in a halfway house. I learned of his charade within a week of the interview but immediately decided to keep the information to myself. If prison authorities became suspicious of him on their own, I had decided, they would have to discover his true identity without my assistance. Not long after his placement in the halfway house, he and the director appeared unannounced at my office and asked when I would interview him for the second and final time. Not wanting to reveal information to someone with power over his post-prison life, I simply told them that I believed we had gathered enough information from his first interview and that his services no longer were needed.

That seemed to satisfy them both for a time. Another member of the research staff, though, casually told someone that we knew this man was not Morini. Word then spread to the halfway house director, who shortly afterward phoned and confronted me with this information. I denied it was true and claimed that he had been misinformed. I lied. I lied and was glad that I did. I lied and today remain happy that I did. Although the director was only one bureaucrat among many, I presumed that he, nonetheless, would be compelled to report the truth as I knew it about Jimmy, and that those with decision-making powers would then have reason to adversely affect his confinement. I thought too about the raw emotional response likely to result from authorities' realization that the entire corrections department had been duped by a three-time loser. Their response, I feared, would be quick, decisive, and repressive. Thus, I intentionally deceived state agents. I deceived them not necessarily because I endorse or practice a conflict methodology, but because I believed providing them with accurate information was (1) irrelevant to the research and (2) not my responsibility, since it was easily available to state managers just as it had been to me. Furthermore, revealing the truth as I knew it to state officials was and is completely contrary to my personal position as a sociologist in the study of crime. These concerns with safeguarding data were heightened during later research.

During a rather lengthy case study that a colleague and I conducted, public defenders, after learning of our research, threatened to subpoena our interview audiotapes, to petition the courts to issue an injunction against us, and to question us under oath about our conversations with our interviewees. Their threats centered on a murder case that we were researching. The defendant, their client, was on death row for the murder. The public defenders had hoped that their appeal, which was in its initial stages, would proceed quietly and remain unknown to the small yet emotionally charged community where the murder had occurred. They feared that our involvement likely would arouse public curiosity about their legal proceedings. When they learned of our case study, they assumed the worst-case scenario and, to prevent our research from becoming known to the wider community, thought it best to silence us—to bring our study to a halt. During a heated two-hour conversation, the attorneys told us that in order to prevent (1) the state's investigation of some of our interview participants, (2) an injunction, and (3) a suit from being filed against us, we must cease the research and, furthermore, deliver to them all materials requested, including specific field notes, interview audiotapes, and interview transcripts. With all of this coming from an office whose work actually had our support and sympathy, we felt we had been blindsided. No matter how much we explained that our raw data simply would not be made available, we had no impact on the attorneys. We left their office having resolved nothing except to reconvene in a few days.

We were faced with a moral dilemma because we had approached the appellate lawyers and elicited their participation in our research, believing that it was important to interview them and hoping that they would arrange an interview with their client. We had intended to win their confidence and support. Suddenly we were confronted with the realization that neither was likely and that they were engaged in an all-out assault on our research and academic freedom.

In the interim, we devised a strategy to minimize risks to our interview participants (to whom we felt indebted; indeed, I had become close with one specific individual), to ourselves, and to the integrity of our study. We had no choice but to refuse to surrender anything—field notes, participants' names, or interview transcripts. We thus decided simply to lie and tell the attorneys that, due to their threats, we had destroyed the tapes and transcripts in question. Furthermore, we decided to let them know that our research would proceed, that their threats of an injunction and lawsuit instilled no fear in us whatsoever, and that if their desire was to have a quiet appeal, then intimidating us likely would produce just the opposite. We believed a good poker face would conceal our nervousness and our concerns that they just might initiate the threatened legal proceedings.

When we later met and stated our position, they were angered but realized we had called their bluff and there was little they could do. We had anticipated this re-action. Still, we had taken a calculated risk, since they very well could have en-gaged in the legal jockeying they had intimated. The risk was especially grave because our university had refused to support our research, having defined the case as a political lightning rod due to public outrage about the murder and its po-sition in the appellate process. This was a painful time during an otherwise re-warding case study, when the potential for risk to our participants, our academic freedom, and ourselves was very real. We proceeded with the case study, and pub-lished three manuscripts from it; the attorneys' client won a new trial on appeal.

Much of our concern during the case study had centered on one specific partic-ipant—an attorney who had first represented their client. Forrest had been the first person interviewed during this case study, and he was the person with whom I had established a long-term friendship. He had given us information that probably violated a lawyer-client confidence (as the appellate lawyers had claimed), but he was committed to this case and to saving the defendant's life. He believed, as did medical professionals, that the offender was insane, that justice had not been served, and that this case represented a story deserving of academic investigation. Forrest was first an interviewee, but he became my friend through-out our several other meetings about this case and also in our time together apart from this research. We had become close, and getting close to participants means confronting, with head and heart, the myth of value-free sociology, for it was no longer possible to be simply objective toward this participant. He had become nonnegotiable. Much of my decision to safeguard him and our secrets was not based on some rational standard of scientific evaluation. Rather, it was based on "emotion work," an "intentional display of affect that is self-induced and man-aged in accordance with others' expectations." We were and are friends, which means emotion was crucial to the ongoing conflicts over this research, the data, our academic freedom, participant protection, and confidentiality. Thus, lying and deceiving those in positions of power over Forrest, the research, and myself became the only choice. There was no calculation, no debate. The decision was a simple one.

Deception, which is central to a sociology of crime, is two-pronged: it involves misleading participants and duping those with only peripheral affiliation to the research. Regarding the first, there is widespread support for being truthful with participants and making them aware of research objectives, confidentiality, and their roles. Some researchers, though, have used deception to gain entree and knowledge not possible otherwise, and have apparently caused no harm to the deceived; without a charade, they were powerless to access the worldview that participants suspiciously guard. Others advocate deception; while they claim that bureaucratic, informed consent and human-rights processes are liberal intrusions into the world of social science, they also maintain the objectives of learning and of avoiding harm, injury, or exposure to participants.

The second form is deceiving those whose positions of official power (e.g., legal authorities) allow them to adversely affect participants, researchers, and researchers' work. Prison guards, university administrators, bureaucrats, and attorneys each possess the power to make life miserable for participants and researchers alike. In some cases, it becomes necessary for researchers to deceive those individuals who are not central to the study; at other times, such deception is not only necessary but also laudable. In both cases, power differentials are at work. And in both scenarios, participants, in the final analysis, are those most at risk and with the most to lose.

I did not have to contemplate deceiving participants to win their co-operation. They assessed the research, its objectives, its legitimacy, and me as one to be or not to be trusted. A precontractual solidarity, so to speak, was at work in our agreeing to certain conditions. I did deceive others who attempted to exercise their power over the research and participants. I believed it necessary, indeed commendable, and in the best interests of the research, the participants, confidentiality, and issues central to academic freedom.

Frontstage/Backstage

Analogous to the theatre, social rituals are composed of interactional performances and are typically stratified within distinct classes and power differentials. Research, like most social rituals, also is stratified and includes the crucial elements of cooperation, negotiation, communication, and power. The qualitative research strategy of interviewing implicitly contains ritualistic behaviors, props, roles, impression management, and frontstage/backstage distinctions. In qualitative inquiries, researchers seek information while participants judge and evaluate the questioning, the questioner, and just what is at stake. Each party engages in frontstage/backstage behavior, assuming a role for the other without revealing the complexities of the whole self, which is managed backstage. Interview research is based, in part, on maintaining this distinction, for while rapport and trust are essential to successful interviews, the conversation is usually unidimensional, as the researcher questions and the participant answers, yielding, submitting, and revealing whatever it may be that the researcher elicits and whatever the participant is willing to bring to center stage. Researchers (in some cases) maintain a professional frontstage appearance that guides directed conversation with a specific objective—vastly different from a conversation among friends, for example. Participants also maintain a frontstage role, fully aware that an interview, rather than a friendly conversation, is in progress. Thus, that which is exposed by participants is no doubt qualitatively different from revelations occurring in more intimate and informal contexts. A participant's presentation of self is guided by the context, purpose, and power differentials at work within the social ritual of interviewing.

Interviewing which is satisfying and fulfilling to researchers and participants involves a process where participants move from the frontstage of presentation of self to the backstage, through the backdrops and heavy curtains of suprapersonal insulation, to yet other backstages. On these backstages are acknowledged those thoughts, actions, motives, and rationales that typically are not revealed on the frontstage, where maintaining an appropriate and ideal image of self is all-important. On these extreme backstages, reflection and rapport in interviewing are at their best. This is where Robert and I traveled—or I should say, where he took me. Making the trip was no easy feat. I could not have forced him along. Nor could I have deceived him into making the passage. I believe the gist of explaining the journey lies in the social moment, the very essence of human interaction that is unique among (to stage only a few) social settings and conditions, individual characteristics, social chemistry, and even mindaltering substances. And perhaps by engaging in the ritual of marijuana smoking with Robert and responding casually to his admitted illegalities, I had been recast from simply "researcher" into someone whom he could trust, a co-participant. Traveling to these backstages is the raison d'être of interview research, and a process where the rich methods of reflexivity and *verstehen* are fundamental.

Reflexivity and *Verstehen*

Reflexivity is a fundamental component of the sociological tradition. Little progress toward developing full understandings of the textures of crime and its seductions is possible without a critical, reflexive methodology. This approach enlightens definitions of crime, revealing dimensions of pleasure, meaning, or expressiveness that otherwise likely would remain unknown. The participant's view (i.e., the emic) and the outsider's perspective, abstractions, and scientific explanations (i.e., the etic) are both essential to a sociology of crime. Good qualitative research is the mixture of the two, as researchers become integrated into the knowledge that is constructed and produced, as the "how" and the "why" of doing sociology become intertwined. As a result, researcher and respondent become co-participants in qualitative strategies that allow movement from frontstages to backstages, that enable rich understandings of the subjects' worldviews to emerge, and that place researchers in arenas where the lines of doing science while maintaining an objective distance from subjects become blurred.

A sociological *verstehen* of crime means accepting the subjective view-point and understanding actors' states of mind while rejecting the notion that science can deliver a complete or ontological reality. It also implicitly means that empirical knowledge is subjective and typically reflects (among other things) investigators' interests, values, and biases. As a result, a sociological *verstehen* of crime recognizes that relativity is central to doing social science. The interpretive requisite for sociology lies in making sense of rational action; for a sociology of crime, the focus is instrumentally rational action (i.e., *Zweckrationalität*), characterized most typically by behaviors aimed at attaining calculated, hedonistic, short-term goals. Understandings of those rich and subtle qualities of behaviors that are subjective, spontaneous, and situationally bounded—actions indicative of property criminals' performances, for example—are best gained through sociological *verstehen*.

Among Weber's dichotomy, it is *"erklarendes verstehen"* (as opposed to *"aktuelles"*) that is central to interviewing strategies regarding crime and criminals, for this methodology places particular acts within "a broader context of meaning involving facts which cannot be derived from immediate observation of a particular act or expression." Although interview accounts are retrospective, we arrive at an explanatory understanding of motives, decisions, and rationales, for example, that emerge within a particular context of meaning and that are significant to and reflective of the individual whose action is being studied. This does not imply that the real and unequivocal truth is attained, for subjective self-reflection is relative. Rather, what is attained is a subjective truth that gets closer to realities and intended meanings, as subjects define them, than does the data generated by other methodologies. Although inherently incomplete, such an approach nonetheless produces rich explanations which represent the defining characteristics of action communicated by researchers' co-participants. In other words, what emerges from a sociological *verstehen* of crime are reflections on backstage behaviors. But as such reflections emerge, researchers often discover, as I did with Robert and Forrest, that sides must be taken.

Taking Sides

Taking sides does not necessarily mean siding with the underdog (as those who take sides are nearly always accused of—such "subjectivity" of course rarely is applied to sociologists who overtly take sides when serving as the system's lackeys). Perhaps those groups most commonly seen as underdogs are oppressed people—racial minorities, women, prisoners of conscience, and the dispossessed and powerless. But the concept is not solely applicable to those groups. Clearly, the new religious right, the moral majority, and antichoice movements all represent underdogs in one fashion or another. There is a distinction then in siding with the underdog and with particular kinds of underdogs. The point with regard to taking sides, as I see it, is advancing a humanist sociology which promotes definitions of crime and criminality that reflect efforts at humanizing the crime control industry, gaining economic parity, and lessening racist, sexist, and oppressive social behaviors. Sociological traditions from Comte to Durkheim, from Marx to Sutherland, from the Schwendingers to current feminist and peace-making sociologies of crime, have called for praxis, that is, for siding with particular kinds of underdogs with the objective of advancing human-centered explanations and solutions for social problems. As this chapter attests, I have done my fair share of taking sides while engaged in the sociology of crime. An additional confession further illustrates this.

In one inhospitable county jail where a research participant found himself incarcerated only three months after his release from prison, I witnessed his confronting the ugly realities of racism. I knew from personal experiences that this county was known for having a racist history and culture. The participant, a black male, expressed anger over his treatment and resentment over the racist policing (as he defined it) in that part of the state. I too was treated unkindly and with grave suspicion by jail officials, because it was he I had come to interview.

Beyond the formal interview, I witnessed this man personally struggle against the injustices of a generations-long tradition, an overtly hostile criminal justice system, and the harsh realities of racist selective incapacitation. During our conversation, we talked more about race than crime; more of injustice than justice; more of empowerment than acquiescence. I surmised that discussing these issues was as important, perhaps more important, than focusing explicitly on the interview. The next day, I ventured out to a local used book store and bought copies of *Manchild in a Promised Land* and *The Autobiography of Malcolm X* and mailed them to him, while wondering if he would receive them or if they would be intercepted by jail authorities. The brief time that we spent together, our common concerns of ongoing racism, our conversations about power and imprisonment, and the simple task of buying him two used books are but modest examples of taking sides on a particular issue and with a particular individual. But beyond that, he had a profound impact on me, reinforcing the axiom that qualitative research is a social process and, as feminist methodologies remind us, is both personal and political. In that situation, not taking sides would have represented a valueless cop-out.

Regarding my choices, one may say, "You sided with known felons who duped state officials"—a point I cannot deny. I sided with those men because I believed I owed them greater allegiance than I did to crime control industry officials. They were co-participants in ongoing studies who had been guaranteed confidentiality and who had placed their faith in my assurances. I had promised state officials nothing. My research sought the cooperation of both authorities and participants, but I only pledged allegiance to the latter. Contrary to the tenets of a conflict-oriented methodology, my purposes were largely benign. My intentions were to avoid conflict with legal authorities and the conditions that would compel me to deceive them intentionally, or to simply withhold information that I determined they had no business knowing. Furthermore, I believed some deception acceptable, especially in cases where being forthright would have adversely affected participants. My decisions to take sides did not simply result from ideology, praxis, or commitment, although each was pertinent to my decisions to engage in the actions described here. My choices were shaped by my own personal limitations, experiences, values, and interpretations. Sociology, happily, is not value free, but is filtered through human qualities and emotions and, as a result, is both limited and liberated by the human state.

Conclusion

These reflections on doing the sociology of crime illustrate some of the benefits and rewards involved in qualitative research—a strategy that is both liberating and restrictive. While survey research certainly minimizes the risks and conundrums described here, the rich, insightful explanations that emerge from qualitative methods remain unparalleled. Doing sociology is greater than simply learning about a particular problem or population. It is an ongoing lesson in how to relate to divergent groups of people, establish rapport, win confidence, and assist participants in opening up and revealing those subtle complexities of social life that are most fully tapped through qualitative methodologies. Such strategies demand that researchers take risks, weigh ethical considerations, ponder just what assurances of confidentiality actually mean, and question just how far they are willing to go to obtain data while at the same time protecting their data, their academic integrity, and their co-participants. Such strategies are the heart and soul of qualitative sociology and are those characteristics that set it apart from other, perhaps less eventful, methodologies.

As I personally have learned, sociologists engaged in the study of crime are particularly vulnerable and often find themselves on the wrong side of the law simply by doing their research. These problems are indicative of the micro-politics of social research and point to political constraints on social scientists' willingness to truly confess revelations about their investigations, their participants, and their interpersonal relationships. Knowledge of criminal/deviant activities alters researchers' performances, as selective revelations are made publicly on the frontstages of scholarly publications, and as allegiances and relationships are maintained on the backstages, all within the negotiated politics of the sociology of crime.

Some sociologists have admitted (sometimes more explicitly than others) that their work has taken them to the edges of crime and, at times, beyond. Others have witnessed crimes as they unfold, and still others have heard admissions of crimes that remain unsolved. Doing the sociology of crime and deviance often places researchers in situations where there is no neutral ground. We become enmeshed in personal contradictions and are caught between dual worlds as values that are not meant to be relevant become germane. Ideological, political, ethical, and scientific decisions are made; choices are weighed; lines are drawn; sides are taken. The choices we make speak loudly about each of us as individuals, our relationships to our participants, and how we choose to live as qualitative researchers—for sociology or off of it.

References

Tunnell, Kenneth D. 1998. Honesty, secrecy, and deception in the sociology of crime: Confessions and reflections from the backstage. Pp 206–220 in Jeff Ferrell and Mark S. Hamm (Eds.) *Ethnography at the Edge: Crime, Deviance, and Field Research.* Boston: Northeastern University Press.

Part 2: Down and Dirty Ethnography: Illustrations of Qualitative Research

The research produced by qualitative methods is often the type of research this may be considered marginal, dangerous, or simply "different." This view is really not accurate, though. Such labels are given to research of this variety because the topics are often outside those that are focused on by quantitative researchers. But, when studying people and communities that are deviant or different, or simply not what everyone is used to interacting with on daily basis, it may be most beneficial to do such a study using qualitative methods. The articles in this section all highlight the ways that qualitative methods can be used, and the different approaches of qualitative methods, for gaining a better understanding of social groups and communities.

The first article in this section by Tewksbury and Gagne focuses on ways in which researchers are perceived by participants in research projects and in communities in which researchers work. The central issues in this discussion are how researchers can manage their behaviors and appearance so as to increase the likelihood that they will be positively perceived and ultimately accepted by those whom they are trying to research. By drawing on their own experiences with a variety of different groups and communities, the arguments in this article suggest that researchers using qualitative methods need to devote a significant amount of attention and energy to managing how they are perceived by the communities in which or with which they work.

The next article, by Wright, Decker, Redfern and Smith, looks at how a group of researchers studied burglars who were actively engaged in breaking into and stealing from homes. The research reported in this article comes from intensive interviews and fieldtrips that were conducted by the research team with persons who were involved in burglaries. In this research, both the persons being studied and the ways that the research were conducted illustrate the different and beneficial ways that qualitative methods can be used. Working with active criminals and doing so in ways that included not only explicit discussions of how, where, when, and why their crimes were committed but also traveling through the community to see the locations where crimes were committed involves a fair amount of danger for the researchers. Also, the creativity that goes into finding and developing trust with such persons is an excellent example of the challenges of qualitative research.

The third article in this section reports on a research endeavor by Miller and Selva that included a researcher actually working undercover in a narcotics market. The research is based on data gathered by way of covert participant observation and shows yet another way that qualitative methods can be used to access the worlds of hard-to-access populations. The activities of both the drug industry participants and law enforcement agencies were observed and compared with publicly stated and endorsed government objectives. In this way the use of qualitative methods provides understandings of people and activities that would not otherwise be accessible.

These same themes can also be seen in the fourth article in this section. In this article Hopper and Moore use interviews and observations to look at the role of women in outlaw motorcycle gangs. These groups, because of their actual activities and the way in which they have historically been treated by law enforcement and other "official" agencies, are difficult to infiltrate, and it is also difficult to gain the trust of their members. But, as this article shows, drawing on one researcher's contacts inside the social world, these authors know how some of the more secretive aspects of biker life transpire. If those being studied in this research had known that they were being studied and that their actions were going to be reported to outsiders, it is likely that they would have barred the researcher(s) from observing them. In this way, the strengths and potential weaknesses of such an approach to conducting research are highlighted in this article.

The use of covert observational techniques and the value of being a known and trusted community member are also highlighted in Nguyen's article on illegal gambling in Vietnamese cafes. Using some innovative approaches to recording data and conducting the research, Nguyen shows that it is possible to use qualitative methods to produce research that outlines the structure and the activities of a social world. Through approaches that could not be replicated using quantitative methods, this article shows how the setting operates as a social world and how the various actors in that world all play important roles in the conduct of the setting's activities.

Finally, in the last article in this section Tewksbury discusses how researchers can navigate the process of disengaging from the settings where they do their research. As this discussion highlights, ending a research project involves much more than just ending interviews or stopping one's attendance in a setting. Instead, the process of curtailing a qualitative research project is likely to involve a number of personal and professional questions about ethics, obligations, and responsibilities. These are issues with which quantitative researchers do not have to contend, and how these issues are addressed and questions answered can clearly impact the outcome of a research project. So too, Tewksbury argues, can these issues and questions have important implications for the researcher.

All in all, these six articles present overviews of the ways that different qualitative methodologies can be used and how these methods can produce different results and outcomes. The important thing to keep in mind as you read these articles is to think about how the actual approaches used by the researchers may or may not have influenced the ultimate conclusions of the research. Ask yourself how quantitative methods might have been able to address these research topics, and if quantitative methods could have produced the knowledge that these qualitative endeavors produced. If we think about how the methods of data collection and analysis influence the content of the research findings, we are moving ourselves to a higher level of analytic and critical thinking.

Questions to Consider

1. How do the actual means by which researchers collect their data influence what the outcomes and conclusions of a research project will be?

2. Would it be possible for any researchers to study any topics using qualitative methods? What are the limitations that some researchers may face when they attempt to study different types of people and communities?

3. What types of information can be learned using qualitative methods that might not be able to be learned using quantitative methods?

4. What are the disadvantages and costs (personal and professional) of using qualitative methods in your research?

1. Assumed and Presumed Identities:

Problems of Self-Presentation in Field Research

**Richard Tewksbury
and Patricia Gagné**

Understanding how qualitative researchers utilize and manage identities in the conduct of field research is a critical, yet underdeveloped, field of inquiry. This article explores the ways that qualitative researchers can facilitate their work through management of their presented identities. Central issues of establishing rapport and gaining trust, especially with stigmatized social groups, are examined in light of the authors' experiences. Drawing upon a diverse range of fieldwork experiences, this article addresses confronting erroneous assumptions about researchers' identities, managing multiple identities, the difficulties of competing field and professional identities, and the stresses that may arise from managing the politics of stigmas. Drawn together, these issues are presented as problematic, yet manageable and constructive influences on the conduct of field research.

Qualitative research often seeks to specify and elaborate on the varieties of identity and identity components that characterize social actors. Qualitative investigations are not explorations of concrete, intact frontiers; rather, they are movements through social spaces that are designed and redesigned as we move through them. The research process is fueled by the raw materials of the physical and social settings and the unique set of personalities, perspectives, and aspirations of those investigating and inhabiting the fluid landscape being explored.

Feminist and postmodern thought has well established that variances in researcher identities yield differing outcomes of the research process. However, it is not only the outcome—the data themselves—that are differentially constructed, but also the tone, direction, composition, and social placement of the research process itself (see Clough 1992). Understanding the ways the process and outcomes of the qualitative endeavor are shaped is not so much a science as an art. It is not a simple calculation of how the predetermined parts mix and congeal, but rather an art of finding, examining, and placing in context the perceptions of those involved in the interactions that inspire the attributes of the interactional process.

Rapport is critical between researchers and those researched. The importance of a strong, positive rapport is intensified when the research endeavor involves a sensitive topic or a stigmatized population (see Lee 1993; Renzetti and Lee 1993). Among those of discredited character, body, or tribe (Goffman 1963), there commonly exists a trepidation concerning the approach of outsiders; however, trust may be facilitated when researchers accept stigma by association (but see also Anderson and Calhoun 1992).

The key to successful research with stigmatized groups is their willingness to "embark on a risky course of action" (Lee 1993, p. 123). This decision is based on trust and the rapport that precedes it. If and when the stigmatized feel accepted and respected and perceive some degree of similarity with their explorers, a relationship can proceed, and the qualitative researcher can pursue investigation of inhabitants' identities, identity components, and experiences (Bergen 1993).

The foundation for any relationship between researcher and researched is the set of perceptions and interpretations that both hold of one another. The social world operates on the basis of attributions, interpretations, and individual self-presentation (Goffman 1959; Berger and Luckman 1966; McCall and Simmons 1978). Self-presentation, however, is not something that field researchers can necessarily always guide to a desired outcome. Even for the most experienced and skilled, it may not be possible to select and completely construct how we are perceived. "We frequently discover that we are being linked with images and backgrounds we cannot hope to maintain. . . . The impressions we project—indeed, sometimes market—are only partially under our own management" (Miller et al. 1993, p. v). Thus, although we may try to present ourselves as accessible, trustworthy, and worthy visitors to the communities we study, we can never be certain of how members of such communities perceive us.

The task, then, becomes to identify how entrée can be gained, rapport established, and trust built, and how one's self-presentation can be managed to optimize the degree and likelihood of these crucial elements of research being completed. On some issues, management is relatively simple: The selection of interviewers should focus on personal and visible physical or social traits that complement those of the population under study (Warren and Rasmussen 1977; Reinharz 1992; Bergen 1993; Coxon et al. 1993). However, more important than simply manipulating the status of the field researcher, and perhaps more costly (in terms of physical, psychic, and scholarly energies), qualitative researchers' presentation of self must be attuned to issues of masking and unmasking actual social identities and constructing and presenting virtual social identities (Goffman 1963).

Within the research terrain, identity management and interpretations encompass both focused and unfocused interactional realms (Goffman 1963). *Focused interactions* are the range of structured contexts where actors reciprocally acknowledge one another and strive to sustain a solitary point of attention. *Unfocused interactions* encompass a broader range of time and space circumstances in which actors may or may not acknowledge one another, yet are nonetheless provided with opportunities to assess one another. Unfocused interactions operate on the basis of interpretation of appearances, artifacts, and presented behaviors. In these circumstances, the actor who is not closely attuned to the management of his or her identity presentation can and often does appear in ways that destroy or weaken the establishment of rapport.

It is important to maintain a focus on the fact that identity management is a process at work among those being researched as well as among researchers

(Douglas 1972; Daniels 1983; El-Or 1992; J. Miller 1995). Furthermore, the interpretation of the researcher by the subjects works to shape and determine the management strategies used by investigators. Interactions rely not only on appearances, but on the meshing of multiple sets of perceptions and interpretations that are complementary (see Goffman 1963).

In a research setting, therefore, it is the researcher's responsibility to seek to construct the research—including gaining entrée, establishing rapport, earning trust, and gathering data—in a way that will result in the collection of valid and complete data. This construction requires a positive relationship, which is the product of the researched arriving at and maintaining particular perceptions of the researcher. Although specifically about ethnographers, Van Maanen's (1982, p. 112) observations are valuable advice in general: "A good part of fieldwork is simply being attentive to the impressions one's presence and activities cast off." Our discussion focuses on the role of the qualitative, interview-based researcher in structuring and managing the research process through the presentation of self. It has been our experience, paradoxically and despite careful management of self in the field and among our colleagues, that erroneous assumptions have been made about our identities and the motivations behind our work. Drawing upon experiences where our identities have been presumed, we seek in this article to identify the ways stigmatized, marginalized groups' perceptions of qualitative researchers influence the possibility of gaining entrée to the community, the establishment of rapport, the earning of trust; and to identify how these three crucial elements of qualitative research in turn affect the ability to gather and report valid and complete data. Our secondary goal is to discuss the strategies we have found to be successful and unsuccessful in facilitating our research on marginalized or highly stigmatized groups.

Background Studies

During the winter and spring of 1986–1987, Gagné conducted ethnographic research to examine the lives of Appalachian women, with a specific focus on their experiences with domestic violence and patriarchal control. The research consisted of part-time residence with a family in the region, participant observation in the community, and semistructured, in-depth interviews with resident women (see Gagné 1992). In a separate project, from 1992 to 1994, Gagné conducted in-depth interviews with battered women who had been convicted of killing or assaulting abusive mates or stepfathers and who, while incarcerated, had been granted clemency for their crimes. In this project, a snowball sampling method was used, with the initial list of contacts provided by Ohio's former First Lady, Dagmar Celeste. Through contacts made while in the field, Gagné ultimately was introduced to and interviewed 12 of the 26 women who had received clemency (see Gagné 1996).

Since 1991, Tewksbury has worked conducting in-depth interviews with more than 70 individuals living with HIV disease. Throughout this work interviewees have been recruited through social service agencies, advertisements, and personal referrals. Following the completion of interviews, averaging 3 to 5 hr in length, interviewees have commonly reported the experience as highly positive and personally beneficial. For Tewksbury the process has been highly productive and very stressful. Not only have there been the numerous usual stresses of recruiting, scheduling, completing, coding, analyzing, and writing up the research, but there have also been the stresses of attending participants' funerals and listening to deathbed discussions of frustrations and dissatisfactions with family, friends, medical providers, social service agencies, and society in general. Whereas many interviewees reported the research experience to be empowering, the exact opposite has been the case for the researcher (see Tewksbury 1994a, 1995a, 1995b).

Tewksbury's previous work has included participant observation in adult bookstore video peepshows and participant observation with traveling troupes of male strippers. In the first project Tewksbury spent afternoons, evenings, and late nights attending and "potentially participating" in the activities of men slowly circulating through the hallways of peepshows, reviewing the posted advertisements for sexually explicit videos playing in individual booths, and cruising for sexual partners (see Tewksbury 1990, 1993a). In the study of male strippers, Tewksbury spent more than 2 years, first interviewing dancers and later traveling and working with one troupe of male dancers (see Tewksbury 1993b, 1994b).

Since 1994, both authors have conducted research on transgendered people, specifically transsexuals, cross-dressers, and gender radicals. The research has consisted primarily of semistructured in-depth interviews ranging from 2 to 4 hr, with participant observation of support groups during times when we were recruiting volunteers for our work. All but one of the people we have interviewed were born male and have adopted temporary or permanent identities as women. We have solicited respondents through actual and virtual (e-mail) support groups, with the assistance of highly visible members of the community. While recruiting volunteers through actual support groups, it has been necessary for one of us to attend meetings and interact with the group. In these settings, we have presented ourselves as outsiders who are interested in and empathetic with the group. Most fieldwork and interviews have been conducted by Gagné, who had limited exposure to the transgender community prior to this research project. Initially, she found the research to be very stressful, in part because of questions about self-presentation and the way she was perceived by others. After beginning to learn the norms of the subculture, she became somewhat relaxed and was able to adopt a persona as a somewhat knowledgeable, empathetic outsider, eager to learn as much as members of the community were willing to teach her about their experiences and lives.

Insider-Outsider Issues

In the work of the present authors, the need for careful management of presented identities—or what Van Maanen (1982) has called "character display"—has been clearly established. In the study of rural Appalachian women living with domestic violence, Gagné (1992) found it necessary to establish herself as a member of the community, attached to and under the control of men who were known and trusted in the region. Tewksbury's (1990) work in adult bookstore video peepshows necessitated the presentation of an appearance suggesting subcultural knowledge and interactional willingness. Without such presented virtual social identities, access, trust, and interactions would not have transpired and the research could not have been accomplished. Examples abound in the literature to show the necessity of managing how qualitative researchers are perceived by inhabitants of the territory of interest. Brief perusal of the debate regarding the ethics of covert participant observation (Roth 1962; Humphreys 1970; Galliher 1973; Bulmer 1980; J.M. Miller 1995) or closed, highly suspicious organizations (Lofland 1966; Berk and Adams 1970; Robbins et al. 1973; Van Maanen 1982; Rochford 1985; Ayella 1993) make the centrality of this issue all too clear.

In pursuing a qualitative research agenda with stigmatized populations, several strategies involving the management of self-presentation may be used to gain access to valid and reliable data. It is well established that trust and rapport may be diminished and bias introduced when interviewer and interviewee are of significantly different social statuses (Berk and Adams, 1970; Landis et al. 1973; Freeman and Butler 1976; El-Or 1992; Johnson and Moore 1993). However, it would be naive to suggest that status congruence or complementarity alone can enhance trust and rapport, leading to a more productive and valid interview. Rather, as Wise (1987) has argued, it is the complex combination of status-based relationships and researcher skills that interact to produce interviews in which the respondents feel comfortable in the act of self-revelation. Or, as Riessman (1987) has suggested, researchers and interviewees can understand one another when they share "cultural patterns." Shared status (such as gender) is not enough. Nonetheless, when researchers share similar or marginally similar experiences with those being investigated, the research process may be enhanced by communicating similarities where they exist. Where researchers and respondents differ in obvious or subtle ways, investigators may establish rapport by communicating empathy for the group based on similar philosophies or world views. In some cases, such communication may simply be impossible for researchers, for example among extremists who advocate or practice violence (Scully 1990; however, see also Mitchell 1993); they must then work harder to establish trust and rapport in other ways, by communicating a commitment to unbiased research, assurances of confidentiality, and reflexive listening. However a researcher ultimately decides to manage a project, the first obstacle to be overcome in any research endeavor is to gain entrée to the group under investigation.

Gaining Entrée

Efforts to overcome the potential or, in some observers' view, likely obstacles to an effective and efficient research process can take any of several forms. Interestingly, however, very little literature exists addressing the problems that accompany efforts to gain entrée and the consequences of the fact that some persons will grant researchers access to settings and others will not (Lee 1993; however, see Herman 1995). Even when researchers clearly are not members of the communities they study, there can be roles constructed or discovered that facilitate research entrée (see Adler and Adler's 1996 discussion of the parent as researcher). Common assumptions (often implicit) in the literature suggest that entrée can be a very difficult task with stigmatized or criminal populations. This, we believe, is a largely faulty assumption. Our research, like Hagedorn's (1988) work with gangs and Wright et al.'s (1992) research with burglars, suggests that although gaining entrée may be a long, sometimes frustrating process, entrée certainly is achievable.

The lack of attention to how entrée is gained, in the eyes of at least one observer, may be for the best: "Nor are researchers necessarily wise while in the field to look too closely at why access has been granted. In so doing they might raise further and unwelcome questions in the minds of gatekeepers about whether the decision to permit the researcher entry was correct in the first place" (Lee 1993, pp. 119–120). We disagree with this view. In the study of stigmatized populations, one must first ask how entrée may be gained and then consider the potential benefits and consequences of any point of entry that is adopted.

In the realm of criminal justice (especially corrections) research, there is a growing movement to incorporate a team research approach in which a community insider and an outsider cooperatively pursue research (Schmid and Jones 1991, 1993; Jones 1995; Taylor and Tewksbury 1995). A second approach centers on presenting oneself as a potential community member, indicating a generally sympathetic view of the group and individuals that are the focus of the study (Lofland, 1966; Robbins et al. 1973; Rochford 1985). Alternatively, one can gain status and present oneself as a marginal member of the community or group, playing on membership in the community but ignorance of the finer points of community membership and life (Stack 1974; Hafley and Tewksbury 1996). Alternatively, it is possible to present oneself as a knowledgeable insider (Styles 1979; Levi Kamel 1980; Ronai and Ellis 1989) or as a semiknowledgeable, empathetic outsider (Smith and Batiuk 1989; Myers 1992; Leinen 1993; J. Miller 1995). Finally, in some instances, especially when negotiating access with a highly closed community or group, it can be beneficial to have a visible and respected individual who holds a position of authority, high respect, or leadership introduce one to the group (Whyte 1955; Boles and Garbin 1974; Foltz 1979; Van Maanen 1982; Herman and Miall 1990; Hopper and Moore 1990; Calhoun 1992; Jacobs 1992; Leinen 1993) or to provide direct referrals (Wright et al. 1992). When such a person takes an active role in facilitating access, he or she is likely to do so in one of three manners: as a bridge to link into a new social world, as a guide who points out what occurs and how culturally different actions are locally meaningful, or as a patron who helps to secure the trust of community members (Lee 1993).

The presentations of self the present authors have used to gain entrée and establish effective status-based relationships are (a) knowledgeable insider, (b) potential participant, (c) marginal member, (d) empathetic outsider, and (e) knowledgeable outsider working with a knowledgeable insider. In conjunction with these strategies, particularly in our investigations of highly closed groups, we have used a visible and respected community member to help us gain entrée, establish rapport, earn trust, and understand locally meaningful events. In Gagné's research on Appalachian women, entrée to the community was gained through a family friend, a member of the community who was known and respected by most in the region. As a marginal member of the community—one who spent weekends in Appalachia and weekdays at graduate school—she needed to gain the trust of men in the community, who served as gatekeepers to their own and other men's wives, daughters, and girlfriends. To persuade her host to sponsor her in the community, she needed to convince him that she was empathetic to the men's world view, that her research report would be unbiased toward men, and that helping her would be a favor to his housemate, her husband. To gain his trust, she presented herself in a manner very foreign to her actual identity, by behaving according to feminine gender norms within the community. Her actions included washing the dishes, cleaning the house, asking permission to leave the house, and deferring to men's decisions about daily activities. In short, she emulated women in the community through presentation of self. (Also, see Warren 1988 for a discussion of how gender may need to be managed for women to gain access to some research settings.) Over time, she gained his trust, and he began to serve as both a guide, explaining the cultural significance of local events and relationships, and as a patron, securing the trust of men in the community. Once contact with women outside the household was established, she needed to gain their trust so interviews could be scheduled and establish enough rapport so that respondents would talk freely about their experiences. To do so, she presented herself as the wife of a new man in the area and a marginal member of the geographic and cultural community, as well as the community of women who had experienced abusive relationships.

Similarly, in a separate project on battered women who received clemency, Gagné was initially dependent on the sponsorship of the former first lady of Ohio, Dagmar Celeste. In an initial exploratory interview, Celeste served as a guide who explained the history of the battered women's movement and how it related to the clemency decisions. By providing permission to "drop" her name, Dagmar Celeste served as a bridge into the world of activism and state decision making. To gain entrée with activists in the battered women's movement, Gagné needed to assure them she was sympathetic to their actions and ideologies. The use of the first lady's name was enough to do so in most cases, although a few feminists required further assurance that Gagné was sympathetic to their activism. To gain entrée with authorities, she needed to convince them either that she was unbiased or that she favored the decision and to imply that she would not write about it unfavorably. To gain entrée with the women granted clemency, she needed an introduction from a trusted insider, and to further establish rapport and engender trust, she needed to convince them she was empathetic to their experiences and the decisions they had made.

Tewksbury's identification and access to persons with HIV disease was enhanced by referrals and initial contacts made by a major, well-known social service agency. In this project, dependence on his role as a highly visible HIV educator in the community allowed him to approach interviewees with a request to have them assist in formalizing "what we all know already." This approach, coupled with his highly visible role, may have led to some selection bias on the part of interviewees: however, whatever costs were encountered are believed to have been offset by his wide acceptance in the HIV community. The employment of the role of "expert" often facilitates entrée. When researching politicized, stigmatized communities, the presentation of self as an empathetic expert (and truly being one) may be the only way to gain full entrée.

In our cooperative work with the transgender community, we gained entrée through our acquaintance with a highly visible and respected community leader who served as a patron, securing trust and providing introductions. Within the transgender community, there is a great deal of overlap in support groups' membership. Once we had gained entrée and established rapport and trust in one group, members who also belonged to or served in leadership positions in other groups served as patrons in the new groups. In essence, we relied on a "snowball patron" approach for facilitating our entrée to new groups. Within each group, our sponsors alerted us to potential social or political factions, making it easier for us to manage the recruitment and interview processes, except when our patrons were part or the cause of such rifts. In such cases, some people were more cautious than others during initial phases of interviews, until they became assured that the patron was simply an acquaintance, not a good friend. To reduce perceptions that we were too closely allied with a particular individual or faction, we publicly reduced our contacts with our patrons once the initial introductions were made. At public meetings, we were always careful to speak to our patron, but then to pursue other contacts quickly. When discussions of other individuals arose, we kept silent, and, if asked for an opinion, simply reminded the group that we needed to maintain our professional neutrality. In private interactions with patrons, we sought information about events and individuals but avoided commenting about them.

In our interactions with transgendered individuals, both in the field and during interviews, we have presented ourselves as empathetic outsiders (although we have been occasionally mistaken for actual or potential group members). When we have been mistaken for insiders or potential insiders, we have used humor when possible, conveyed our empathy with the group, and drawn upon our theoretical belief that gender is a social construction.

Despite the obvious benefits of having a high profile insider facilitate access and introductions, there are less obvious pitfalls. In all of these projects, some community members voiced hesitancy to consent to interviews or to disclose experiences and feelings fully because of the initial referral or contact from a visible—and sometimes disliked—community member. As Stack (1974) has argued, gaining entrée through authorities provides a biased view of the community under study. Clearly, some communities (especially stigmatized communities) may be distrustful of authorities and "professionals"; therefore, as many feminist researchers advocate, it may be advantageous to minimize one's professional status in interactions (Reinharz 1992). Although we acknowledge such concerns, we believe that all points of entrée produce potentially different phenomenological realities and, therefore, result in bias. In our own research, the authoritative introduction was facilitative, but in a minority of instances political maneuverings internal to the community under study introduced additional obstacles to be overcome. To engender trust and establish rapport with less trustful group members, we carefully selected and managed our self-presentations. This management resulted in a broader sample than would otherwise have been possible, leading to a broader phenomenological reality being revealed.

Community Perceptions of Researchers

When seeking entrée to work with stigmatized others, we found that it was not uncommon for community members to assume, or ask if, we shared the statuses that stigmatized members. Assumed identities are common; they are frequently deduced through one's interests, associates, or appearance. The fact that researchers possess virtual social identities is unavoidable, and needs to be recognized as such. "The mistaken belief that the researcher's role is unmitigated by those whom he or she studies remains the positivist's unachievable hope" (Mitchell 1993, p. 13). The ways that researchers present themselves to communities of study can shape and direct the expectations others have of the researchers. Similarly, the information not shared can also influence others' constructed identities for researchers (Mitchell 1993). Assumptions regarding researchers' identities can also be made in the absence of active identity management efforts on the part of researchers. In unfocused interactions, when researchers are attentive to instrumental task completion, community members may very well be attentive to the reasons researchers give for pursuing their line of research, whom the researchers know in the community, and details of physical appearance and interactional styles. From such cues, whether given intentionally or unintentionally, assumptions are made and expectations formed. In short, "any aspect of a researcher's identity can impede or enhance the research process" (Reinharz 1992, p. 26).

Letters of introduction and telephone calls requesting interviews are frequently the earliest impressions researchers make on potential respondents. Although most of us are careful to write a well-crafted letter or to explain ourselves clearly on the telephone, it is essential to remain aware that the names of associates one drops to engender trust or establish rapport become central cues in the presentation of self. This technique may create the dilemma of requiring the researcher to know about group factions and the affiliations of members while she or he is in the process of learning about the political landscape under investigation. In her research on the clemency decisions, Gagné gained permission to mention the names of those people who identified further potential respondents. She naively assumed that anyone who would grant permission for his or her name to be used would probably be on good terms with those to whom she was referred. Therefore, in all initial contacts, she mentioned the name of the person who had suggested she contact the respondent. In all but two instances, the contact person was one with whom the respondent was friendly or in philosophical agreement. In those two cases, however, authorities who thought the clemencies were politically inexpedient for the governor declined to be interviewed when the name of the person who suggested they be included was mentioned. In much the same way, Tewksbury's work with persons with AIDS, in which most introductions included mention of his professional affiliation with the social service agency, occasionally resulted in refusals to participate and active avoidance. Tewksbury quickly realized that it was necessary to investigate individuals' roles in the community so as to anticipate how best to make introductions and structure initial contacts.

When soliciting interviewees during the course of fieldwork involving face-to-face interaction, the cues one gives are often inadvertent—or "given off" (Goffman 1959)—unless one is extremely conscious in impression management and knowledgeable about the group under study. Almost without exception, when Tewksbury first encountered new members of the HIV community he would be offered food, a glass of water, or a hug. Although initially the participants seemed simply to be a very gracious and warm set of individuals, it soon became apparent that by such acts of kindness they were actually testing his comfort and knowledge of HIV. Somewhat differently, upon entrance to transgender support groups for the first time, we found that members were extremely attentive to the actions and reactions of the researcher(s) present. During interviews, group members explained that they watch all women closely to learn their mannerisms and other aspects of social presentation. However, it was Gagné's perception that during initial, and particularly public, interactions, members were scrutinizing and assessing her to see if she was, in fact, comfortable with the group and sympathetic to their experiences. For example, upon walking into a group meeting for the first time, one member approached and introduced herself, saying, "Hi, I'm 'Jane.' Are you here for the freak show?" At another meeting, held in a restaurant, Gagné arrived early with her patron, a cross-dresser. As members arrived, everyone looked closely at Gagné's face when approaching and attended closely to her clothing, voice, and mannerisms. After being introduced, several asked her hostess, "So, is she one of us?" Later that evening, the group adjourned to a bar, where they were joined by other transgenderists. Gagné went around the bar introducing herself, explaining our research, and asking for volunteers to be interviewed. During the process, she was approached several times by people asking, "So, are you a guy, or what?" In these interactions, it was imperative that Gagné (a genetic female) use humor to defuse awkward situations, admit when she did not know or understand part of the subculture, and convey empathy with the experiences and worldviews of the group. By presenting herself as a somewhat naive but empathetic outsider she was able to establish rapport with the group as one they would educate so that she could, in turn, educate others. Nonetheless, it is not enough for one to be able to fall back on naiveté. Although it is imperative to admit ignorance, rather than feign knowledge, the researcher must carefully manage the impression being made and base the presentation of self on as complete information as is available.

A diversity of interviewees in any project can make the management of self-presentations a tricky and stressful activity. This problem was made abundantly clear in Tewksbury's interviews with persons with AIDS when, one day after completing an interview with a self-defined punk performance artist, Tewksbury was "jokingly" told that he probably could not understand much of what the multiple-pierced man with barbed wire tattooed across his body had said, because Tewksbury was "such a conservative, middle-class type." Immediately following this exchange he drove to a second interview, where the 27-year-old medical student greeted him and commented, "You're a lot more liberal-seeming than I expected." Even managed identities can be interpreted very differently, and no matter how careful researchers may be about self-presentations, we can never be in total control of the impressions we make on others.

Ethical Dilemmas of Presumed Identity

When researchers know, or strongly suspect, that research subjects have attributed identities to them that are in fact different from their actual social identities, the question of whether to self-disclose information that would "correct" these assumptions is raised. This question rests on the more general issue of whether researchers should engage in any form of significant self-disclosure with interviewees. As is common with such issues, the answer is that it depends on the situation.

Daniels (1983) has argued that self-disclosures can be beneficial to the process and has suggested that it establishes a relationship based on exchanges of information. More adamantly, Hosie (1986, p. 206) has argued, "it is conversely unfair to expect a person to bare his/her soul without reciprocity." Such a position suggests that researchers hold a moral obligation to self-disclose. However, in some situations, the exchange of information may, in fact, act to dissuade subjects from open discussion (See Bombyk et al. 1985, cited in Reinharz 1992). In his work with persons with HIV disease, when interviewees assumed that Tewksbury was HIV-positive, they would often discuss at length their positive and negative experiences with a variety of health care providers. In reality, Tewksbury was HIV-negative at the time of the interviews, and many of the doctors, nurses, and therapists being discussed were his associates. When respondents entered interviews knowing of his organizational affiliations, only brief, superficial, and almost always positive comments were offered regarding health care providers. Obviously, disclosure quieted some subjects: it did not establish a relationship based on mutual exchange.

When the researched believe they have something to gain from the researcher, including simple knowledge, the offer of such disclosures after the completion of the formal interview can facilitate the research process. However, while respondents may be willing to trade information or favors, such offers of information may put researchers in the awkward situation of having to tell the truth. For example, at the end of our interviews with transgendered individuals, we always ask whether respondents have any questions they would like to ask us. Typically, we are asked how we became interested in the topic, when the research will be published, and how respondents may obtain a copy of our work. Occasionally we have been challenged with comments indicating that interviewees "know" we must be cross-dressers. Such challenges must be handled carefully, because the misinterpretation must be corrected without appearing to distance ourselves from the stigma. On occasion we have been asked to comment on the "convincingness" of interviewees' self-presentations as women. Particularly with those new to transgenderism, this situation can be very awkward. However, we have learned that constructive criticism is appreciated.

In summary, the dynamics of the situation need to be assessed, as well as the expectations and needs interviewees show for interactions, in determining whether researchers should engage in self-disclosure. In considerations of the special circumstances where self-disclosure would serve to alter assumptions held about researchers' identities, these issues become yet more complex. Not only must subjects' expectations and needs be assessed in general, but they must also be examined in terms of stigma politics. In our interviews with transgenderists, we have been unable to draw upon any status similarities between ourselves and our subjects. During interviews and other interactions when our research motives have been questioned or respondents have become defensive or reticent, we have been able to reestablish empathy by explaining that we believe gender is socially constructed and exists along a continuum. In all of our collaborative and individual research projects, when we have disagreed with the moral or ethical nature of our respondents' actions, we have reminded ourselves that we are not there to argue or judge, only to listen or observe. In short, we temporarily suspended judgement while in the field. It has been our strategy to play up similarities of status and worldview and downplay differences. When respondents' interpretations have clearly been based on untruths, we have corrected the mistake by explaining the degree of similarity, not difference, with the group under investigation.

Stated slightly differently, it is not necessarily the presentation of a virtual social identity in accord with one's actual social identity that is critical to the efficient and productive interview; rather, it is the presentation of commitment that matters. Although perhaps presenting ethical concerns in some instances, one does not always have to present oneself wholly and exclusively "accurately." A managed, and generally accurate, presentation of self that emphasizes similarities with interviewees and that displays empathy is more likely to be fruitful. Researchers can benefit from presenting themselves as having a strong commitment to the goals of their research (Berk and Adams 1970; Shaffir et al. 1980) and to the interviewee. As put forth by Daniels (1983, p. 199), in the interview situation, "Reciprocity, generosity, sympathy, and responsibility to informants are rewarded." It appears to be more important to present oneself as a caring, concerned person, and as a researcher who is dedicated to the research issue, than to concoct false status similarities to convince the stigmatized individual to trust one.

The Pragmatism of Presumed Identity

From our experiences, it appears that when a researcher seeks and gains entrée to stigmatized populations, members often assume or believe that the researcher is actually or potentially a member of the community. It is not uncommon for questions, both direct and indirect, to be posed to determine if the reading the community members have of the researcher's virtual social identity is accurate (Bergen 1993). This assumption may well be because of the strength of the stigmas felt by community members. Because they themselves are discredited in society, it is not surprising that such individuals may believe that only similarly stigmatized persons would be interested in them and their experiences.

It may well also be that their readings of appearances—physical, reputational, status-based, and managed—lead to community members' presumptions. When entering new and perhaps threatening interactions, interviewees bring with them interaction needs. One way to perceive the interview setting and process with less apprehension is to believe that the setting is "safe." For stigmatized individuals, the safest environments are those in which co-presenting others are similarly situated.

However, not only interviewees bring interactional needs to the interview setting; so do researchers. By way of identity management—manipulation of identity cues—researchers can and actively do construct virtual social identities (see Daniels 1983). Although researcher management of identity presentations may facilitate gaining entrée, some may question whether it is ethical for researchers actively to manipulate such aspects of self. On one hand, there is a degree of deception that is practiced in such instances. However, identities and appearances are always socially constructed, and the process of interpretation and reaction to appearances occurs, anyway. Because the investigator is necessarily going to be interpreted, it behooves the research process for the investigator to consider carefully his or her self-presentation and maximize its potential to garner entrée and facilitate rapport and trust. However, although one may "stretch" a marginal or potential identity, the researcher must carefully avoid fabricated virtual identities that simply do not exist. Interviewees can and do actively respond to what they perceive as researcher identities, based on presentations of self.

As social knowledge, the "truthful" answer to the question of whether a researcher is a community member may not be as simple as expected on first glance. Recognizing that membership in a stigmatized community comes in varying degrees and that statuses are interpretations of "facts," it may well be that, even if researchers do not actively define themselves as members of the communities under study, members may perceive the facts of researchers' biographies as indicating some degree of group membership. In some instances, both identity definitions may, in fact, be accurate. For example, Tewksbury was and is an activist in the HIV community although at the time of his fieldwork not HIV-positive. Similarly, while observing in bookstores, he was, in a sense, cruising: Although not following through on received sexual propositions, he was carefully watching others, just as the sexually interested patrons were doing. Because Gagné had never been seriously beaten, had never killed anyone, and had never been incarcerated, her self-revelations to some in the community that she had in fact been in an abusive relationship became very awkward when it became apparent that respondents had overinterpreted them. The dilemma of this overinterpreted identity was never more evident than when she was introduced to a support group for women who had killed or attempted to kill their abusers as, "This is Dr. Gagné. She's one of us."

What, then, if anything, should be done in response when researchers recognize that they are being perceived as a member of the community to which they are seeking research access or continued access? As we see it, there are four basic responses that may be used. First, researchers can let the incorrect assumption stand and use it to their benefit. Second, the attribution can be corrected, either directly with those with whom the researcher interacts or by informing members of the community's communication network and allowing the information to filter back to previous interviewees at a later date. Third, the assumption can be allowed to stand until the time that (more) interviews are conducted and corrections can be among the initial conversation topics at that time. Or, fourth, researchers can approach the dilemma as a nonissue, letting the assumption stand and not attending to whether corrections are made. Decisions on how to handle this dilemma can be based on whether the perceptions are true, the researchers' comfort with the "gray areas" of their similarities with group members, and the degree to which such misperceptions are overtly expressed. Particularly among highly stigmatized or marginal groups, it is imperative that corrections be made in such a way that respondents do not perceive that researchers are distancing themselves, either from the group or from the stigma. Even after interviews are completed, community members may talk to other potential respondents, conveying their perceptions of researchers' discomfort or efforts to distance themselves from stigma. Maintaining entrée, rapport, and trust within a community, even when interviews are completed, is an essential part of the process of managing a qualitative project. Even as they leave one geographic area for another, researchers must be ever mindful that there may be considerable overlap of membership among groups, and the impressions they make with a single respondent may make it easier or more difficult to gain access to the next group.

The Dilemma of Field Identities and Professional Persona

Qualitative researchers have devoted relatively little attention to the explicit stresses of their work, and especially to their need to manage identities in conducting fieldwork while simultaneously maintaining (or attaining) professional status (however, see Zigarmi and Zigarmi 1980; Warren 1988; Ronai 1992). In all qualitative research, decisions about the presentation of self are an inherent part of managing the project. In some cases, researchers may find it necessary to present different identities to varying audiences in one field of investigation while simultaneously wondering if those being presented are the "right" or "best" ones. At the same time, researchers must continue to manage their professional identities. Such worries as how public knowledge may affect one's private life and how courtesy stigmas may affect professional attainment or standing are an additional source of strain. For example, in her efforts to gain entrée to women in a small Appalachian community, Gagné had to convince men who could provide introductions in the

·

area that she was no threat to them and that it was safe for their wives to be interviewed. She did so by always introducing herself as the wife of one of the men who lived in the region, and if his name was not recognized, she mentioned that they stayed with "John," a long-time, trusted community member. The key to acceptance was convincing people that, were it not for her college career—which was probably a waste of time—she would be living there with her husband. This method brought up the obvious dilemma of presenting herself as someone she could have become, had she chosen not to pursue an advanced degree. During this period, she was also seeking to attain the status of sociologist by presenting herself at the university as a (potentially) knowledgeable professional. In the field, particularly around men, she had to be careful not to talk or know too much and always to defer to men's judgment. In interview settings, when she was alone with women, she needed to convince them that she was, in fact, knowledgeable about life in Appalachia, women's issues, and wife abuse, and she had to consider how much of her own abusive history to reveal. At the university, when discussing her research, she obscured her personal ties to the community in an effort to downplay her membership in a stigmatized group and to emphasize her professional standing. Being a chameleon in a diverse landscape is one skill an investigator must acquire; learning to discern the proper presentation of self based on knowledge of the landscapes and cues provided by research subjects and professional colleagues is another.

Identity construction and management can push researchers to question and reformulate their "true" identities. Those who conduct research in communities where they already have a significant degree of familiarity and involvement are most likely to encounter identity-based dilemmas. Adler and Adler (1996) have reported that the parent-as-researcher role can be very complex and presents numerous potential ethical questions. Whittier (1991) reported that by listening to the stories of lesbian feminist activists she came to recognize that her research and other activities qualified her as an activist. Similarly, in the midst of interviewing persons with AIDS, Tewksbury was approached by a researcher requesting an interview about his "HIV activism." It was not until this time that he realized he was an activist, and apparently so defined by others. To recognize that one is perceived differently than assumed is usually at least somewhat disturbing. Whereas feminist methodology accepts the breakdown of the "subject/object" dichotomy (Cook and Fonow 1990), positivism demands objectivity and the separation of researcher and respondent. Even among those who are trained in feminist methodologies, researchers frequently recognize, and at some level internalize, the higher status afforded positivist research methods. As an academic striving to be, and be seen as, an objective scientist, indisputable evidence of others' perceptions of one as a politicized actor can be disheartening. Recognition of his or her own activism can lead the neophyte researcher to question his or her legitimacy as a scientist—which is exactly what Tewksbury did.

Managing multiple identities may be a primary source of stress for field researchers. While touring with male strippers, Tewksbury was also a doctoral student and adjunct faculty member at several colleges and universities. Numerous awkward situations arose when students saw their sociology teacher arrive and work with the dancers. Similarly, even well-seasoned fieldworkers may add to the stresses of those managing multiple identities. Such was the case when a feminist qualitative methodologist in Tewksbury's department insisted that he "must be dancing" and reacted angrily when he "wouldn't invite her to one of his shows." Succeeding in both worlds can sometimes be interpreted as being a member of both.

On top of these stresses are the ethical dilemmas of the ethnographic "white lie," implied when one acts differently among varying groups and the stress involved in getting it right each time. Unless one is experienced in the field under investigation, we advise against the management of multiple identities.

Identity and Project Politics

Our experience in the field suggests that when researchers emphasize similarities of status or worldview to gain entrée to a community, members hold a tacit, or frequently overt, assumption that research reports will depict them in a favorable and uncritical fashion. Similarly, Mitchell (1993, p. 14) has suggested that "whatever fieldworkers intend their roles to be they are most often perceived initially as naive sympathizers." Such assumptions have the potential to create a moral dilemma for researchers.

The dilemma of respecting the trust of group members may be resolved in two ways. The first is to use the research report as praxis (see Lather 1986). Based on assumptions and goals of critical and feminist theory, research-based praxis seeks to decenter privileged groups and assumptions, holds a deep respect for the intellectual and political capacities of the dispossessed, and works toward social change and the empowerment of marginal or stigmatized groups (Lather 1986). For example, in her work with Appalachian women, Gagné conceptualized a continuum of methods used by men to control women and discussed women's efforts to assert autonomy in a patriarchal social setting. Similarly, rather than examining the lives of AIDS "victims," Tewksbury analyzed the sexual adaptations of persons *living with* HIV and their efforts to resist externally imposed stigmatizing labels by reclaiming the language used to construct their identities.

The second means of balancing the expectations of community members with researchers' needs is based in interpretive theory's goal for social research, which is simply to enhance understanding of a community. Weber's ([1913] 1981) concept of *verstehen* is particularly useful here. Although researchers may personally condemn or approve of the behaviors, lifestyles, and worldviews of communities under investigation, interpretive theory demands that descriptions of the group be written from the perspectives of community members. Analyses that help readers understand the community and the unusual behaviors or worldviews of its members are likely to be accepted by the community under study. For example, respondents in our research on transgenderism have frequently expressed the belief that we will write research reports advocating transgenderism. In the field, we have corrected such misperceptions by explaining that we believe gender is socially constructed and exists along a continuum and that our goal is to understand the transition process from the perspectives of those who have lived it. We have also explained that once we have described the transformation processes, we will also analyze the sociological factors that encourage or impede the transition from one gender category to another (see Gagné and Tewksbury 1996).

Researchers need not agree with or depict in a favorable light all aspects of group beliefs or behaviors, but it is imperative that they make an effort to include the perspectives of those under investigation. By providing a critical examination of the social context of the community under investigation, researchers may advance understandings about the social factors that lead to group members' behaviors. Respondents may or may not agree with researchers' analyses of their situations, but if the perspective of the group is depicted accurately and completely, analyses are likely to be respected, if not held in agreement. In short, whereas researchers may emphasize similarities in status or worldview to gain entrée to a community, they must demonstrate commitment to the research project without violating the trust of the community in reporting their findings.

Conclusion

In any qualitative examination of stigmatized groups, gaining entrée, establishing rapport, and building trust are essential to the success of the research project. Among stigmatized groups, rapport and trust are most likely to be engendered when researchers emphasize their similarities with the group members. However, managing what the researched perceive about the researchers is not always easy, efficient, or even possible. It is not uncommon for those being studied to presume identities of researchers, often erroneously. This problem may very possibly result in ethical dilemmas and practical difficulties for those seeking to pursue a research agenda efficiently.

When trying to manage the research setting and their own identity presentations, researchers may encounter uncertainties regarding how individual members of researched communities will, in fact, construct virtual social identities for them. Although this goal is perhaps not entirely possible, it is critical that all qualitative field researchers carefully attend to the cues—both obvious and subtle—that the researched give off (Goffman 1959). Both direct and indirect interactional markers need to be observed, especially in unfocused interactions, where the attributions and identity definitions held by the researched concerning researchers may best be discerned. Both verbal and nonverbal communications can be instructive for identifying how one is being constructed in the eyes of others.

What we find in the end is an affirmation of the belief that qualitative fieldwork is more of an art than a science (if we apply traditional definitions). To know *how* to do fieldwork, one must experience fieldwork. To understand if, when, where, and with whom approaches are efficient and effective may require experimentation. To know when a piece of fieldwork is "good" requires the observer to know what it is like to be in the field. Knowing about fieldwork means knowing about what it is like to be in the field.

We hope this discussion has accomplished two tasks. First, it has been our intention to make clear that identity management is something that simply must be done, something of which researchers must be aware at all times in pursuing qualitative fieldwork. Identities are constructed, and continually reconstructed, throughout the fieldwork process. Knowing that how they wish to be perceived may not be how they really are perceived can attune researchers to both practical and ethical dilemmas in their work.

Second, we hope that this discussion will reinvigorate a dialogue about the pragmatic issues involved in conducting qualitative fieldwork. By sharing our experiences, and discussing them in the above outlined conceptual framework, we hope we have shed some light on issues of identity management of which other (both novice and experienced) qualitative researchers may be unaware. To discuss the theoretical, philosophical, and political underpinnings of qualitative methods can be fruitful; but so can frank, honest discussions of what works, and what does not work, in the field.

At the core of the fieldwork experience, we believe, is the identity management process. Here is the art, not the science, of qualitative work. Despite the difficulties of constantly attending to identity management, with the researchers required to make rapid "gut-level" judgements on the courses of action to take, successful management of assumed and presumed identities will continue to yield important sociological data that would be impossible to gather under more rigidly imposed positivist rules.

References

Adler, P., and P. Adler. 1996. "Parent-as-Researcher: The Politics of Researching in the Personal Life." *Qualitative Sociology* 19(1):35–58.

Anderson, Leon, and Thomas C. Calhoun. 1992. "Facilitative Aspects of Field Research with Deviant Street Populations." *Sociological Inquiry* 62:490–498.

Ayella M. 1993. " 'They Must Be Crazy': Some of the Difficulties in Researching 'Cults'." Pp. 108–124 in *Researching Sensitive Topics*, edited by C. M. Renzetti and R. M. Lee. Newbury Park, CA: Sage.

Bergen, R. K. 1993. "Interviewing Survivors of Marital Rape: Doing Feminist Research on Sensitive Topics." Pp. 197–211 in *Researching Sensitive Topics*, edited by C. M. Renzetti and R. M. Lee. Newbury Park, CA: Sage.

Berger, P. L., and T. L. Luckman. 1966. *The Social Construction of Reality.* New York: Doubleday.

Berk, R. A., and J. A. Adams. 1970. "Establishing Rapport with Deviant Groups." *Social Problems* 18:102–117.

Boles, J., and A. P. Garbin. 1974. "The Strip Club and Stripper: Customer Patterns of Interaction." *Sociology and Social Research* 58:136–144.

Bombyk, M., M. Bricker-Jenkins, and M. Wedenoja. 1985. "Reclaiming our Profession Through Feminist Research: Some Methodological Issues in the Feminist Practice Project." Paper presented at the annual meeting of the Council on Social Work Education.

Bulmer, M. 1980. "Comment on the Ethics of Covert Methods." *British Journal of Sociology* 31:59–65.

Calhoun, T. C. 1992. "Male Street Hustling: Introduction Processes and Stigma Containment." *Sociological Spectrum* 12:35–52.

Clough, P. 1992. *The End(s) of Ethnography.* Newbury Park, CA: Sage.

Cook, J., and M. M. Fonow. 1990. "Knowledge and Women's Interests: Issues of Epistemology and Methodology in Feminist Sociological Research." Pp. 69–93 in *Feminist Research Methods: Exemplary Readings in the Social Sciences,* edited by J. M. Nielsen. Boulder, CO: Westview Press.

Coxon, T., P. M. Davies, A. J. Hunt, T.J. McManus, C. M. Rees, and P. Weatherburn. 1993. "Research Note: Strategies in Eliciting Sensitive Sexual Information: The Case of Gay Men." *The Sociological Review* 41:537–555.

Daniels, A. K. 1983. "Self-Deception and Self-Discovery in Fieldwork." *Qualitative Sociology* 6:195–214.

Douglas, D. 1972. "Managing Fronts in Observing Deviance." Pp. 93–115 in *Research on Deviance,* edited by J. D. Douglas, New York: Random House.

El-Or, T. 1992. "Do You Really Know How They Make Love? The Limits on Intimacy with Ethnographic Informants." *Qualitative Sociology* 15:53–72.

Foltz, T. 1979. "Escort Services: An Emerging Middle Class Sex-for-Money Scene." *California Sociologist* 2:105–133.

Freeman, J., and E. W. Butler. 1976. "Some Sources of Interviewer Variance in Surveys." *Public Opinion Quarterly* 40:79–92.

Gagné, P. 1992. "Appalachian Women: Violence and Social Control." *Journal of Contemporary Ethnography* 20:387–415.

Gagné, P. 1996. "Identity, Strategy, and Feminist Politics: Clemency for Battered Women who Kill." *Social Problems* 43:77–93.

Gagné, P., and R. Tewksbury. 1996, August. "Hiding in Plain Sight: Conformity Pressures in the Transgender Community." Paper presented at the annual meetings of the Society for the Study of Social Problems, New York.

Galliher, J. F. 1973. "The Protection of Human Subjects: A Reexamination of the Professional Code of Ethics." *The American Sociologist* 8:93–100.

Goffman, E. 1959. *The Presentation of Self in Everyday Life.* Garden City, NY: Doubleday Anchor Books.

Goffman, E. 1963. *Stigma: Notes on the Management of Spoiled Identity.* Englewood Cliffs, NJ: Prentice-Hall.

Hafley, S. R., and R. Tewksbury, 1996, "Reefer Madness in Bluegrass County: Community Structure and Roles in the Rural Kentucky Marijuana Industry." *Journal of Crime and Justice* 19(1):75–94.

Hagedorn, J. M. 1988. *People and Folks: Gangs, Crime and the Underclass in a Rustbelt City.* Chicago, IL: Lake View Press.

Herman, N. J. 1995. "Accessing the Stigmatized: Gatekeeper Problems, Obstacles, and Impediments to Social Research." Pp. 132–145 in *Deviance: A Symbolic Interactionist Approach,* edited by N. J. Herman, Dix Hills, NY: General Hall.

Herman, N. J., and C. Miall. 1990. "The Positive Consequences of Stigma: Two Case Studies in Mental and Physical Disability." *Qualitative Sociology* 13:251–269.

Hopper, C., and J. Moore. 1990. "Women in Outlaw Motorcycle Gangs." *Journal of Contemporary Ethnography* 18:363–387.

Hosie, P. 1986. "Some Theoretical and Methodological Issues To Consider When Using Interviews for Naturalistic Research." *Australian Journal of Education* 30:200–211.

Humphreys, L. 1970. *Tearoom Trade: Impersonal Sex in Public Places.* New York: Aldine.

Jacobs, B. 1992. "Undercover Drug Evasion Tactics: Excuses and Neutralization." *Symbolic Interaction* 15:435–453.

Johnson, T. P., and R. W. Moore. 1993. "Gender Interactions Between Interviewer and Survey Respondents: Issues of Pornography, and Community Standards." *Sex Roles* 28:243–261.

Jones, R. 1995. "Prison as a Hidden Social World." *Journal of Contemporary Criminal Justice* 11:106–118.

Landis, J. R., D. Sullivan, and J. Sheley. 1973. "Feminist Attitudes as Related to Sex of the Interviewer." *Pacific Sociological Review* 16:305–314.

Lather, P. 1986. "Research as Praxis." *Harvard Educational Review* 56:257–277.

Lee, R. 1993. *Doing Research on Sensitive Topics.* Newbury Park, CA: Sage.

Leinen, S. 1993. *Gay Cops.* New Brunswick, NJ: Rutgers University Press.

Levi Kamel, G. W. 1980. "Leathersex: Meaningful Aspects of Gay Sadomasochism." *Deviant Behavior* 1:171–191.

Lofland, J. 1966. *Doomsday Cult.* Englewood Cliffs, NJ: Prentice-Hall.

McCall, G. J., and J. L. Simmons. 1978. *Identities and Interactions: An Examination of Human Associations in Everyday Life,* Rev. ed. New York: Free Press.

Miller, J. 1995. "Gender and Power on the Streets: Street Prostitution in the Era of Crack Cocaine." *Journal of Contemporary Ethnography* 23:427–452.

Miller, J. M. 1995. "Covert Participant Observation: Reconsidering the Least Used Method." *Journal of Contemporary Criminal Justice* 11:97–105.

Miller, M. L., P. K. Manning, and J. Van Maanen. 1993. "Editors' Introduction." Pp. v–vi in *Secrecy and Fieldwork* (Qualitative Research Methods Series, Vol. 29), edited by R. G. Mitchell. Newbury Park, CA: Sage.

Mitchell, R. G. (Ed.) 1993. *Secrecy and Fieldwork* (Qualitative Research Methods Series, Vol. 29), Newbury Park, CA: Sage.

Myers, J. 1992. "Nonmainstream Body Modification: Genital Piercing, Branding, Burning, and Cutting." *Journal of Contemporary Ethnography* 21:267–306.

Reinharz, S. 1992. *Feminist Methods in Social Research.* New York: Oxford University Press.

Renzetti, C. M., and R. M. Lee (Eds.). 1993. *Researching Sensitive Topics.* Newbury Park, CA: Sage.

Riessman, C. 1987. "When Gender is Not Enough: Women Interviewing Women." *Gender & Society* 2(1):172–207.

Robbins. T., D. Anthony, and T. Curtis. 1973. "The Limits of Symbolic Realism: Problems of Empathetic Field Observation in a Secretive Context." *Journal for the Scientific Study of Religion* 12:259–272.

Rochford, E. B. 1985. *Hare Krishna in America.* New Brunswick, NJ: Rutgers University Press.

Ronai, C. R. 1992. "The Reflexive Self Through Narrative: A Night in the Life of an Erotic Dancer/Researcher." Pp. 102–124 in *Investigating Subjectivity: Research on Lived Experience*, edited by C. Ellis and M. G. Flaherty. Newbury Park, CA: Sage.

Ronai, C. R., and C. Ellis, 1989. "Turn-Ons for Money: Interactional Strategies of the Table Dancer." *Journal of Contemporary Ethnography* 18:271–298.

Roth, J. A. 1962. "Comments on Secret Observation." *Social Problems* 9:283–284.

Schmid, T. J., and R. S. Jones, 1991. "Suspended Identity: Identity Transformation in a Maximum Security Prison." *Symbolic Interaction* 14:415–432.

Schmid, T. J., and R. S. Jones, 1993. "Ambivalent Actions: Prison Adaptation Strategies of First-Time, Short-Term Inmates." *Journal of Contemporary Ethnography* 21:439–463.

Scully, D. 1990. *Understanding Sexual Violence.* Boston, MA: Unwin Hyman.

Shaffir, W., V. Marshall, and J. Haas. 1980. "Competing Commitments: Unanticipated Problems of Field Research." *Qualitative Sociology* 2(3):56–71.

Smith, N. E., and M. E. Batiuk, 1989. "Sexual Victimization and Inmate Social Interaction." *The Prison Journal* 69(2):29–38.

Stack, C. 1974. *All Our Kin: Strategies for Survival in a Black Community.* New York: Harper and Row.

Styles, J. 1979. "Outsider/Insider: Researching Gay Baths." *Urban Life* 8:135–152.

Taylor, J. M., and R. Tewksbury, 1995. "From the Inside Out and Outside In: Team Research in the Correctional Setting." *Journal of Contemporary Criminal Justice* 11:119–136.

Tewksbury, R. 1990. "Patrons of Porn: Research Notes on the Clientele of Adult Bookstores." *Deviant Behavior* 11:259–271.

Tewksbury, R. 1993a. "Peepshows and 'Perverts': Men and Masculinity in an Adult Bookstore." *The Journal of Men's Studies* 2:53–67.

Tewksbury, R. 1993b. "Male Strippers: Men Objectifying Men." Pp. 168–181 in *Doing "Women's Work": Men in Nontraditional Occupations,* edited by C. Williams, Newbury Park, CA: Sage.

Tewksbury, R. 1994a; " 'Speaking of Someone with AIDS': Identity Constructions of Persons with HIV Disease." *Deviant Behavior* 15:337–355.

Tewksbury, R. 1994b. "A Dramaturgical Analysis of Male Strippers." *The Journal of Men's Studies* 2:325–342.

Tewksbury, R. 1995a. "Sexuality of Men with HIV Disease." *The Journal of Men's Studies* 3:205–228.

Tewksbury, R. 1995b. "Sexual Adaptations among Gay Men with HIV Disease." Pp. 222–245 in *Men's Health & Illness: Gender, Power and the Body,* edited by D. Sabo and D. Gordon, Newbury Park, CA: Sage.

Van Maanen, J. 1982. "Fieldwork on the Beat." In *Varieties of Qualitative Research,* edited by J. Van Maanen, J. M. Dobbs. Jr., and R. R. Faulkner. Beverly Hills, CA: Sage.

Warren, C. 1988. *Gender Issues in Field Research* (Qualitative Research Methods Series Vol. 9). Newbury Park, CA: Sage.

Warren, C., and Rasmussen, P. 1977. "Sex and Gender in Field Research." *Urban Life* 6:349–369.

Weber, M. [1913] 1981. "Some Categories of Interpretive Sociology." *The Sociological Quarterly* 22:151–180.

Whittier, N. 1991. *Identity Construction in Interviewing: Feminist Postmodern Methodological Dilemmas in Research in Lesbian Feminist Communities.* Paper presented at the annual meetings of the North Central Sociological Association, April, Dearborn, MI.

Whyte, W. F. 1955. *Street Corner Society.* Chicago: University of Chicago Press.

Wise, S. 1987. "A Framework for Discussing Ethical Issues in Feminist Research: A Review of the Literature." *Studies in Sexual Politics* 19:47–88.

Wright, R., S. H. Decker, A. K. Redfern, and D. L. Smith, 1992. "A Snowball's Chance in Hell: Doing Fieldwork with Active Residential Burglars." *Journal of Research in Crime and Delinquency* 29:148–161.

Zigarmi, D., and P. Zigarmi, 1980. "The Psychological Stresses of Ethnographic Research." *Education and Urban Society* 12:291–322.

2. A Snowball's Chance in Hell:

Doing Fieldwork with Active Residential Burglars

Richard Wright, Scott H. Decker,
Allison K. Redfern, and Dietrich L. Smith

Criminologists long have recognized the importance of field studies of active offenders. Nevertheless, the vast majority of them have shied away from researching criminals "in the wild" in the belief that doing so is impractical. This article, based on the authors' fieldwork with one-hundred five currently active residential burglars, challenges that assumption. Specifically, it describes how the authors went about finding these offenders and obtaining their cooperation. Further, it considers the difficulties involved in maintaining an on-going field relationship with those who lead chaotic lives. And lastly, the article outlines the characteristics of the sample, noting important ways in which it differs from one collected through criminal justice channels.

Criminologists long have recognized the importance of field studies of active offenders. More than 2 decades ago, for example, Polsky (1969, p. 116) observed that "we can no longer afford the convenient fiction that in studying criminals in their natural habitat, we would discover nothing really important that could not be discovered from criminals behind bars." Similarly, Sutherland and Cressey (1970) noted that:

> Those who have had intimate contacts with criminals "in the open" know that criminals are not "natural" in police stations, courts, and prisons, and that they must be studied in their everyday life outside of institutions if they are to be understood. By this is meant that the investigator must associate with them as one of them, seeing their lives and conditions as the criminals themselves see them. In this way, he can make observations which can hardly be made in any other way. Also, his observations are of unapprehended criminals, not the criminals selected by the processes of arrest and imprisonment. (p. 68)

And McCall (1978, p. 27) also cautioned that studies of incarcerated offenders are vulnerable to the charge that they are based on "unsuccessful criminals, on the supposition that successful criminals are not apprehended or at least are able to avoid incarceration." This charge, he asserts, is "the most central bogeyman in the criminologist's demonology" (also see Cromwell, Olson, and Avery 1991; Hagedorn 1990; Watters and Biernacki 1989).

Richard Wright et al. in *Journal of Research in Crime and Delinquency*, Vol. 29 No. 2, May 1992 148–161 © 1992 Sage Publications, Inc. Reprinted by permission by Sage Publications, Inc.

Although generally granting the validity of such critiques, most criminologists have shied away from studying criminals, so to speak, in the wild. Although their reluctance to do so undoubtedly is attributable to a variety of factors (e.g., Wright and Bennett 1990), probably the most important of these is a belief that this type of research is impractical. In particular, how is one to locate active criminals and obtain their cooperation?

The entrenched notion that field-based studies of active offenders are unworkable has been challenged by Chambliss (1975) who asserts that:

> The data on organized crime and professional theft as well as other presumably difficult-to-study events are much more available than we usually think. All we really have to do is to get out of our offices and onto the street. The data are there; the problem is that too often [researchers] are not. (p. 39)

Those who have carried out field research with active criminals would no doubt regard this assertion as overly simplistic, but they probably would concur with Chambliss that it is easier to find and gain the confidence of such offenders than commonly is imagined. . . .

We recently completed the fieldwork for a study of residential burglars, exploring, specifically, the factors they take into account when contemplating the commission of an offense. The study is being done on the streets of St. Louis, Missouri, a declining "rust belt" city. As part of this study, we located and interviewed 105 active offenders. We also took 70 of these offenders to the site of a recent burglary and asked them to reconstruct the crime in considerable detail. In the following pages, we will discuss how we found these offenders and obtained their cooperation. Further, we will consider the difficulties involved in maintaining an on-going field relationship with these offenders, many of whom lead chaotic lives. Lastly, we will outline the characteristics of our sample, suggesting ways in which it differs from one collected through criminal justice channels.

Locating the Subjects

In order to locate the active offenders for our study, we employed a "snowball" or "chain referral" sampling strategy. As described in the literature (e.g., Sudman 1976; Watters and Biernacki 1989), such a strategy begins with the recruitment of an initial subject who then is asked to recommend further participants. This process continues until a suitable sample has been "built."

The most difficult aspect of using a snowball sampling technique is locating an initial contact or two. Various ways of doing so have been suggested. . . . In attempting to find active offenders for our study, we avoided seeking referrals from criminal justice officials for both practical and methodological reasons. From a practical standpoint, we elected not to use contacts provided by police or probation officers, fearing that this would arouse the suspicions of offenders that the research was the cover for a "sting" operation. One of the offenders we interviewed, for example, explained that he had not agreed to participate earlier because he was worried about being set up for an arrest: "I thought about it at first because I've seen on T.V. telling how [the police] have sent letters out to people telling 'em they've won new sneakers and then arrested 'em." We also did not use referrals from law enforcement or corrections personnel to locate our subjects owing to a methodological concern that a sample obtained in this way may be highly unrepresentative of the total population of active offenders. It is likely, for instance, that such a sample would include a disproportionate number of unsuccessful criminals, that is, those who have been caught in the past (e.g., Hagedorn 1990). Further, this sample might exclude a number of successful offenders who avoid associating with colleagues known to the police. Rengert and Wasilchick (1989, p. 6) used a probationer to contact active burglars, observing that the offenders so located "were often very much like the individual who led us to them."

A commonly suggested means of making initial contact with active offenders other than through criminal justice sources involves frequenting locales favored by criminals (see Chambliss 1975; Polsky 1969; West 1980). This strategy, however, requires an extraordinary investment of time as the researcher establishes a street reputation as an "all right square" (Irwin 1972, p. 123) who can be trusted. Fortunately, we were able to short-cut that process by hiring an ex-offender (who, despite committing hundreds of serious crimes, had few arrests and no felony convictions) with high status among several groups of Black street criminals in St. Louis. This person retired from crime after being shot and paralyzed in a gangland-style execution attempt. He then attended a university and earned a bachelor's degree, but continued to live in his old neighborhood, remaining friendly, albeit superficially, with local criminals. We initially met him when he attended a colloquium in our department and disputed the speaker's characterization of street criminals.

Working through an ex-offender with continuing ties to the underworld as a means of locating active criminals has been used successfully by other criminologists (see e.g., Taylor 1985). This approach offers the advantage that such a person already has contacts and trust in the criminal subculture and can vouch for the legitimacy of the research. In order to exploit this advantage fully, however, the ex-offender selected must be someone with a solid street reputation for integrity and must have a strong commitment to accomplishing the goals of the study.

The ex-offender hired to locate subjects for our project began by approaching former criminal associates. Some of these contacts were still "hustling," that is, actively involved in various types of crimes, whereas others either had retired or remained involved only peripherally through, for example, occasional buying and selling of stolen goods. Shortly thereafter, the ex-offender contacted several street-wise law-abiding friends, including a youth worker. He explained the research to the contacts, stressing that it was confidential and that the police were not involved. He also informed them that those who took part would be paid a small sum (typically $25.00). He then asked the contacts to put him in touch with active residential burglars.

• • •

Throughout the process of locating subjects, we encountered numerous difficulties and challenges. Contacts that initially appeared to be promising, for example, sometimes proved to be unproductive and had to be dropped. And, of course, even productive contact chains had a tendency to "dry up" eventually. One of the most challenging tasks we confronted involved what Biernacki and Waldorf (1981, p. 150) have termed the "verification of eligibility," that is, determining whether potential subjects actually met the criteria for inclusion in our research. In order to take part, offenders had to be both "residential burglars" and "currently active." In practice, this meant that they had to have committed a residential burglary within the past 2 weeks. This seems straightforward, but it often was difficult to apply the criteria in the field because offenders were evasive about their activities. In such cases, we frequently had to rely on other members of the sample to verify the eligibility of potential subjects.

We did not pay the contacts for helping us to find subjects and, initially, motivating them to do so proved difficult. Small favors, things like giving them a ride or buying them a pack of cigarettes, produced some cooperation, but yielded only a few introductions. Moreover, the active burglars that we did manage to find often were lackadaisical about referring associates because no financial incentive was offered. Eventually, one of the informants hit on the idea of "pimping" colleagues, that is, arranging an introduction on their behalf in exchange for a cut of the participation fee (also see Cromwell et al. 1991). This idea was adopted rapidly by other informants and the number of referrals rose accordingly. In effect, these informants became "locators" (Biernacki and Waldorf 1981), helping us to expand referral chains as well as vouching for the legitimacy of the research, and validating potential participants as active residential burglars.

The practice of pimping is consistent with the low level, underworld economy of street culture, where people are always looking for a way to get in on someone else's deal. One of our contacts put it this way: "If there's money to make out of something, I gotta figure out a way to get me some of it." Over the course of the research, numerous disputes arose between offenders and informants over the payment of referral fees. We resisted becoming involved in these disputes, reckoning that such involvement could only result in the alienation of one or both parties (e.g., Miller 1952). Instead, we made it clear that our funds were intended as interview payments and thus would be given only to interviewees.

Field Relations

The success of our research, of course, hinged on an ability to convince potential subjects to participate. Given that many of the active burglars, especially those located early in the project, were deeply suspicious of our motives, it is reasonable to ask why the offenders were willing to take part in the research. Certainly the fact that we paid them a small sum for their time was an enticement for many, but this is not an adequate explanation. After all, criminal opportunities abound and even the inept "nickel and dime" offenders in the sample could have earned more had they spent the time engaged in illegal activity. Moreover, some of the subjects clearly were not short of cash when they agreed to participate; at the close of one interview, an offender pulled out his wallet to show us that it was stuffed with thousand dollar bills, saying:

> I just wanted to prove that I didn't do this for the money. I don't need the money. I did it to help out [the ex-offender employed on our project]. We know some of the same people and he said you were cool.

Without doubt, many in our sample agreed to participate only because the ex-offender assured them that we were trustworthy. But other factors were at work as well. Letkemann (1973, p. 44), among others, has observed that the secrecy inherent in criminal work means that offenders have few opportunities to discuss their activities with anyone besides associates—which many of them find frustrating. As one of his informants put it: "What's the point of scoring if nobody knows about it." Under the right conditions, therefore, some offenders may enjoy talking about their work with researchers.

We adopted several additional strategies to maximize the cooperation of the offenders. First, following the recommendations of experienced field researchers (e.g., Irwin 1972; McCall 1978; Walker and Lidz 1977; Wright and Bennett 1990), we made an effort to "fit in" by learning the distinctive terminology and phrasing used by the offenders. Here again, the assistance of the ex-offender proved invaluable. Prior to entering the field, he suggested ways in which questions might be asked so that the subjects would better understand them, and provided us with a working knowledge of popular street terms (e.g., "boy" for heroin, "girl" for cocaine) and pronunciations (e.g., "hair ron" for heroin). What is more, he sat in on the early interviews and critiqued them afterwards, noting areas of difficulty or contention and offering possible solutions.

A second strategy to gain the cooperation of the offenders required us to give as well as take. We expected the subjects to answer our questions frankly and, therefore, often had to reciprocate. Almost all of them had questions about how the information would be used, who would have access to it, and so on. We answered these questions honestly, lest the offenders conclude that we were being evasive. Further, we honored requests from a number of subjects for various forms of assistance. Provided that the help requested was legal and fell within the general set "of norms governing the exchange of money and other kinds of favors" (Berk and Adams 1970, p. 112) on the street, we offered it. For example, we took subjects to job interviews or work, helped some to enroll in school, and gave others advice on legal matters. We even assisted a juvenile offender who was injured while running away from the police, to arrange for emergency surgery when his parents, fearing that they would be charged for the operation, refused to give their consent.

One other way we sought to obtain and keep the offenders' confidence involved demonstrating our trustworthiness by "remaining close-mouthed in regard to potentially harmful information" (Irwin 1972, p. 125). A number of the offenders tested us by asking what a criminal associate said about a particular matter. We declined to discuss such issues, explaining that the promise of confidentiality extended to all those participating in our research.

Much has been written about the necessity for researchers to be able to withstand official coercion (see Irwin 1972; McCall 1978; Polsky 1969) and we recognized from the start the threat that intrusions from criminal justice officials could pose to our research. The threat of being confronted by police patrols seemed especially great given that we planned to visit the sites of recent successful burglaries with offenders. Therefore, prior to beginning our fieldwork, we negotiated an agreement with police authorities not to interfere in the conduct of the research, and we were not subjected to official coercion.

Although the strategies described above helped to mitigate the dangers inherent in working with active criminals (see e.g., Dunlap et al. 1990), we encountered many potentially dangerous situations over the course of the research. For example, offenders turned up for interviews carrying firearms including, on one occasion, a machine gun; we were challenged on the street by subjects who feared that they were being set up for arrest; we were caught in the middle of a fight over the payment of a $1 debt. Probably the most dangerous situation, however, arose while driving with an offender to the site of his most recent burglary. As we passed a pedestrian, the offender became agitated and demanded that we stop the car: "You want to see me kill someone? Stop the car! I'm gonna kill that motherfucker. Stop the fuckin' car!" We refused to stop and actually sped up to prevent him jumping out of the vehicle; this clearly displeased him, although he eventually calmed down. The development of such situations was largely unpredictable and thus avoiding them was difficult. Often we deferred to the ex-offender's judgment about the safety of a given set of circumstances. The most notable precaution that we took involved money; we made sure that the offenders knew that we carried little more than was necessary to pay them.

Characteristics of the Sample

Unless a sample of active offenders differs significantly from one obtained through criminal justice channels, the difficulties and risks associated with the street-based recruitment of research subjects could not easily be justified. Accordingly, it seems important that we establish whether such a difference exists. In doing so, we will begin by outlining the demographic characteristics of our sample. In terms of race, it nearly parallels the distribution of burglary arrests for the City of St. Louis in 1988, the most recent year for which data are available. The St. Louis Metropolitan Police Department's Annual Report (1989) reveals that 64% of burglary arrestees in that year were Black, and 36% were White. Our sample was 69% Black and 31% White. There is divergence for the gender variable, however; only 7% of all arrestees in the city were female, while 17% of our sample fell into this category. This is not surprising. The characteristics of a sample of active criminals, after all, would not be expected to mirror those of one obtained in a criminal justice setting.

Given that our research involved only currently active offenders, it is interesting to note that 21 of the subjects were on probation, parole, or serving a suspended sentence, and that a substantial number of juveniles—27 or 26% of the total—were located for the study. The inclusion of such offenders strengthens the research considerably because approximately one third of arrested burglars are under 18 years of age (Sessions 1989). Juveniles, therefore, need to be taken into account in any comprehensive study of burglars. These offenders, however, seldom are included in studies of burglars located through criminal justice channels because access to them is legally restricted and they often are processed differently than adult criminals and detained in separate facilities.

Prior contact with the criminal justice system is a crucial variable for this research. . . .

More than one-quarter of the offenders (28%) claimed never to have been arrested. (We excluded arrests for traffic offenses, "failure to appear" and similar minor transgressions, because such offenses do not adequately distinguish serious criminals from others.) Obviously, these offenders would have been excluded had we based our study on a jail or prison population. Perhaps a more relevant measure in the context of our study, however, is the experience of the offenders with the criminal justice system for the offense of burglary, because most previous studies of burglars not only have been based on incarcerated offenders, but also have used the charge of burglary as a screen to select subjects (e.g., Bennett and Wright 1984; Rengert and Wasilchick 1985). Of the 105 individuals in our sample, 44 (42%) had no arrests for burglary, and another 35 (33%) had one or more arrests, but no convictions for the offense. Thus 75% of our sample would not be included in a study of incarcerated burglars.

• • •

Conclusion

By its nature, research involving active criminals is always demanding, often difficult and occasionally dangerous. However, it is possible . . . [that] some of the offenders included in such research may differ substantially from those found through criminal justice channels. It is interesting, for example, that those in our sample who had never been arrested for anything, on average, offended *more* frequently and had committed *more* lifetime burglaries than their arrested counterparts. These "successful" offenders, obviously, would not have shown up in a study of arrestees, prisoners, or probationers—a fact that calls into question the extent to which a sample obtained through official sources is representative of the total population of criminals.

Beyond this, researching active offenders is important because it provides an opportunity to observe and talk with them outside the institutional context. As Cromwell et al. (1991) have noted, it is difficult to assess the validity of accounts offered by institutionalized criminals. Simply put, a full understanding of criminal behavior requires that criminologists incorporate field studies of active offenders into their research agendas. Without such studies, both the representativeness and the validity of research based on offenders located through criminal justice channels will remain problematic.

References

Bennett, Trevor and Richard Wright. 1984. *Burglars on Burglary: Prevention and the Offender*, Aldershot, England: Gower.

Berk, Richard and Joseph Adams. 1970. "Establishing Rapport with Deviant Groups." *Social Problems* 18:102–17.

Biernacki, Patrick and Dan Waldorf. 1981. "Snowball Sampling: Problems and Techniques of Chain Referral Sampling." *Sociological Method & Research* 10:141–63.

Chambliss, William. 1975. "On the Paucity of Research on Organized Crime: A Reply to Galliher and Cain." *American Sociologist* 10:36–39.

Cromwell, Paul, James Olson, and D' Aunn Avery. 1991. *Breaking and Entering: An Ethnographic Analysis of Burglary:* Newbury Park, CA: Sage.

Dunlap, Eloise, Bruce Johnson, Harry Sanabria, Elbert Holliday, Vicki Lipsey, Maurice Barnett, William Hopkins, Ira Sobel, Doris Randolph, and Ko-Lin Chin. 1990. "Studying Crack Users and Their Criminal Careers: The Scientific and Artistic Aspects of Locating Hard-to-Reach Subjects and Interviewing Them about Sensitive Topics" *Contemporary Drug Problems* 17:121–44.

Hagedorn, John. 1990. "Back in the Field Again: Gang Research in the Nineties." Pp. 240–59 in *Gangs in America*, edited by C. Ronald Huff. Newbury Park, CA: Sage.

Irwin, John. 1972. "Participant Observation of Criminals." Pp. 117–37 in *Research on Deviance*, edited by Jack Douglas. New York: Random House.

Letkemann, Peter. 1973. *Crime as Work*. Englewood Cliffs, NJ: Prentice-Hall.

McCall, George. 1978. *Observing the Law*. New York: Free Press.

Miller, S. M. 1952. "The Participant Observer and Over-Rapport." *American Sociological Review* 17:97–99.

Polsky, Ned. 1969. *Hustlers, Beats, and Others*. Garden City, NJ: Anchor.

Rengert, George and John Wasilchick. 1985. *Suburban Burglary: A Time and a Place for Everything*. Springfield, IL: Thomas.

———. 1989. *Space, Time and Crime: Ethnographic Insights into Residential Burglary*. Final report submitted to the National Institute of Justice, Office of Justice Programs, U.S. Department of Justice.

Sessions, William. 1989. *Crime in the United States—1988*. Washington, DC: U.S. Government Printing Office.

St. Louis Metropolitan Police Department. 1989. *Annual Report—1988/89.* St. Louis, MO: St. Louis Metropolitan Police Department.

Sudman, Seymour. 1976. *Applied Sampling.* New York: Academic Press.

Sutherland, Edwin and Donald Cressey. 1970. *Criminology—8th Edition.* Philadelphia, PA: Lippincott.

Taylor, Laurie. 1985. *In the Underworld.* London: Unwin.

Walker, Andrew and Charles Lidz. 1977. "Methodological Notes on the Employment of Indigenous Observers." Pp. 103–23 in *Street Ethnography,* edited by Robert Weppner, Beverly Hills, CA: Sage.

Watters, John and Patrick Biernacki. 1989. "Targeted Sampling: Options for the Study of Hidden Populations." *Social Problems* 36:416–30.

West, W. Gordon. 1980. "Access to Adolescent Deviants and Deviance." Pp. 31–44 in *Fieldwork Experience. Qualitative Approaches to Social Research,* edited by William Shaffir, Robert Stebbins, and Allan Turowitz., New York: St. Martin's.

Wright, Richard and Trevor Bennett. 1990. "Exploring the Offender's Perspective: Observing and Interviewing Criminals." Pp. 138–51 in *Measurement Issues in Criminology,* edited by Kimberly Kempf. New York: Springer-Verlag.

3. Drug Enforcement's Double-Edged Sword:

An Assessment of Asset Forfeiture Programs

J. Mitchell Miller
and Lance H. Selva

• • •

The 1988 Anti-Drug Abuse Bill created new legal tools to handle the special enforcement problems presented by crack cocaine, gang-related violence, and domestic marijuana production, all of which appeared to be increasing steadily (Weisheit 1991). The bill provided for additional allocation of resources for equipment and manpower, as well as stiffer legal penalties for drug law offenders. It also created an Asset Forfeiture Fund. This fund is modeled after the Racketeer-Influenced and Corrupt Organizations (RICO) and the Continuing Criminal Enterprise statutes as well as the Federal Criminal Forfeiture Act of 1984, which legalized seizing the fruits of criminal activities (Moore 1988).

The Asset Forfeiture Fund is much more than a depository for income generated by liquidating seized assets, whether cash, automobiles, jewelry, art, or real estate. It is the central component in a reciprocal relationship between law enforcement agencies and federal and state treasury departments, from which the attorney general may authorize

> payment of any expenses necessary to seize, detail/inventory, safeguard, maintain, advertise or sell property under seizure or detention pursuant to any law enforced. . . . Payments from the fund can be used for awards for information or assistance related to violation of criminal drug laws. . . . Deposits to the fund will be from the forfeiture of property under any law enforced or administered (Lawrence 1988:2).

The Asset Forfeiture Fund was created with the intention of helping law enforcement agencies to combat drug lords whose wealth gave them refuge from traditional enforcement tactics. Proponents were optimistic that seizing assets would limit the amount of working capital available to drug dealers, thereby reducing their ability to facilitate criminal activity (Drug Policy Foundation 1992; Fried 1988).

The fund calls on federal agencies to form special units for conducting operations to make seizures. Most state law enforcement agencies and several metropolitan police departments soon noted the monetary benefits of the fund and

J. Mitchell Miller and Lance H. Selva. *Justice Quarterly*, Vol. 11 No. 2, June 1994. © 1994 Academy of Criminal Justice Sciences.

copied the federal approach, making asset seizure and forfeiture a sweeping narcotics policing strategy (United States Department of Justice 1988). Like any legal innovation, however, it had the potential for unintended consequences.

Critics contend that seizing assets and money has become a concern of vice divisions in smaller enforcement agencies, primary to the exclusion of traditional enforcement goals of deterrence and punishment (Stuart 1990; Trebach 1987). The routinization of seizure and forfeiture, others allege, has prompted enforcement agencies to develop new strategies of narcotics policing that are directed more toward asset hunting than toward reducing illegal drug use (Miller 1991; Trebach and Zeese 1990). Furthermore, this new policing strategy appears to be increasingly intrusive. A number of journalistic accounts describe civil liberties violations related directly to asset forfeiture enforcement (Jacobs 1992; Morganthau and Katel 1990). A series published by the Pittsburgh Press, titled *Presumed Guilty: The Law's Victims in the War on Drugs* (Schneider and Flaherty 1991), portrays the frequent, severe victimization of ordinary citizens through forfeiture. These excellent reports, based on reviews of 25,000 DEA seizures and 510 court cases, reveal that "enormous collateral damage to the innocent" is the effect of a new standard of presumed guilt. Other information on asset forfeiture comes from legal critiques dissecting the language of the 1988 Anti-Drug Abuse Act and surveying its feasibility as an effective drug enforcement initiative (Goldstein and Kalant 1990; Krauss and Laezear 1991). No grounded studies have been conducted, however, to examine asset forfeiture in the field and to assess whether it is fair practice or foul play.

This study is an empirical examination of asset forfeiture as a tool of drug enforcement policy. It differs from previous work in this area in that it examines the implementation of the laws from within forfeiture programs, explaining experimentally rather than speculatively why and how one aspect of the drug war has gone astray. We begin with a survey of the literature, focusing on the legal basis of forfeiture policy and describing the extent of its use. This section also highlights major criticisms regarding problematic aspects of asset forfeiture programs. This discussion is followed by an explanation of the study. Next, we present observations. We conclude with an assessment of asset forfeiture.

Background

An initial assessment of the 1988 Anti-Drug Abuse Bill might suggest that it is little more than an intensification of preexisting laws and enforcement programs. Most of the provisions are either replicas or renovations of previous initiatives, but closer examination of the component establishing the Asset Forfeiture Fund reveals new developments. A brief survey of the use of forfeiture in the United States provides a framework for examining these recent changes.

The seizing of assets, both as an enforcement tactic and as a sanction, was practiced long before the creation of the 1988 Anti-Drug Abuse Bill. Historically, a felony was defined as a crime for which a person could be required to forfeit all property (Reid 1991). The power of forfeiture was recognized and approved by the American colonies and was used by the First Congress of the United States to confiscate smuggling, pirate, and slave ships (Greek 1992; Myers and Brzostowski 1982). Hundreds of forfeiture laws have been created and are now enforced by both state and federal governments.

The strategy of asset forfeiture was first used against drug dealers in 1970, when persons operating a trafficking organization were required to forfeit illegally acquired profits and assets according to the Comprehensive Drug Abuse Prevention and Control Act of 1970 (*United States Code* V.21). Subsequently Congress authorized federal attorneys to file *in rem* actions, civil lawsuits staking the government's claim to property and money related to the illicit drug industry. This step potentially enabled the government to obtain legal possession of property and currency even despite dismissal of criminal charges based on a legal technicality such as a faulty search warrant or a *Miranda* rights violation. In addition, prosecutors enjoyed the reduced burden of proof required under civil law; a simple preponderance of the evidence, as opposed to the "beyond a reasonable doubt" standard recognized in criminal courts.

The consequences were considerable. During 1979, the first full year of implementation, the DEA seized close to $10 million in assets; this figure reached $54.4 million in 1981 (Myers and Brzostowski 1982). In 1983 more than $100 million in cash and property was forfeited to the government (Stellwagen 1985); an astronomical $460 million was forfeited in 1990 (Bureau of Justice Statistics 1991). Despite these impressive statistics, advocates of asset forfeiture considered the power to be seriously underutilized.

In the early 1980s all states were seizing illicit substances during routine narcotics operations, but few were following the federal example of seizing drug profits. In 1982, to encourage states that had yet to pass laws attacking the profits of drug trafficking, the DEA developed a Model Forfeiture of Drug Profits Act and published a training manual titled "Drug Agents" Guide to Forfeiture of Assets (Myers and Brzostowski 1982). The federal agency suggested that states adopting the Act, or a similar provision, allocate revenue generated through seizure and forfeiture to drug enforcement. By 1985, 47 states had passed legislation resembling the 1982 DEA Act (Stellwagen 1985). Federal policy recommendations, formulated in a 1985 U.S. Department of Justice study of 50 prosecutors, including extending statutes to condemn additional types of property and hiring staff for financial investigations and asset management (U.S. Department of Justice 1988). The practice of returning seized money to drug enforcers was incorporated in the 1988 Anti-Drug Abuse Bill and is the heart of the controversy surrounding asset forfeiture and its offspring, a seizure-based style of narcotics policing.

The importance of the Asset Forfeiture Fund, and the element that makes it more than a mere intensification of previous seizure laws, centers on the redirection of the income produced by asset forfeiture (Osborne 1991). Before provision was made for an Asset Forfeiture Fund, income raised by liquidating assets was generally channeled into treasury departments for redistribution into the national or state budgets. Under the present provision, however, a percentage of the funds generated by asset seizures is returned Government treasury departments to law enforcement agencies to supplement their budgets. In 1988, in fact, the United States Justice Department shared $24.4 million with state and local law enforcement agencies that participated in investigations and arrests producing forfeitures (Burden 1988:29). A cycle was created, which allowed narcotics operations to make seizures that could be used to finance other operations in which yet more assets might be seized.

Proponents of asset seizure claim that it is necessary for enforcing the law and could turn the tide in the war on drugs. Substantial cash seizures, they argue, cripple large drug trafficking operations. The Los Angeles County Sheriff's Department, for example, seized more than $26 million in drug money in 1987 and another $33 million in 1988 (Stuart 1990). Forfeitures have included a Chevrolet dealership, a recording studio, a thousand-acre plantation, and numerous luxury homes, cars, boats, and planes (Wrobleski and Hess 1990:429). The distribution of the proceeds varies among federal agencies and from state to state. Under Louisiana's Drug Racketeering and Related Organizations law, all property associated with illegal drug activity is subject to forfeiture. Division of the spoils in Louisiana are 50 percent to the state, 25 percent to the district attorney's office; and 25 percent to the narcotics division of the seizing law enforcement agency. The Illinois Narcotics Profit Forfeiture Act allocates 50 percent for local drug policing, 25 percent for narcotics prosecution, and 25 percent to the State Drug Traffic Prevention Fund (U.S. Department of Justice 1988).

Problems

Success in drug work traditionally has been measured by the protection it provides society through ferreting out drugs and drug dealers, eradicating the substances, and apprehending offenders (Carter 1990; Moore 1977). The goal has been to diminish drug use and trafficking. Despite a problematic history, narcotics policing has employed strategies and tactics that at least appeared to be consistent with policy objectives (Carter and Stephens 1988; Klockars 1983; Manning and Redlinger 1977; Wilson 1961). Many of the traditional problems of drug control, such as exposure to pressures and invitations to corruption (Carter 1990: Chambliss 1988; Wilson 1978), still must be addressed, but new problems have developed since the implementation of asset forfeiture programs.

Journalistic accounts suggest that seizing assets has become a high-priority objective in drug enforcement (Dortch 1992; Shaw 1990; Willson 1990). According to Dan Garner, an undercover narcotics agent in southern California, drug enforcement success is measured by the amount of money seized:

> You see that there's big money out there, you want to seize the big money for your department. For our unit, the sign of whether you were doing good or poorly was how much money you seized, and the kind of cases you did. And my supervisor made it extremely clear that big money cases were a lot more favorable for your overall evaluation than big dope cases (Stuart 1990).

Garner and some of his fellow agents were accused of stealing drug profits during seizure operations. Their story has called attention to a growing problem, as have other highly publicized drug related police scandals such as the Miami River murders of drug dealers by officers who stole their profits, and the arrest of more than half of the Sea Girt, New Jersey Police Department by the DEA on drug trafficking charges (Dombrink 1988).

Asset forfeiture was designed to be used against major dealers involved heavily in criminal activity. In practice, however, suspects not associated significantly with criminal activity often become the targets of operations because they have valuable assets. Under forfeiture laws, the potential value of assets strongly affects the priority of cases, thus determining who the suspects will be. The goal of raising revenue encourages selection of cases according to the suspect's resources. Targets of police surveillance thus are chosen for their resources rather than for their criminal activity, giving credence to frequent insinuations that the police facilitate crime (Block 1993; Braithwaite, Fisse, and Geis 1987; Marx 1988).

Observers argue that when narcotics officers become revenue producers, the system itself becomes corrupt (Carter 1990; McAlary 1987; Trebach 1987). As one critic points out,

> Once you focus on cash as the goal for the officers, they accept that and they forget about the ultimate goal of eliminating dope dealers. Seizure operations are simply revenue raising devices for departments, and divert officers' attention from the real goal, stopping dope (Stuart 1990).

According to one study, police in both Los Angeles and Miami routinely took assets from dealers but did not arrest them. Officers seized money from individuals and asked them to sign a disclaimer form before release. The disclaimer form stated that the suspect was not the owner of the seized money, had no knowledge of where it came from, and would not attempt to claim it. Such forms were used in investigations where money was seized but no drugs were found. The purpose, according to agency memos, "was to assist the department in gaining legal possession of the money" (Stuart 1990).

Examination of the forfeiture process from seizure to revenue highlights the steps involved in liquidating assets. Seized currency moves through the system more rapidly than do assets such as automobiles and real estate, which must be warehoused (when appropriate), advertised, and auctioned. By seizing cash, law enforcement agencies obtain their percentage of the revenue produced much sooner than by seizing property. For this reason, narcotics operations employ strategies designed to generate cash.

The "reverse sting" (Miller 1991) has emerged as the predominant choice of narcotics divisions. This type of operation features undercover agents as the sellers of drugs, rather than as buyers who seek out illicit substances. This controversial method involves negotiation, frequently through confidential informants, aimed at arranging a time and place at which undercover agents posing as drug dealers will provide felonious resale quantities of an illicit substance for a predetermined price. After the transaction has been completed, a "take-down" team of agents arrests the suspect and seizes any assets than can be associated with the deal (frequently an automobile) as well as any cash involved. The reverse sting is the preferred approach because agents can control and calculate the amount of money a deal will involve before they commit time and resources.

Traditional tactics, such as executing search warrants, often may produce arrests and confiscation of illegal substances, but no certain cash seizure. Narcotics enforcement is becoming a business, in which officers and equipment are allocated so as to maximize profits rather than to control or eradicate drugs. Efficiency is measured by the amount of money seized rather than by the impact on drug trafficking. In achieving efficiency, however, law enforcement has so misused the power of seizure that the Supreme Court recently has limited the scope of forfeiture laws.

In *Austin v. United States* (1993) the high court examined whether the Excessive Fines Clause of the Eighth Amendment applies to forfeitures of property. Although the court declined an invitation to establish a multifactor test for determining whether a forfeiture is excessive, it held that the principle of proportionality serves as a basis by which lower courts may decide individual cases. Thus the court determined that the government exacted too high a penalty (forfeiture of a home, $4,500, and an auto body shop) for the offense (sale of two grams of cocaine). Also, in *U.S. v. A Parcel of Land* (1993), some protection was provided to innocent owners of property related to the drug industry. Although these cases may slow the momentum of future asset-gathering operations, they address only a few of the real and potential dangers presented by forfeiture laws. Observations of undercover reverse sting operations point out these dangers and evidence the contradictions of such an approach.

The Study: A Year Under Cover

The data for this study come from the observations and experiences of one of the authors, who assumed the role of confidential informant in undercover narcotics operations in a southern state. This position provided a rare opportunity to examine, through covert participant observation, the clandestine work of narcotics operations units and to observe undercover narcotics agents, typically an inaccessible subject group.

While the researcher was a graduate student in a criminal justice program, he became friendly with fellow students who were drug enforcement agents. They invited him to participate in narcotics cases as a confidential informant. Although these fellow graduate students enabled his initial entry, the researcher then interacted with drug agents who did not know him and who had no knowledge of his research objectives. The label *confidential informant* should not be misconstrued; the position typically involves undercover work more often than the revealing of privileged knowledge to narcotics agents. The primary functions of a confidential informant are negotiating with and manipulating suspects so as to involve them in reverse sting operations.

The sense of police fraternity (Wilson 1961) is intensified in narcotics units, making them neither open nor receptive to research. As a confidential informant, the researcher was not accepted fully in the group. Nevertheless, his position allowed him to penetrate the hidden activities of narcotics operations and provided an excellent vantage point for conducting a study of drug enforcement. Informants interact with agent and criminal alike, often serving as a communication link between the two. This position allows proximity to the thoughts, feelings, motives, and strategies of both agents and suspects, thus permitting an investigation of asset forfeiture as implemented at the street level.

The researcher remained in this position for one year; he participated in 28 narcotics cases with agents and officers from very small city police departments, larger county sheriffs departments, urban and metropolitan forces, and two state law enforcement agencies. Here a case is defined operationally as a series of events that culminated in arrest, seizure of assets, or both. Cases often overlapped because they ranged in duration from a few days to several months. The events of each case were recorded upon leaving the various field settings, maintained in separate files, and updated as each case progressed.

As a "complete-member-researcher" (Adler and Adler 1987), the author conducted "opportunistic research" (Ronai and Ellis 1989) by studying phenomena in a setting in which he participated as a full member. This method also has been called "disguised observation" (Erikson 1967). Its distinguishing feature is that the research objectives are not made known to others in the field setting. The use of disguised or covert observational techniques often has been regarded as ethically controversial, as evidenced by the "deception debate" (Bulmer 1980; Galliher 1973; Humphreys 1970; Roth 1962). Participants in the debate tend to assume one of two polarized positions: moralistic condemnation or responsive justification. Opponents of this method hold that covert strategies should be banned from social science research (Erikson 1967). Their major objection is that these techniques often violate basic ethical principles such as informed consent, invasion of privacy, and the obligation to avoid causing harm to subjects. Specifically, the critics allege that misrepresentation can cause irreparable damage to subjects, to the researcher, and to science by evoking negative public scrutiny and by making subject populations wary of future researchers (Galliher 1973; Polsky 1967).

Justifications for the use of covert techniques have been presented on both practical and philosophical levels. One practical argument is that persons engaged in illegal or unconventional behavior, such as drug dealers and users, simply will not submit to or participate in study by overt methods. Similarly, those in powerful and authoritative positions, such as drug enforcement agents, have been considered secretive and difficult to observe openly (Shils 1975). From a philosophic perspective, Denzin (1968) argues, following Goffman (1959), that all researchers wear masks and ethical propriety thus depends on the context. Denzin suggests that

> the sociologist has the right to make observations on anyone in any setting to the extent that he does so with scientific intents and purposes in mind (1968:50).

The basis for this disguise in this study, however, is "the end and the means" position stated first by Roth (1962) and later by Homan (1980). That the end may justify the means also is acknowledged by the British Sociological Association, which allows the convert approach "where it is not possible to use other methods to obtain essential data" (1973:3); such is the case in the present situation. We believe that the benefits of investigating and reporting on this expensive and dysfunctional drug enforcement strategy outweigh its potential costs. Failure to study how this strategy is implemented on the street would condemn other citizens to the misfortunes and abuses we describe below. In addition, scarce resources in the war on drugs would continue to be misused.

Drug enforcers' use of asset forfeiture has been questioned by the press and media so frequently and with such intensity that scholarly examination is warranted. The very nature of the allegations, however, has prompted the police fraternity to close ranks, thus making disguised entry a necessity. To rule out study of covert behavior, whether by the powerful or by the powerless, simply because it cannot be studied openly imposes artificial limits on science and prevents study of what may be important and consequential activities in society. The propriety and the importance of research activities always must be judged case by case. In this particular case, abandoning the study because it could not be conducted with overt techniques would cause the potential misconduct and betrayal of public trust by government officials to remain unexposed. We hope others will agree not only that the end justifies the means in the context of this research, but that it takes ethical precedence.

Observations: Some Typical Cases

The following examples of cases involve acts and decisions by narcotics agents that illustrate several troubling aspects of asset forfeiture. These concern the impact of forfeiture on both the type of cases selected for undercover operations and the function of covert policing in society.

The researcher first came to understand how cases were assigned priority while he was working with the police department of a medium-sized city in 1989. Still unaware of the profit-seeking nature of narcotics divisions, he began undercover work by "feeling out" possible deals and meeting with an undercover agent to discuss potential cases. The researcher mistakenly believed that a large quantity of drugs or a "known" dealer made a case desirable, and accordingly proposed two possible deals. The first deal involved 2 ½ pounds of marijuana that a dealer was willing to sell to the researcher's buyer (the agent). The second involved a factory worker who was shopping for a half-pound of marijuana to resell to friends and co-workers. The agent asked the researcher to note the license plate numbers of the suspects' vehicles. The researcher believed the plate numbers were to be used for gathering information such as the suspects' ages, addresses, and arrest records. The primary purpose, however, was to learn whether the suspect owned the vehicle or whether a lien holder was involved. This information enabled the agent to determine the amount of equity in a suspect's vehicle.

The equity in a vehicle represented potential profit that officers could expect to receive if the vehicle was seized. If a person whose car had been seized had a clear title, he or she was likely to lose the car. It would be sold later at auction, and the seizing agency would receive a percentage of the money. If a person was still making payments, the situation was more complex. Normally the defendant was given the option of making a "contribution" to the arresting department's drug fund, equal to the level of equity, in exchange for the seized vehicle.

The agent in charge of this case compared the two proposed deals in order to assess which one would generate more income. The first case involved five times as much marijuana as the second. Also, by working the first deal, officers would take 2 ½ pounds of marijuana out of circulation because the dealer would be selling. The seller was a full-time drug dealer with two prior drug-related convictions, and was on probation at the time of this case. The suspect in the second deal had no arrest record and appeared to be a relatively small-time user who hoped to make a modest profit by selling quarter-ounce bags of marijuana. Although the first deal seemed more serious, the second would guarantee seizure of at least $700 when the suspect purchased drugs from the agent. In addition, the latter suspect owned a truck, whereas the professional dealer had only a little equity in a late-model sports car. The officer explained that the first deal simply was not profitable and would not be pursued.

The researcher was instructed to arrange for the latter suspect to meet the "seller." When he expressed concern that the officer was encouraging the suspect to commit a crime, the officer justified the operation by contending that the suspect would secure marijuana elsewhere and eventually would become a major dealer. In this way, according to the officer, the problem would be "nipped in the bud" because the suspect would be deterred from future criminal activity. The purchase was consummated with the agent, the suspect was arrested, and his cash and vehicle were seized.

This case provided the agent's department with a small profit. The buyer may or may not have been deterred from future criminal behavior. On the other hand, no drugs were taken out of circulation, and the buyer might never have acted on his intentions to purchase a felonious quantity of drugs if the researcher and the agent had not presented him with such an opportunity.

The strategy involved in this case was termed a "reverse" sting because the visual undercover function of buying narcotics was the opposite of this arrangement: here, officers became sellers. This strategy was preferred by every agency and department with which the researcher was associated because it allowed agents to gauge potential profit before investing a great deal of time and effort. Reverses occurred so regularly that the term *reverse* became synonymous with the word *deal*.

This case was not an isolated incident; it was one of many such cases in which the operational goal was profit rather than the incapacitation of drug dealers. The pursuit of profit clearly influenced policies on case selection.

The researcher was told that only exchanges involving a certain amount of money or narcotics would be acceptable. It was apparent that these guidelines came from supervisors who did not want squads to work comparatively small cases or those of low monetary value, when more profitable options existed. These standards proved to be contrary to the notion of taking distributors off the street.

The drug trade, an illicit market, is similar to licit markets in several ways. One likeness is natural price regulation through the mechanics of supply and demand (Manning and Redlinger 1977). Upon seeing a large bust, supervisors tended mistakenly to believe that the drug markets in their jurisdictions were flooded with a particular substance. Consequently they imposed limits for agents and informants. Ironically, the arrest that prompted the decision was often an isolated incident that did not accurately reflect local drug trading activity.

These limits were a constant source of annoyance for both the researcher and the officers with whom he worked. One case, in which the researcher and an agent had spent a week preparing a suspect for a deal, provides a revealing example.

The researcher had established a relationship with the suspect, having bought marijuana from him on one occasion and cocaine on another. The suspect was informed that he could discuss business with the researcher's connection, who could supply quantities of marijuana at a low price. Having gained the suspect's confidence and whetted his appetite for a substantial bargain, the researcher arranged a conference between his supplier (an undercover agent) and the suspect. A deal was struck whereby the agent would sell two pounds of marijuana to the suspect for $2,500. The deal was canceled before the transaction, however, because the agent's supervisor decided that only reverses of five pounds or more would be worked. The researcher was told to give the suspect a reason why the deal could not take place.

After two unproductive weeks, the supervisor realized that he had been unrealistic in setting a five-pound limit. He lowered the limit to the previous level of one pound and then ordered the agent to try to recover the deal he had canceled two weeks earlier. The deal could not be saved, however, because the suspect no longer trusted the researcher. The undercover work and the money spent on compensating the researcher had been wasted. In addition, the suspect, a recidivist with criminal intent, remained free to solicit illicit substances.

Another case that was lost because of imposed limits involved a well-known suspect whom an agent had kept under surveillance for more than a year. The suspect, a college student, dealt primarily in "ECSTASY", a hallucinogenic drug in tablet form. The agent told the researcher that previously he had served a search warrant at the suspect's apartment, but had found nothing to warrant an arrest. The student had abused the agent verbally and threatened to sue his department for harassment. Later the researcher learned when and where this suspect was to deliver a quantity of ECSTASY and marijuana. Although the agent wanted to arrest this suspect, largely for revenge, his supervisor was reluctant to pursue the case because it was not regarded as profitable.

Episodes such as these not only involved nonenforcement of narcotics' laws, but also promoted cynicism among officers, a troublesome aspect of police work (Carter 1990; Manning 1980). The ever-changing limits on deals magnified this problem as some officers began to question the nature and the true purpose of their occupation.

Other drug agents, however, demonstrated acceptance of asset forfeiture operations. When asked why a search warrant would not be served on a suspect known to have resale quantities of marijuana in his apartment, one officer replied: "Because that would just give us a bunch of dope and the hassle of having to book him (the suspect). We've got all the dope we need in the property room. Just stick to rounding up cases with big money and stay away from warrants."

Selecting cases on the basis of potential gain creates another problem, one that not only causes neglect of obligatory police functions but also tampers with civil rights. To raise revenue, asset gathering operations must focus on suspects with money and other resources. Large-scale dealers could not have achieved their status without connections and suppliers. Their ties and their discretion make them largely inaccessible to seizure operations because they are not easily "reversible." Many of these dealers value safety more, than profit, and work by selling drugs on credit in an operation known as "fronting." They recognize the legal advantage of keeping cash separate from illegal drugs. The big dealers do not make natural suspects for seizure strategies, nor are they easy prey. Consequently agents take the suspects they can get, namely lower-level dealers and ordinary users who fall victim to enterprising informants.

Another incident involved a 19-year-old male college sophomore, who came under surveillance while making routine deliveries of various drugs in a certain county jurisdiction. To obtain information, the researcher arranged and made an authorized purchase of two ounces of marijuana from the suspect. This individual turned out to be a "mule," a person who transports drugs but usually does not make buys or negotiate deals. The regular procedure in situations such as this was to arrest the suspect and then coerce him into cooperating with law enforcement by setting up the bigger dealer with whom he was working.

The researcher was surprised when the agent requested that a meeting be arranged with the suspect. A few days later, the researcher brought the suspect to a bar where the agent was waiting. The agent, having gained the suspect's confidence through conversation and by paying for drinks, persuaded him to secure a personal loan from a bank by using his vehicle as collateral so that he might purchase five pounds of marijuana. The ploy was successful and the suspect was arrested a few days later. This student was not searching for a large quantity of drugs, nor did he view himself as a dealer until the agent showed him how to become one. Thus, at times, undercover policing actually may promote crime by manipulating individuals who are naive, suggestible, or corruptible. Such activity not only victimizes ordinary people but also affects the conduct of police and their function in society.

The Impact of Forfeiture on Police Conduct

The following example demonstrates how the seizure motive can undermine police interest of service to the community. The suspect, one of the larger "players" whom the researcher encountered, dealt in marijuana, barbiturates, cocaine, and stolen property. The researcher had conducted two "buy-walks" with the suspect in order to establish a relationship. A buy-walk occurs when officers or their assistants purchase illegal substances, but officers do not make an arrest so that they may observe a situation and determine whether it will lead them higher in a drug ring's hierarchy.

The state agent wanted to reverse the suspect, but realized that a reverse strategy was impractical for this situation. The alternative was to serve a search warrant that ideally would occur when the suspect possessed a large amount of cash that could be seized. As a result, the researcher was required to stay in close contact with the suspect for two days; during that time the dealer received a quarter-kilogram of cocaine, a large shipment. This shipment was worth about $7,000 in bulk and as much as $13,000 on the street. The researcher relayed this information to the agent in charge of the operation.

In this case the researcher felt that the only decision to be made was when the warrant should be served. He believed that the narcotics division of the involved state agency would wish to intervene before the drugs could be resold. Proper police procedure does not mandate that agents act immediately on information which makes an arrest possible. If that were so, valuable periods of surveillance could not be conducted. The researcher, however, was surprised when he was instructed to observe the suspect's transactions to determine the rate at which the cocaine was being resold. Less drugs meant more cash, and the agent's objective was to seize currency rather than cocaine. The case was successful as to proceeds, but perhaps not in view of the quantity of cocaine that officers knowingly permitted to reach consumers. This incident illustrates that a focus on revenue requires police to compromise law enforcement in a manner that may harm rather than protect society.

The pressure created by a demand for productivity created competition among agents from nearby jurisdictions. This was magnified in rural county agencies that also had a city or town police force. Agents consequently became "turf conscious," regarding negatively the arrests of mutual suspects by agents from other agencies because those agents had taken away potential profit and had nullified the time and effort invested in surveillance. Thus operations often disintegrated because of a general lack of interagency cooperation, and numerous suspects were left at large.

One large case collapsed for this reason. A well-known drug dealer, who traded crack and cocaine in a small rural town, had been frequenting a neighboring jurisdiction to visit a woman with whom the researcher became acquainted. The suspect had been delivering drugs on weekly visits and was said to always have a large supply on his person. A city narcotics agent arranged for the researcher and a second undercover informant, a female posing as the researcher's date, to meet with the suspect for a small party at a residence approximately two miles from the city limit, the agent's jurisdictional boundary. The researcher notified the agent when the suspect was coming and described the route he would take.

The researcher and his associate noticed that the suspect possessed a kilogram of cocaine and had an unknown amount of cash in a gallon-sized plastic freezer bag. They attempted to manipulate the dealer into entering the city police department's jurisdiction by suggesting various bars that the group might patronize. The suspect refused to go, and the deal stalled.

Other agents learned what was happening by monitoring surveillance equipment, hidden wires fixed to each informant, but they were powerless to act because of the jurisdictional dilemma. Nothing prevented them, however, from contacting the county sheriff's department or notifying the state agency, who might have conducted a vehicle stop. Even so, the agents took no action, and the suspect slipped away with his bag of money and cocaine.

Even in cases involving children's welfare, officers sometimes failed to notify other agencies. In one such case, officers of a state agency monitored the daily activities of a marijuana and cocaine dealer for a long period because he was a vital link in an interstate drug ring. On one occasion, while the researcher was waiting with the suspect late at night for a phone call regarding a shipment of cocaine, he saw the suspect overdose; he had been injecting cocaine repeatedly for two hours. The man came staggering from a bathroom and muttered something unintelligible as he walked toward a patio. He forgot to open a sliding glass door and rammed his body through the glass, cutting his face and arms badly. His wife called for an ambulance and then revealed that he had overdosed twice before.

Less than a week later, the researcher was invited to a party to celebrate the suspect's release from the hospital. The party was disrupted when a friend of the suspect brought warning of a possible raid, thus prompting the suspect to retreat to a motel room with his wife and her 12-year-old son from a previous marriage. Suffering from intense paranoia, they remained there for eight days where the researcher visited them twice.

The boy in this family had failed three grades in school and was permitted to smoke pot and drink beer. The case was unfolding in late September, when he should have been attending school. This issue was raised by the suspect's wife, who had received warnings of legal action due to the boy's excessive absences. Furthermore, during this period, the suspect traveled with his wife to a bordering state to secure drugs, leaving the youth alone in the motel room for two days.

The researcher relayed the details of this situation to the agents working the case, who listened with indifference. The researcher recommended that the agents contact the Department of Human Services (DHS), but was told that such action would only disrupt the case; DHS would be notified after an arrest was made.

This case dragged on for another month before the suspect was arrested in a marijuana field in another county. When the researcher inquired about the boy, two agents explained that the time required to contact a social worker and complete the paperwork associated with that step could be better spent in making another case.

During the summer of 1990, the researcher spent several weeks concentrating on locating marijuana patches. This task was difficult because of the secretive nature of marijuana farming and the suspicion among farmers who previously had lost crops to thieves. To induce growers to reveal the location of their crops, the researcher joined suspects in planting other patches, thus becoming a "partner." This act fostered a common bond, which often produced the information that agents desired. The researcher observed that marijuana growers took a great deal of pride in their work and often bragged about their botanical abilities. When he expressed doubt about the truthfulness of growers' claims, occasionally they showed him a patch as proof of their cultivation skills.

One eradication case demonstrated how the objective of raising revenue undermined the police functions of apprehending criminals and enforcing narcotics laws. The researcher traveled with a suspect to a rural county, while six state agents in three vehicles tailed the suspect's truck to the site where the researcher had visited twice. Another group of state agents, the "take-down" team, waited in the woods at the edge of a marijuana field. This was the researchers's largest case in terms of the number of agents involved, the amount of marijuana (approximately 50 pounds), and the potential value of the plants. The marijuana grew in three loosely connected rectangular patches, each containing approximately 30 plants 12 to 16 feet high.

The researcher and the suspect arrived at the location and hiked two miles to reach the patches. This period was very suspenseful because armed, camouflaged agents were filming every move. The suspect was armed with a semi-automatic shotgun and a nine-millimeter pistol: the researcher carried a rifle. The possibility of gunfire and the size of the deal created a great deal of anxiety.

The suspect had come to the patches on this occasion to fertilize the plants with a liquid nitrogen solution. After he and the researcher had tended to about half of the plants, agents emerged from the brush, pointing automatic weapons. Both the suspect and the researcher were ordered to lie on the ground, and were handcuffed. To protect the researcher's identity, the agents subjected him to everything that was done to the suspect, such as frisking and interrogating. The agents cut down the plants, seized the suspect's firearms, took approximately $300 in cash, which was in his wallet, and another $200 from the glove box in his truck. A quick records check on the truck showed that the grower did not own it; thus seizure of this vehicle was an unattractive option.

After taking everything of value, the agents ordered the grower to enter his truck and leave, without formally arresting him for cultivating marijuana. In effect they appeared to rob the suspect. When the researcher inquired about this questionable use of discretion, an agent replied that the grower was subject to being indicted at a later date. The suspect had not been charged formally when this study was concluded.

In several cases that the researcher observed, members of the law enforcement community compromised legitimate police functions to secure profits. This last case is significant because the pursuit of higher goals was completely abandoned. Usually the objectives of seizure operations were disguised and mixed with traditional activities, including arrests, but in this case the taking of assets was displayed boldly as the foremost concern.

An Assessment of Asset Forfeiture

Before asset forfeiture policies were established, narcotics cases were assigned priority by the amount of drugs involved and the level of threat to society posed by suspects. The observations made here, however, show that asset seizure has become the primary objective of drug enforcement. The problematic nature of asset forfeiture policy became apparent when the development of specific narcotics cases was observed. Before the procedural stage of the observed cases, the fundamental function of narcotics divisions was made clear to officers and agents through supervisors' decisions as to which cases would be pursued.

Selection of cases on the basis of seizure policy creates two basic problems. First, the process of raising revenue through asset forfeiture often requires police to concentrate on cases that offer little or no direct social benefit. Second, the suspects involved in these cases often are not engaged in serious criminal activity. Their personal profiles differ greatly from those of the drug lords, for whom asset forfeiture strategies were designed.

Equally disturbing is the effect of asset-hunting operations on police conduct; they elevate both the image and the reality of the private soldier over those of the public servant. Too often the tactics required to generate regular seizures conflict with the ideals of protecting and serving the public. A situation has developed, which allows narcotics supervisors to choose justifiably between strategies that produce revenue and those which acknowledge the demands of justice.

The recent Supreme Court decisions have done little to alter the present approach of forfeiture programs. Both *Austin v. United States* (1993) and *U.S. v. A Parcel of Land* (1993) set limits on forfeiture, thus protecting citizens' civil liberties. These restrictions, however, will not necessarily limit the scope of victimization and intrusion; they may even worsen the present condition. The principle of proportionality, for example, confines law enforcement to less property per seizure, but may invite more frequent application of the tactic so as to maintain revenue levels already fixed in agency budgets.

In certain cases, asset forfeiture has proved to be a valuable enforcement tool. This potential benefit, however, must be weighed against unfavorable consequences. This study addresses what recently has been considered a primary question concerning forfeiture laws: "What impact will asset forfeiture have on police operations and management?" (Holden 1993:1). It is apparent that asset forfeiture is already being institutionalized within law enforcement; this process is influencing its disposition. Although the narcotics units observed in this study were confined to one general locale, the mid-south, neither empirical studies nor journalistic accounts suggest that seizure-based policing tactics differ elsewhere. Certainly, further examinations of asset forfeiture programs should be pursued. Interrelated topics to be addressed include comparative analysis of the levels of assets seized by federal and state agencies, by regions of the country; the relationship of forfeiture to the fiscal autonomy of the police (Miller and Bryant Forthcoming); the soundness of conceptualizing forfeiture as legitimized police deviance; and selective targeting by race and class.

The redirection of narcotics enforcement is manifested theoretically in broader implications for the entire interaction of law enforcement with society at large. The inherent contradictions of asset seizure practices have surfaced as highly controversial civil liberties violations which increasingly have eroded our sense of fairness and have caused drug enforcers to subordinate justice to profit. This insidious redirection is rooted in and propelled by American values of success, specifically profit. Societal and governmental opposition rarely succeeds in deterring means of income generation. The enforcers' inability to combat the pervasive illicit drug market does not justify legal mechanisms whereby law enforcement agencies share the wealth of drug trafficking under the guise of "service" to society.

Asset forfeiture has given drug enforcers a powerful incentive to maintain and manage economic mechanisms that allow the illegal drug market to continue. In this market, the drug enforcers and the drug traffickers become symbiotic beneficiaries of the "War on Drugs." Ironically, in its failure to reduce the marketing of illegal drugs, drug enforcement has succeeded in profiteering. Unfortunately, continued "success" in this area portends further and more widespread subversion of our ideals of fairness and justice.

References

Adler, P. A. and P. Adler (1987) "The Past and Future of Ethnography." *Journal of Contemporary Ethnography* 16:4–24.

Block, A. (1993) "Issues and Theories on Covert Policing." *Crime, Law and Social Change: An International Journal* (special issue) 18:35–60.

Braithwaite, J. B. Fisse, and G. Geis (1987) "Covert Facilitation and Crime: Restoring Balance to the Entrapment Debate." *Journal of Social Issues* 43:5–42.

British Sociological Association (1973) *Statement of Ethical Principles and Their Application to Sociological Practice.*

Bugliosi, V. T. (1991) *Drugs in America: The Case for Victory.* New York: Knightsbridge.

Bulmer, M. (1980) "Comment on the Ethics of Covert Methods." *British Journal of Sociology* 31:59–65.

Burden, O. P. (1988) "Finding Light at the End of the Drug War Tunnel." *Law Enforcement News*, December 15, pp. 8.

Bureau of Justice Statistics (1991) *Sourcebook of Criminal Justice Statistics.* Washington. DC: National Institute of Justice.

Carter, D. L. (1990) "Drug Related Corruption of Police Officers: A Contemporary Typology." *Journal of Criminal Justice* 18:85–98.

Carter, D. L. and D. W. Stephens (1988) *Drug Abuse by Police Officers: An Analysis of Policy Issues.* Springfield, IL: Thomas.

Chambliss, W. (1988) *On the Take: From Petty Crooks to Presidents.* Bloomington, IN: Indiana University Press.

Denzin, N. (1968) "On the Ethics of Disguised Observation." *Social Problems* 115:502–504.

Dombrink, J. (1988) "The Touchables: Vice and Police Corruption in the 1980's." *Law and Contemporary Problems* 51:201–32.

Dortch, S. (1992) "356 Marijuana Plants, House, Weapons Seized." *Knoxville News-Sentinel*, August 29, pp. 1.

Drug Policy Foundation (1992) "Asset Forfeiture: Fair Practice or Foul Play?" (Film) *Drug Forum*, Date Not Available.

Erikson, K. T. (1967) "Disguised Observation in Sociology." *Social Problems* 14:366–72.

Fried, D. J. (1988) "Rationalizing Criminal Forfeiture." *Journal of Criminal Law and Criminology* 79:328–36.

Galliher, J. F. (1973) "The Protection of Human Subjects: A Reexamination of the Professional Code of Ethics." *The American Sociologist* 8:93–100.

Goffman, E. (1959) *The Presentation of Self in Everyday Life.* New York: Doubleday.

Goldstein, A. and H. Kalant (1990) "Drug Policy: Striking the Right Balance." *Science*, September 28, pp. 9–13.

Greek, C. (1992) "Drug Control and Asset Seizures: A Review of the History of Forfeiture in England and Colonial America." In Thomas Mieczkowski (eds.), *Drugs, Crime, and Social Policy*, pp. 4–32 Boston, MA: Allyn & Bacon.

Holden, R. N. (1993) "Police and the Profit-Motive: A New Look at Asset Forfeiture." *ACJS Today* 12:2.

Humphreys, L. (1970) *Tearoom Trade: Impersonal Sex in Public Places.* New York: Aldine.

Jacobs, D. (1992) "Police Take $700 from Man, Calling It Drug Money." *Knoxville News-Sentinel*, February 23, pp. 1.

Klockars, C. (1983) *Thinking About Police.* New York: McGraw-Hill.

Krauss, M. B. and E. P. Laezear, eds. (1991) *Searching for Alternatives: Drug-Control Policy in the United States.* Stanford, CA: Hoover Institution Press.

Lawrence, C. C. (1988) "Congress Clears Anti-Drug Bills." *Congressional Quarterly Weekly Report*, October 29, pp. 3145.

Manning, P. K. (1980) *The Narc's Game: Organizational and Informational Limits on Drug Enforcement.* Cambridge, MA: MIT Press.

Manning, P. K. and L. J. Redlinger (1977) "Invitational Edges of Corruption: Some Consequences of Narcotic Law Enforcement." In P. Rock (ed.), *Drugs and Politics*, pp. 279–310. Rutgers, NJ: Transaction Books.

Marx, G. (1988) *Undercover: Police Surveillance in America.* Los Angeles: Twentieth Century Fund Books.

McAlary, M. (1987) *Buddy Boys: When Cops Turn Bad.* New York: Putnam's.

Miller, J. M. (1991) "Inside Narcotics Policing Operations." Master's thesis, Middle Tennessee State University.

Miller, J. M. and K. Bryant (Forthcoming) Predicting Police Behavior: Ecology, Class, and Autonomy." *American Journal of Criminal Justice*.

Moore, M. (1977) *Buy and Bust: The Effective Regulation of an Illicit Market in Heroin*, Lexington, MA: Lexington Books.

—. (1988) "Drug Trafficking." In *Crime File*, pp. 1–4. Washington National Institute of Justice.

Morganthau, T. and P. Katel (1990) "Uncivil Liberties? Debating Whether Drug-War Tactics Are Eroding Constitutional Rights." *Newsweek*, April 29, pp. 18–21.

Myers, H. L. and J. Brzostowski (1982) "Dealers, Dollars, and Drugs: Drug Law Enforcement's Promising New Program." *Drug Enforcement* (Summer): 7–10.

Osborne, J. (1991) *The Spectre of Forfeiture*. Frazier Park, CA: Access Unlimited.

Polsky, N. (1967) *Hustlers, Beats, and Others*. New York: Anchor.

Reid. S. T. (1991) *Crime and Criminology:* San Francisco, CA: Holt, Rinehart, and Winston.

Ronai, C. R. and C. Ellis (1989) "Turn-Ons for Money: Interactional Strategies of the Table Dancer." *Journal of Contemporary Ethnography* 18:271–98.

Roth, J. A. (1962) "Comments on Secret Observation." *Social Problems* 9:283–84.

Schneider, A. and M. P. Flaherty (1991) "Presumed Guilty. The Law's Victims in the War on Drugs." *Pittsburgh Press*, August 11–16.

Shaw, B. (1990) "Fifth Amendment Failures and RICO Forfeitures." *American Business Law Journal* 28:169–200.

Shils, E. A. (1975) In *Center and Periphery: Essays in Macrosociology;* Chicago, IL: University of Chicago Press.

Stellwagen, L. D. (1985) "Use of Forfeiture Sanctions in Drug Cases." *Research in Brief* (July).

Stuart, C. (1990) "When Cops Go Bad." (Film) *Frontline*, July 18.

Trebach, A. S. (1987) *The Great Drug War*, Washington, DC: Drug Policy Foundation.

Trebach, A. S. and K. B. Zeese (1990) *Drug Prohibition and the Conscience of Nations*. Washington, DC: Drug Policy Foundation.

United States Department of Justice (1988) *Research Brief*. Washington, DC: National Institute of Justice.

Weisheit, R. A. (1991) "Drug Use Among Domestic Marijuana Growers." *Contemporary Drug Problems* 17:191–217.

Willson, E. (1990) "Did a Drug Dealer Own Your Home? (Criminal assets may be seized)." *Florida Trend*. February, pp. 6–9.

Wilson, J. Q. (1961) *Varieties of Police Behavior.* Cambridge, MA: Harvard University Press.

—. (1978) *The Investigators: Managing the F.B.I. and the Drug Enforcement Administration.* New York: Basic Books.

Wrobleski, H. M. and K. M. Hess (1990) *Introduction to Law Enforcement and Criminal Justice,* St. Paul, MN: West.

Cases Cited

Austin v. United States 113 S. Ct. 2801 (1993)

U.S. v. A Parcel of Land 113 S. Ct. 1126 (1993)

4. Women in Outlaw Motorcycle Gangs

Columbus B. Hopper
and Johnny Moore

This article is about the place of women in gangs in general and in outlaw motorcycle gangs in particular. Street gangs have been observed in New York dating back as early as 1825 (Asbury, 1928). The earliest gangs originated in the Five Points district of lower Manhattan and were composed mostly of Irishmen. Even then, there is evidence that girls or young women participated in the organizations as arms and ammunition bearers during gang fights.

The first gangs were of two types: those motivated primarily as fighters and those seeking financial gain. Women were represented in both types and they shared a remarkably similar reputation with street gang women more than 100 years later (Hanson, 1964). They were considered "sex objects" and they were blamed for instigating gang wars through manipulating gang boys. The girls in the first gangs were also seen as undependable, not as loyal to the gang, and they played inferior roles compared to the boys.

The first thorough investigation of youth gangs in the United States was carried out by Thrasher (1927) in Chicago. Thrasher devoted very little attention to gang girls but he stated that there were about half a dozen female gangs out of 1,313 groups he surveyed. He also said that participation by young women in male gangs was limited to auxiliary units for social and sexual activities.

Short (1968) rarely mentioned female gang members in his studies, which were also carried out in Chicago, but he suggested that young women became gang associates because they were less attractive and less socially adequate compared to girls who did not affiliate with gangs.

According to Rice (1963), girls were limited to lower status in New York street gangs because there was no avenue for them to achieve power or prestige in the groups. If they fought, the boys thought them unfeminine; if they opted for a passive role, they were used only for sexual purposes.

Ackley and Fliegel (1960) studied gangs in Boston in which girls played both tough roles and feminine roles. They concluded that preadolescent girls were more likely to engage in fighting and other typically masculine gang actions, while older girls in the gangs played more traditionally feminine roles.

Miller (1973, 1975) found that half of the male gangs in New York had female auxiliaries but he concluded that the participation of young women in the gangs

Columbus B. Hopper and J. Moore. *Journal of Contemporary Ethnography*, Vol. 18 No. 4, January 1990 383–387 © 1990 Sage Publications, Inc. Reprinted by permission of Sage Publications, Inc.

did not differ from that which existed in the past. Miller also pointed out that girls who formed gangs or who were associates of male gangs were lower-class girls who had never been exposed to the women's movement. After studying black gangs in Los Angeles, Klein (1971) believed that, rather than being instigators of gang violence, gang girls were more likely to inhibit fighting.

The most intensive studies of female gang members thus far were done by Campbell (1984, 1986, 1987) on Hispanic gangs in New York City. Although one of the three gangs she studied considered itself a motorcycle gang, it had only one working motorcycle in the total group. Therefore, all of the gangs she discussed should be thought of as belonging to the street gang tradition.

Campbell's description of the gang girls was poignant. The girls were very poor but not anomic; rather, they were true believers in American capitalism, aspiring to success as recent immigrants always have. They were torn between maintaining and rejecting Puerto Rican values while trying to develop a "cool" streetwise image.

As Campbell reported, girl gang members shared typical teenage concerns about proper makeup and wearing the right brands of designer jeans and other clothing. Contrary to popular opinion, they were also concerned about being thought of as whores or bad mothers, and they tried to reject the Latin ideal that women should be totally subordinate to men. The basic picture that came out of Campbell's work was that gang girls had identity problems arising from conflicting values. They wanted to be aggressive and tough, and yet they wished to be thought of as virtuous, respectable mothers.

Horowitz (1983, 1986, 1987) found girls in Chicano gangs to be similar in basic respects to those that Campbell described. The gang members, both male and female, tried to reconcile Latin cultural values of honor and violence with patterns of behavior acceptable to their families and to the communities in which they existed.

The foregoing and other studies showed that girls have participated in street gangs as auxiliaries, as independent groups, and as members in mixed-gender organizations. While gangs have varied in age and ethnicity, girls have had little success in gaining status in the gang world. As reported by Bowker (1978, Bowker and Klein, 1983), however, female street gang activities were increasing in most respects; he thought that independent gangs and mixed groups were increasing more than were female auxiliary units.

Unlike street gangs that go back for many years, motorcycle gangs are relatively new. They first came to public attention in 1947 when the Booze Fighters, Galloping Gooses, and other groups raided Hollister, California (Morgan, 1978). This incident, often mistakenly attributed to the Hell's Angels, made headlines across the country and established the motorcycle gangs' image. It also inspired *The Wild Ones*, the first of the biker movies released in 1953, starring Marlon Brando and Lee Marvin.

Everything written on outlaw motorcycle gangs has focused on the men in the groups. Many of the major accounts (Eisen, 1970; Harris, 1985; Montegomery, 1976; Reynolds, 1967; Saxon, 1972; Thompson, 1967; Watson, 1980; Wilde, 1977;

Willis, 1978; Wolfe, 1968) included a few tantalizing tidbits of information about women in biker culture but in none were there more than a few paragraphs, which underscored the masculine style of motorcycle gangs and their chauvinistic attitudes toward women.

Although the published works on outlaw cyclists revealed the fact that gang members enjoyed active sex lives and had wild parties with women, the women have been faceless: they have not been given specific attention as functional participants in outlaw culture. Indeed, the studies have been so onesided that it has been difficult to think of biker organizations in anything other than a masculine light. We have learned that the men were accompanied by women, but we have not been told anything about the women's backgrounds, their motivations for getting into the groups, or their interpretations of their experiences as biker women.

From the standpoint of the extant literature, biker women have simply existed; they have not had personalities or voices. They have been described only in the contemptuous terms of male bikers as "cunts," "sluts," "whores," and "bitches." Readers have been given the impression that women were necessary nuisances for outlaw motorcyclists. A biker Watson (1980:118) quoted, for example, summed up his attitude toward women as follows: "Hell," he said, "if I could find a man with a pussy, I wouldn't fuck with women. I don't like 'em. They're nothing but trouble."

In this article, we do four things. First, we provide more details on the place of women in arcane biker subculture, we describe the rituals they engage in, and we illustrate their roles as money-makers. Second, we give examples of the motivations and backgrounds of women affiliated with outlaws. Third, we compare the gang participation of motorcycle women to that of street gang girls. Fourth, we show how the place of biker women has changed over the years of our study, and we suggest a reason for the change. We conclude by noting the impact of sex role socialization on biker women.

Methods

The data we present were gathered through participant observation and interviews with outlaw bikers and their female associates over the course of 17 years. Although most of the research was done in Mississippi, Tennessee, Louisiana, and Arkansas, we have occasionally interviewed bikers throughout the nation, including Hawaii. The trends and patterns we present, however, came from our study in the four states listed.

During the course of our research, we have attended biker parties, weddings, funerals, and other functions in which outlaw clubs were involved. In addition, we have visited in gang clubhouses, gone on "runs," and enjoyed cookouts with several outlaw organizations.

It is difficult to enumerate the total amount of time or the number of respondents we have studied because of the necessity of informal research procedures. Bikers would not fill out questionnaires or allow ordinary research methods such as tape recorders or note taking. The total number of outlaw motorcyclists we studied over the years was certainly several hundred. In addition to motorcycle gangs in open society, we also interviewed and corresponded with male and female bikers in state and federal prisons.

The main reason we were able to make contacts with bikers was the background of Johnny Moore, who was once a biker himself. During the 1960s, "Big John" was president of Satan's Dead, an outlaw club on the Mississippi Gulf Coast. He participated in the rituals we describe, and his own experiences and observations provided the details of initiation ceremonies that we relate. As a former club president. Moore was able to get permission for us to visit biker clubhouses, a rare privilege for outsiders.

Most of our research was done on weekends because of our work schedules and because the gangs were more active at this time. The bikers usually had a large party one weekend a month, or more often when the weather was nice, and we were invited to many of these.

At some parties, such as the "Big Blowout" each spring in Gulfport, there were a variety of nonmembers present to observe the motorcycle shows and "old lady" contests as well as to enjoy the party atmosphere. These occasions were especially helpful in our study because bikers were "loose" and easier to approach while partying. We spent more time with three particular "clubs," as outlaw gangs refer to themselves, because of their proximity.

In addition to studying outlaw bikers themselves, we obtained police reports, copies of Congressional hearings that deal with motorcycle gangs, and indictments that were brought against prominent outlaw cyclists. Our attempt was to study biker women and men in as many ways as possible. We were honest in explaining the purpose of our research to our respondents. They were told that our goal was only to learn more about outlaw motorcycle clubs as social organizations.

Dilemmas of Biker Research

Studying bikers was a conflicted experience for us. It was almost impossible to keep from admiring their commitment, freedom, boldness, and fearlessness; at the same time, we saw things that caused us discomfort and consternation because bikers' actions were sometimes bizarre. We saw bikers do things completely foreign to our personal values. Although we did not condone these activities, we did not express our objections for two reasons. First, we would not have been able to continue our study. Second, it was too dangerous to take issue with outlaws on their own turf.

Studying bikers was a risky undertaking for us, even without criticizing them. At times when we were not expecting any problems, conditions became hazardous. In Jackson, Tennessee, for example, one morning in 1985 we walked into an area where bikers had camped out all night. Half asleep and hung over, several of them jumped up and pulled guns on us because they thought we might be members of a rival gang that had killed five of their "brothers" several years earlier. If Grubby, a biker who recognized us from previous encounters, had not interceded in our behalf, we could have been killed or seriously injured.

Bikers would not humor many questions, and they did not condone uninvited comments. Even seemingly insignificant remarks sometimes caused a problem. In Biloxi on one occasion, we had an appointment to visit a biker clubhouse late on a Saturday afternoon in 1986. When we were admitted into the main room of the building, two women picked up four pistols that had been on a coffee table and scurried into a bedroom. Several men remained in front of a television set, watching a wrestling match.

Because we looked upon professional wrestling as a humorous sham, one of us made a light reference to it. Immediately the bikers became tense and angry; it was clear that another sarcastic comment would have resulted in our being literally thrown out of the clubhouse. In this way, we accidentally learned that some bikers take television wrestling seriously. It would have been a bad mistake to have questioned them about their reasons for liking the dubious sport. There was a human skull on a pole in front of their clubhouse but we thought it better to ignore it!

For practical purposes, both male and female bikers worship the Harley Davidson motorcycle. One Mississippi group that we studied extensively had an old flat-head "Hog" mounted on a high tree stump at the entrance to their clubhouse. When going in or out, members bowed to the old Harley or saluted it as an icon of the highest order. They took it very seriously. Had we not shown respect for their obeisance, our relationship would have been terminated, probably in a violent manner.

It was hard to fathom the chasm between bikers and the rest of us. Outlaw cyclists have no constraints except those their club mandates. When a biker spoke of something being "legal," he was referring to the bylaws of his club rather than to the laws of a state or nation. A biker's "legal" name was his club name that was usually inscribed on his jacket or "colors." Club names were typically one word, and this was how other members and female associates referred to a biker. Such descriptive names as Trench Mouth, Grimy, Animal, Spooky, and Red sufficed for most bikers we studied. As we knew them, bikers lived virtually a tribal life-style with few restraints. The freedom they enjoyed was not simply being "in the wind"; it was also emotional. Whereas conventional people fear going to prison, the bikers were confident that they had many brothers who would look for them inside the walls. Consequently, the threat of confinement had little influence on a biker's behavior, as far as we could tell.

Perhaps because society gave them so little respect, the bikers we studied insisted on being treated with deference. They gave few invitations to nonmembers or "citizens," and they were affronted when something they offered was refused. Our respondents loved to party, and they did not understand anyone who did not. Once we were invited to a club party by a man named Cottonmouth. The party was to begin at 9:00 p.m. on a Sunday night. When we told Cottonmouth that we had to leave at seven in the evening to get back home, we lost his good will and respect entirely. He could not comprehend how we could let anything take precedence over a "righteous" club party.

Bikers were suspicious of all conversations with us and with other citizens; they were not given to much discussion even among themselves. They followed a slogan we saw posted in several clubhouses: "One good fist is worth a thousand words." Studying outlaw cyclists became more difficult rather than easier over the course of our study. They grew increasingly concerned about being investigated by undercover agents. . . . At times, over the last years of our study, respondents whom we had known for months would suddenly accuse us of being undercover "pigs" when we seemed overly curious about their activities.

Our study required much commitment to research goals. We believed it was important to study biker women and we did so in the only way open to us—on the terms of the bikers themselves. We were field observers rather than critics or reformers, even when witnessing things that caused us anguish.

Problems in Studying Biker Women

Although it was difficult to do research on outlaw motorcycle gangs generally, it was even harder to study the women in them. In many gangs, the women were reluctant to speak to outsiders when the men were present. We did not hear male bikers tell the women to refrain from talking to us. Rather, we often had a man point to a woman and say, "Ask her," when we posed a question that concerned female associates. Usually, the woman's answer was, "I don't know." Consequently, it took longer to establish rapport with female bikers than it did with the men.

Surprisingly, male bikers did not object to our being alone with the women. Occasionally, we talked to a female biker by ourselves and this is when we were able to get most of our information and quotations from them. In one interview with a biker and his woman in their home, the woman would not express an opinion about anything. When her man left to help a fellow biker whose motorcycle had broken down on the road, the woman turned into an articulate and intelligent individual. Upon the return of the man, however, she resumed the role of a person without opinions.

The Place of Women in Outlaw Motorcycle Gangs

Although national outlaw motorcycle clubs of the 1980s had restricted their membership to adult males (Quinn, 1983), women were important in the outlaw lifestyle we observed. We rarely saw a gang without female associates sporting colors similar to those the men wore.

To the casual observer, all motorcycle gang women might have appeared the same. There were, however, two important categories of women in the biker world: "mamas" and "old ladies." A mama belonged to the entire gang. She had to be available for sex with any member and she was subject to the authority of any brother. Mamas wore jackets that showed they were the "property" of the club as a whole.

An old lady belonged to an individual man; the jacket she wore indicated whose woman she was. Her colors said, for example, "Property of Frog." Such a woman was commonly referred to as a "patched old lady." In general terms, old ladies were regarded as wives. Some were in fact married to the members whose patches they wore. In most instances, a male biker and his old lady were married only in the eyes of the club. Consequently, a man could terminate his relationship with an old lady at any time he chose, and some men had more than one old lady.

A man could require his old lady to prostitute herself for him. He could also order her to have sex with anyone he designated. Under no circumstances, however, could an old lady have sex with anyone else unless she had her old man's permission.

If he wished to, a biker could sell his old lady to the highest bidder, and we saw this happen. When a woman was auctioned off, it was usually because a biker needed money in a hurry, such as when he wanted a part for his motorcycle or because his old lady had disappointed him. The buyer in such transactions was usually another outlaw.

Rituals Involving Women

Outlaw motorcycle gangs, as we perceived them, formed a subculture that involved rituals and symbols. Although each group varied in its specific ceremonies, all of the clubs we studied had several. There were rites among bikers that had nothing to do with women and sex but a surprising number involved both.

The first ritual many outlaws were exposed to, and one they understandably never forgot, was the initiation into a club. Along with other requirements, in some gangs, the initiate had to bring a "sheep" when he was presented for membership. A sheep was a woman who had sex with each member of the gang during an initiation. In effect, the sheep was the new man's gift to the old members.

Group sex, known as "pulling a train," also occurred at other times. Although some mamas or other biker groupies (sometimes called "sweetbutts") occasionally volunteered to pull a train, most instances of train pulling were punitive in nature. Typically, women were being penalized for some breach of biker conduct when they pulled a train.

An old lady could be forced to pull a train if she did not do something her old man told her to do, or if she embarrassed him by talking back to him in front of another member. We never observed anyone pulling a train but we were shown clubhouse rooms that were designated "train rooms," and two women told us they had been punished in this manner.

One of the old ladies who admitted having pulled a train said her offense was failing to keep her man's motorcycle clean. The other had not noticed that her biker was holding an empty bottle at a party. (A good old lady watched her man as he drank beer and got him another one when he needed it without having to be told to do so.) We learned that trains were pulled in vaginal, oral, or anal sex. The last was considered to be the harshest punishment.

Another biker ritual involving women was the earning of "wings," a patch similar to the emblem a pilot wears. There were different types of wings that showed that the wearer had performed oral sex on a woman in front of his club. Although the practice did not exist widely, several members of some groups we studied wore wings.

A biker's wings demonstrated unlimited commitment to his club. One man told us he earned his wings by having oral sex with a woman immediately after she had pulled a train; he indicated that the brothers were impressed with his abandon and indifference to hygiene. Bikers honored a member who laughed at danger by doing shocking things

The sex rituals were important in many biker groups because they served at least one function other than status striving among members. The acts ensured that it was difficult for law enforcement officials, male or female, to infiltrate a gang.

Biker Women as Money-Makers

Among most of the groups we studied, biker women were expected to be engaged in economic pursuits for their individual men and sometimes for the entire club. Many of the old ladies and mamas were employed in nightclubs as topless and nude dancers. Although we were not able to get exact figures on the proportion of "table dancers" who were biker women, in two or three cities almost all of them were working for outlaw clubs.

A lot of the dancers were proud of their bodies and their dancing abilities. We saw them perform their routines in bars and at parties. At the "Big Blowout" in Gulfport, which is held in an open field outside of the city, in 1987 and 1988 there was a stage with a sound system set up for the dancers. The great majority of the 2,000 people in attendance were bikers from around the country so the performances were free.

Motorcycle women who danced in the nightclubs we observed remained under the close scrutiny of the biker men. The men watched over them for two reasons. First, they wanted to make sure that the women were not keeping money on the side; second, the cyclists did not want their women to be exploited by the bar owners. Some bikers in one gang we knew beat up a nightclub owner because they thought he was "ripping off" the dancers. The man was beaten so severely with axe handles that he had to be hospitalized for several months.

While some of the biker women limited their nightclub activities to dancing, a number of them also let the customers whose tables they danced on know they were available for "personal" sessions in a private place. As long as they were making good money regularly, the bikers let the old ladies choose their own level of nightclub participation. Thus some women danced nude only on stage; others performed on stage and did table dances as well. A smaller number did both types of dances and also served as prostitutes.

Not all of the money-making biker women we encountered were employed in such "sleazy" occupations. A few had "square" jobs as secretaries, factory workers, and sales persons. One biker woman had a job in a bank. A friend and fellow biker lady described her as follows: "Karen is a chameleon. When she goes to work, she is a fashion plate; when she is at home, she looks like a whore. She is every man's dream!" Like the others employed in less prestigious labor, however, Karen turned her salary over to her old man on payday.

A few individuals toiled only intermittently when their bikers wanted a new motorcycle or something else that required more money than they usually needed. The majority of motorcycle women we studied, however, were regularly engaged in work of some sort.

Motivations and Backgrounds of Biker Women

In view of the ill treatment the women received from outlaws, it was surprising that so many women wanted to be with them. Bikers told us there was never a shortage of women who wanted to join them, and we observed this to be true. Although it was unwise for men to draw conclusions about the reasons mamas and old ladies chose their life-styles, we surmised three interrelated factors from conversations with them.

First, some women, like the male bikers, truly loved and were excited by motorcycles. Cathy was an old lady who exhibited this trait. "Motorcycles have always turned me on," she said. "There's nothing like feeling the wind on your titties. Nothing's as exciting as riding a motorcycle. You feel as free as the wind."

Cathy did not love motorcycles indiscriminately, however. She was imbued with the outlaw's love for the Harley Davidson. "If you don't ride a Hog," she stated, "you don't ride nothing. I wouldn't be seen dead on a rice burner" (Japanese model). Actually, she loved only a customized bike or "chopper." Anything else she called a "garbage wagon."

When we asked her why she wanted to be part of a gang if she simply loved motorcycles, Cathy answered:

> There's always someone there. You don't agree with society so you find someone you like who agrees with you. The true meaning for me is to express my individuality as part of a group.

Cathy started "putting" (riding a motorcycle) when she was 15 years old and she dropped out of school shortly thereafter. Even with a limited education, she gave the impression that she was a person who thought seriously. She had a butterfly tattoo that she said was an emblem of the freedom she felt on a bike. When we talked to her, she was 26 and had a daughter. She had ridden with several gangs but she was proud that she had always been an old lady rather than a mama.

The love for motorcycles had not dimmed for Cathy over the years. She still found excitement in riding and even in polishing a chopper. "I don't feel like I'm being used. I'm having fun," she insisted. She told us that she would like to change some things if she had her life to live over, but not biking. "I feel sorry for other people; I'm doing exactly what I want to do," she concluded.

A mama named Pamela said motorcycles thrilled her more than anything else she had encountered in life. Although she had been involved with four biker clubs in different sections of the country, she was originally from Mississippi and she was with a Mississippi gang when we talked to her. Pamela said she graduated from high school only because the teachers wanted to get rid of her. "I tried not to give any trouble, but my mind just wasn't on school."

She was 24 when we saw her. Her family background was a lot like most of the women we knew. "I got beat a lot," she remarked. "My daddy and my mom both drank and ran around on each other. They split up for good my last year in school. I ain't seen either of them for a long time."

Cathy described her feelings about motorcycles as follows:

> I can't remember when I first saw one. It seems like I dreamed about them even when I was a kid. It's hard to describe why I like bikes. But I know this for sure. The sound a motorcycle makes is really exciting—it turns me on, no joke. I mean really! I feel great when I'm on one. There's no past, no future, no trouble. I wish I could ride one and never get off.

The second thing we thought drew women to motorcycle gangs was a preference for macho men. "All real men ride Harleys," a mama explained to us. Generally, biker women had contempt for men who wore suits and ties. We believed it was the disarming boldness of bikers that attracted many women.

Barbara, who was a biker woman for several years, was employed as a secretary in a university when we talked to her in 1988. Although Barbara gradually withdrew from biker life because she had a daughter she wanted reared in a more conventional way, she thought the university men she associated with were wimps. She said:

> Compared to bikers, the guys around here (her university) have no balls at all. They hem and haw, they whine and complain. They try to impress you with their intelligence and sensitivity. They are game players. Bikers come at you head on. If they want to fuck you, they just say so. They don't care what you think of them. I'm attracted to strong men who know what they want. Bikers are authentic. With them, what you see is what you get.

Barbara was an unusual biker lady who came from an affluent family. She was the daughter of a highly successful man who owned a manufacturing and distributing company. Barbara was 39 when we interviewed her. She had gotten into a motorcycle gang at the age of 23. She described her early years to us:

I was rebellious as long as I can remember. It's not that I hated my folks. Maybe it was the times (1960s) or something. But I just never could be the way I was expected to be. I dated "greasers," I made bad grades; I never applied myself. I've always liked my men rough. I don't mean I like to be beat up, but a real man. Bikers are like cowboys; I classify them together. Freedom and strength I guess are what it takes for me.

Barbara did not have anything bad to say about bikers. She still kept in touch with a few of her friends in her old club. "It was like a family to me," she said. "You could always depend on somebody if anything happened. I still trust bikers more than any other people I know." She also had become somewhat reconciled with her parents, largely because of her daughter. "I don't want anything my parents have personally, but my daughter is another person. I don't want to make her be just like me if she doesn't want to," she concluded.

A third factor that we thought made women associate with biker gangs was low self-esteem. Many we studied believed they deserved to be treated as people of little worth. Their family backgrounds had prepared them for subservience.

Jeanette, an Arkansas biker woman, related her experience as follows:

My mother spanked me frequently. My father beat me. There was no sexual abuse but a lot of violence. My parents were both alcoholics. They really hated me. I never got a kind word from either of them. They told me a thousand times I was nothing but a pain in the ass.

Jeanette began hanging out with bikers when she left home at the age of 15. She was 25 when we talked to her in 1985. Although he was dominating and abusive, her old man represented security and stability for Jeanette. She said he had broken her jaw with a punch. "He straightened me out that time," she said. "I started to talk back to him but I didn't get three words out of my mouth." Her old man's name was tattooed over her heart.

In Jeanette's opinion, she had a duty to obey and honor her man. They had been married by another biker who was a Universal Life minister. "The Bible tells me to be obedient to my husband," she seriously remarked to us. Jeanette also told us she hated lesbians. "I go in lesbian bars and kick ass," she said. She admitted she had performed lesbian acts but she said she did so only when her old man made her do them. The time her man broke her jaw was when she objected to being ordered to sleep with a woman who was dirty. Jeanette believed her biker had really grown to love her. "I can express my opinion once and then he decides what I am going to do," she concluded.

In the opinions of the women we talked to, a strong man kept a woman in line. Most old ladies had the lowly task of cleaning and polishing a motorcycle every day. They did so without thanks and they did not expect or want any praise. To them, consideration for others was a sign of weakness in a man. They wanted a man to let them know who was boss.

Motorcycle Women versus Street Gang Girls

The motorcycle women in our study were similar to the street gang girls described by Campbell and Horowitz because their lives were built around deviant social organizations that were controlled by members of the opposite sex. There were, however, important differences that resulted from the varying natures of the two subcultures.

As our terminology suggests, female associates of motorcycle gangs were women as opposed to the teenage girls typically found in street gangs. The biker women who would tell us their age averaged 26 years, and the great majority appeared to be in their mid-20s. While some biker women told us they began associating with outlaws when they were teenagers, we did not observe any young girls in the clubs other than the children of members.

Male bikers were older than the members of street gangs and it followed that their female companions were older as well. In one of the outlaw clubs we surveyed, the men averaged 34 years old. Biker men also wanted women old enough to be legally able to work in bars and in other jobs.

All of the biker women we studied were white, whereas street gang girls in previous studies were predominantly from minority groups. We were aware of one black motorcycle gang in Memphis but we were unable to make contact with it.

Biker women were not homogeneous in their backgrounds. While street gangs were composed of "home boys" and "home girls" who usually grew up and remained in the areas in which their gangs operated, the outlaw women had often traveled widely. Since bikers were mobile, it was rare for us to find a woman who had not moved around a lot. Most of the biker women we saw were also high school graduates. Two had attended college although neither had earned a degree.

While Campbell found girls in street gangs to be interested in brand name clothes and fashions, we did not notice this among motorcycle women. In fact, it was our impression that biker ladies were hostile toward such interests. Perhaps because so many were dancers, they were proud of their bodies but they did not try to fit into popular feminine dress styles. As teenagers they may have been clothes-conscious, but as adults biker women did not want to follow the lead of society's trend setters.

• • •

As another consequence of the age difference, biker women were not torn between their families and the gang. Almost all of the old ladies and mamas were happy to be rid of their past lives. They had made a clean break and they did not try to live in two worlds. The motorcycle gang was their focal point without rival. Whereas street gang girls often left their children with their mothers or grandparents, biker women did not, but they wanted to be good mothers just the same. The children of biker women were more integrated into the gang. Children went with their mothers on camping trips and on brief motorcycle excursions or "runs." When it was necessary to leave the children at home, two or three old ladies alternately remained behind and looked after all of the children in the gang.

The biker men were also concerned about the children and handled them with tenderness. A biker club considered the offspring of members as belonging to the entire group, and each person felt a duty to protect them. Both male and female bikers also gave special treatment to pregnant women. A veteran biker woman related her experience to us as follows:

> Kids are sacred in a motorcycle club. When I was pregnant, I was treated great. Biker kids are tough but they are obedient and get lots of love. I've never seen a biker's kid who was abused.

As mentioned, the average biker woman was expected to be economically productive, a trait not emphasized for female street gang members or auxiliaries. It appeared to us that the women in motorcycle gangs were more thoroughly under the domination of their male associates than were girls described in street gang studies.

The Changing Role of Biker Women

During the 17 years of our study, we noticed a change in the position of women in motorcycle gangs. In the groups we observed in the 1960s, the female participants were more spontaneous in their sexual encounters and they interacted more completely in club activities of all kinds. To be sure, female associates of outlaw motorcycle gangs have never been on a par with the men. Biker women have worn "property" jackets for a long time, but in the outlaw scene of 1989, the label had almost literally become fact.

Bikers have traditionally been notoriously active sexually with the women in the clubs. When we began hanging out with bikers, however, the men and the women were more nearly equal in their search for gratification. Sex was initiated as much by the women as it was by the men. By the end of our study, the men had taken total control of sexual behavior, as far as we could observe, at parties and outings. As the male bikers gained control of sex, it became more ceremonial.

While the biker men we studied in the late 1980s did not have much understanding of sex rituals, their erotic activities seemed to be a means to an end rather than an end in themselves, as they were in the early years of our study. That is to say, biker sex became more concerned with achieving status and brotherhood than with "fun" and physical gratification. We used to hear biker women telling jokes about sex but even this had stopped.

The shift in the position of biker women was not only due to the increasing ritualism in sex; it was also a consequence of the changes in the organizational goals of motorcycle gangs as evidenced by their evolving activities. As we have noted, many motorcycle gangs developed an interest in money; in doing so, they became complex organizations with both legal and illegal sources of income (McGuire, 1986).

When bikers became more involved in illegal behavior, they followed the principles of sex segregation and sex typing in the underworld generally. The low place of women has been well documented in the studies of criminal organizations (Steffensmeier, 1983). The bikers did not have much choice in the matter. When they got involved in financial dealings with other groups in the rackets, motorcycle gangs had to adopt a code that had prevailed for many years; they had to keep women out of "the business."

Early motorcycle gangs were organized for excitement and adventure; money-making was not important. Their illegal experiences were limited to individual members rather than to the gang as a whole. In the original gangs, most male participants had regular jobs, and the gang was a part-time organization that met about once a week. At the weekly gatherings, the emphasis was on swilling beer, soaking each other in suds, and having sex with the willing female associates who were enthusiastic revelers themselves. The only money the old bikers wanted was just enough to keep the beer flowing. They did not regard biker women as sources of income; they thought of them simply as fellow hedonists.

Most of the gangs we studied in the 1980s required practically all of the members' time. They were led by intelligent presidents who had organizational ability. One gang president had been a military officer for several years. He worked out in a gym regularly and did not smoke or drink excessively. In his presence, we got the impression that he was in control, that he led a disciplined life. In contrast, when we began our study, the bikers, including the leaders, always seemed on the verge of personal disaster.

A few motorcycle gangs we encountered were prosperous. They owned land and businesses that had to be managed. In the biker transition from hedonistic to economic interests, women became defined as money-makers rather than companions. Whereas bikers used to like for their women to be tattooed, many we met in 1988 and 1989 did not want their old ladies to have tattoos because they reduced their market value as nude dancers and prostitutes. We also heard a lot of talk about biker women not being allowed to use drugs for the same reason. Even for the men, some said drug usage was not good because a person hooked on drugs would be loyal to the drug, not to the gang.

When we asked bikers if women had lost status in the clubs over the years, their answers were usually negative. "How can you lose something you never had?" a Florida biker replied when we queried him. The fact is, however, that most bikers in 1989 did not know much about the gangs of 20 years earlier. Furthermore, the change was not so much in treatment as it was in power. It was a sociological change rather than a physical one. In some respects, women were treated better physically after the transition than they were in the old days. The new breed did not want to damage the "merchandise."

An old lady's status in a gang of the 1960s was an individual thing, depending on her relationship with her man. If her old man wanted to, he could share his position to a limited extent with his woman. Thus the place of women within a gang was variable. While all women were considered inferior to all men, individual females often gained access to some power, or at least they knew details of what was happening.

By 1989, the position of women had solidified. A woman's position was no longer influenced by idiosyncratic factors. Women had been formally defined as inferior. In many biker club weddings, for example, the following became part of the ceremony:

> You are an inferior woman being married to a superior man. Neither you nor any of your female children can ever hold membership in this club or own any of its property.

Although the bikers would not admit that their attitudes toward women had shifted over the years, we noticed the change. Biker women were completely dominated and controlled as our study moved into the late 1980s. When we were talking to a biker after a club funeral in North Carolina in 1988, he turned to his woman and said, "Bitch, if you don't take my dick out, I'm going to piss in my pants." Without hesitation, the woman unzipped his trousers and helped him relieve himself. To us, this symbolized the lowly place of women in the modern motorcycle gang.

Conclusion

Biker women seemed to represent another version of what Romenesko and Miller (1989) have referred to as a "double jeopardy" among female street hustlers. Like the street prostitutes, most biker women came from backgrounds in which they had limited opportunities in the licit or conventional world, and they faced even more exploitation and subjugation in the illicit or deviant settings they had entered in search of freedom.

It is ironic that biker women considered themselves free while they were under the domination of biker men. They had the illusion of freedom because they lived with men who were bold and unrestrained. Unlike truly liberated women, however, the old ladies and mamas did not compete with men; instead, they emulated and glorified male bikers. Biker women thus illustrated the pervasive power of socialization and the difficulty of changing deeply ingrained views of the relations between the sexes inculcated in their family life. They believed that they should be submissive to men because they were taught that males were dominant. While they adamantly stated that they were living the life they chose, it was evident that their choices were guided by values that they had acquired in childhood. Although they had rebelled against the strictures of straight society, their orientation in gender roles made them align with outlaw bikers, the epitome of macho men.

References

Ackley, E. and B. Fliegel (1960) "A social work approach to street-corner girls." *Social Problems* 5: 29–31.

Asbury, H. (1928) *The Gangs of New York.* New York: Alfred A. Knopf.

Bowker, L (1978) *Women. Crime, and the Criminal Justice System.* Lexington, MA: D. C. Health.

Bowker, L. and M. Klein (1983) "The etiology of female juvenile delinquency and gang membership: a test of psychological and social structural explanations." *Adolescence* 8: 731–751.

Campbell, A. (1984) *The Girls in the Gang.* New York: Basil Blackwell.

Campbell, A. (1986) "Self report of fighting by females." *British J. of Criminology* 26: 28–46.

Campbell, A. (1987) "Self-definition by rejection: the case of gang girls." *Social Problems* 34: 451–466.

Eisen, J. (1970) *Altamont.* New York: Avon Books.

Hanson, K. (1964) *Rebels in the Streets.* Englewood Cliffs, NJ: Prentice-Hall.

Harris, M. (1985) *Bikers.* London: Faber & Faber.

Horowitz, R. (1983) *Honor and the American Dream.* New Brunswick, NJ: Rutgers Univ. Press.

Horowitz, R. (1986) "Remaining an outsider: membership as a threat to research rapport." *Urban Life* 14: 238–251.

Horowitz, R. (1987) "Community tolerance of gang violence." *Social Problems* 34: 437–450.

Klein, M. (1971) *Street Gangs and Street Workers.* Englewood Cliffs. NJ: Prentice Hall.

McGuire, P. (1986) "Outlaw motorcycle gangs: organized crime on wheels." *National Sheriff* 38: 68–75.

Miller, W. (1973) "Race, sex and gangs." *Society* 11: 32–35.

Miller, W. (1975) *Violence by Youth Gangs and Youth Groups as a Crime Problem in Major American Cities.* Washington, DC: Government Printing Office.

Montegomery, R. (1976) "The outlaw motorcycle subculture." *Canadian J. of Criminology and Corrections* 18: 332–342.

Morgan, R. (1978) *The Angels Do Not Forget.* San Diego: Law and Justice.

Quinn, J. (1983) "Outlaw Motorcycle Clubs: A Sociological Analysis." M.A. thesis: University of Miami.

Reynolds, F. (1967) *Freewheeling Frank.* New York: Grove Press.

Rice, R. (1963) "A reporter at large: the Persian queens." *New Yorker* 39: 153.

Romenesko, K. and E. Miller (1989) "The second step in double jeopardy: appropriating the labor of female street hustlers." *Crime and Delinquency* 35: 109–135.

Saxon, K. (1972) *Wheels of Rage.* (privately published)

Short, J. (1968) *Gang Delinquency and Delinquent Subcultures.* Chicago, IL: University of Chicago Press.

Steffensmeier, D. (1983) "Organization properties and sex-segregation in the underworld: building a sociology theory of sex differences in crime." *Social Forces* 61: 1010–1032.

Thompson, H. (1967) *Hell's Angels.* New York: Random House.

Thrasher. F. (1927) *The Gang: A Study of 1,313 Gangs in Chicago.* Chicago, IL: University of Chicago Press.

Watson, J. (1980) "Outlaw motorcyclists as an outgrowth of lower class values." *Deviant Behavior* 4: 31–48.

Wilde, S. (1977) *Barbarians on Wheels.* Secaucus, NJ: Chartwell Books.

Willis, P. (1978) *Profane Culture.* London: Routledge & Kegan Paul.

Wolfe, T. (1968) *The Electric Kool-Aid Acid Test.* New York: Farrar. Straus & Giroux.

5. The Business of Illegal Gambling:

An Examination of the Gambling Business of Vietnamese Cafés

Tomson H. Nguyen

Since the mid-1990s, a new type of a video poker machine appeared in Vietnamese cafés in southern California. These machines change from video game mode to gambling mode using a remote control, therefore making it difficult for law enforcement to detect gambling. This study was conducted to better understand the social structure and gambling procedures of one Vietnamese café in southern California that uses these gambling machines. Data were collected throughout a 12-week period of covert observations. The findings detailed and described the gambling process and indicated that the social structure plays an important role in maintaining the café community.

Literature Review

Gambling is a universal cultural phenomenon that has existed for at least 4,000 years, and virtually every culture has some form of gambling in which its members participate (Abt, Smith, and Christiansen 1985). It is a phenomenon that has been increasingly accepted by mainstream America. According to a survey conducted by the Minnesota State Lottery (1998) from 1989 to 1997, 80%–90% of respondents reported that they have gambled in their lifetime. Today, legal gambling is practically the norm in the United States. According to the North American Association of State and Provincial Lotteries, lotteries are offered in 38 states, including the District of Columbia. In addition, a casino, whether it is on land, on river, or on an ocean, is usually within driving distance from most major American cities (2004).

The public's acceptance of gambling, both the public and agents of social control, maintain that legal sanctions will not stop gambling, that people will continue to gamble regardless of the legality of such activities, and that enforcement is an ineffective deterrent (Rosecrance 1988). Gambling, whether legal or illegal, remains an important presence on the American scene. It occurs everywhere: in the workplace, in schools, in the home, and even in churches. Illegal gambling is indeed widespread (Abt et al. 1985). This also can be said about the type of individuals who illegally gamble. Rosecrance noted in his study that a 65-year-old bookmaker who has been in the business for over 40 years had two police officers who were regular customers!

Deviant Behavior, 25: 451–464, 2004.

Illegal gambling using video poker machines is a new criminal phenomenon (McSkimming 1999). Due to its secretive nature, there has been no research specially aimed at studying the gambling behavior associated with these machines as well as the way these machines operate. There is, on the other hand, a considerable amount of research done on gaming activities in taverns, but only focused on horse racing, sports competition, and shuffle board playing (Devereaux 1949; Zola 1963; Katovich and Reese 1987). As society has entered the technological age, gaming has taken on a whole new appearance. These electronic poker machines have been able to stay one step ahead of law enforcement by using technology to elude detection.

Methodology

The setting for this study was a Vietnamese café in southern California. The café was chosen because it catered to regulars who were also locals, and was expected to have a more established social structure as opposed to non-neighborhood taverns whose main customers are transients.

Another reason that this café was chosen was because the researcher had an already existing relationship with the owner. Typically, to reduce the chances of detection by law enforcement, Vietnamese cafés that offer their patrons the service of illegal gambling are very strict about to whom they allow access. For this reason, accessibility to such areas for the purpose of conducting research is nearly impossible. However, due to the relationship the researcher had with the owner, the researcher was granted full access to the café.

The researcher spent several days per week in order to be accepted as part of the social structure of the café. Each visit lasted approximately 45 minutes to 1 hour although, at times, observations lasted more than an hour and a half. The research lasted 12 weeks. In total, approximately 30 hours were spent in the field.

Methodologically, the decision was made to use covert non-participant observations as the main data collection technique. Although the owner of the café knew the researcher's purpose, no other patrons were informed about the study; therefore, the researcher was able to minimize subject reactivity. Since the social structure of the café was under scrutiny, covert observation was necessary to truly view the natural behavior of patrons in their environment. Observations were conducted while sitting inside the café within close proximity to the video poker gambling machines. The researcher observed behavioral patterns and social processes by watching and listening to what was being said and what the gamblers in the café were doing. No interactions with the gamblers were necessary.

In order to discreetly take notes, a wireless phone was utilized. Within the environment of the café, the use of a wireless phone attracts very little unwarranted attention. As a matter of fact, wireless phones are commonly used in cafés and do not distract from patrons' activities. Notes were taken using a special voice memo feature, which is similar to a handheld recording device. The researcher was able to use the voice memo feature of the phone to record notes while in the field, simply appearing as if he was making a telephone call.

Another method used for taking notes was jotting words or phrases on paper napkins while inside the café. Prior to the beginning of the research, a determination was made that this note-taking strategy may be required to take place in the restroom or outside the café in order to prevent other patrons from noticing any unusual activities. During observations, however, it was quite normal to write down words or phrases on the hands of the researcher, napkins, or lottery tickets without having to leave the immediate area. None of the patrons of the café seemed the least interested in the behavior of the researcher.

While conducting this study, there were potential risks or concerns for the safety of the researcher. One such risk is that cafés like the one observed have been known for attracting gang violence in southern California, particularly from Asian gangs. Aside from gang violence, Vietnamese cafés, similar to taverns and bars, are locations in which social conflicts may occur. Although Vietnamese cafés do not serve alcohol, as taverns and bars do, there is still a high potential for physical altercations between patrons.

The results of this study in regards to café patrons are likely to be limited to the Vietnamese population. However, the research findings regarding the social structure within the café may have strong relevance in Vietnamese cafés across the United States.

Social Structure Within Vietnamese Cafés

Similar to what McSkimming (1996) found in his study of tavern gaming and gambling, a fairly clear social structure does exist in the Vietnamese gambling café. The actors in this structure include gamblers, regular patrons, friends and family members of patrons or gamblers, new patrons (potential gamblers), and strangers.

The Gambler

Gamblers enter the café mainly for the purposes of gambling. Although gamblers may engage in certain activities similar to the regular, such as purchasing drinks and socializing with other café patrons, their main purpose in the café is to gamble. A gambler, for example, may spend up to 90% of his or her time in the café gambling.

Gamblers are highly trusted individuals within the café. They have gained this trust by developing a relationship with the owner as well as other patrons of the café. As such, they are given full access to all the services that the café offers. And since gamblers are the primary source of income, they are treated with much courtesy by the owner of the café.

The Regular

Regulars engage in normal café activities and maintain a certain atmosphere or community within the café (McSkimming 1996). Regular customer activities within Vietnamese cafés include purchasing drinks, playing video games, pool, or chess; watching sports; and socializing with waitresses, other regular patrons, and the owner. Although regulars may occasionally gamble a small amount of money from time to time, gambling is not the purpose of their presence in the café. The regulars' purpose of frequenting the café is to enjoy the atmosphere and the community that the café offers.

The Family/Friend

Friends or family members are those individuals who are either close friends or family members of the owner of the café. These individuals frequent the café as a place to hang out. Friends and family members are similar to regulars as to their purpose in the café with one minor difference: friends and family members are discouraged from gambling by the owner of the café. These individuals are highly trusted and respected members of the café due to their relationship with the owner. On occasion, they may even help out with the daily operations of the business (running the register, operating the gambling machines, and socializing with other patrons to maintain positive customer relations).

New Patrons (Potential Trusted Gamblers)

New patrons are always viewed with much caution. Since they are unknown to the established patrons of the café (i.e., gamblers, regulars, family/friend members, and owners), they are restricted from even being informed that gambling is available in the café. New patrons generally enter the café primarily for the purpose of engaging in normal café activities such as ordering drinks and watching a sports game. Although new patrons are viewed with much caution prior to being trusted, they also are considered potential trusted gamblers if their presence at the café increases.

New patrons can frequent the cafés to become familiar faces. When trust is developed, new patrons are then allowed to engage in all the services that the café offers, including gambling. At that time, regulars and gamblers guide new patrons on how to gamble.

The Stranger

The types of strangers who enter the café are dichotomized into two groups. The first type of stranger is an individual who is of Vietnamese ethnic background. The second type of stranger is a person of non-Vietnamese ethnic background—a genuine outsider.

Strangers of Vietnamese descent, especially those who speak Vietnamese, may enter the café to enjoy the social atmosphere without raising much, if any, suspicion. When these individuals enter the café and conduct normal café activities, such as ordering drinks, socializing with other members of the café community, or watching a sports game on television, very little attention is paid to them. However, although these strangers are not considered a major threat to the café, they are viewed cautiously until they reach the status of trusted café patron. Although caution tends to be exercised by all of the patrons, it is especially noticeable with the owner. For example, the owner usually does not initiate a gambling session while a "new face" is in the café. However, when a Vietnamese stranger acts suspicious by snooping around gambling tables or questioning individuals, the owner starts to take measures to protect the business such as switching gambling machines to video game mode and hiding gambling-related devices such as remote controls and records of winnings and losses.

On the other hand, when a stranger of non-Vietnamese ethnic background enters the café, all the individuals who make up the social structure of the café (regulars, gamblers, friend/family members, and owners) may feel an obligation to protect the café community. Since taverns and bars can be construed as "small societies" (Spradley and Mann 1975), one may expect the members of the "society" to protect it. In these cases, patrons may try to warn the owner by yelling his name so that the owner can switch the machines to video game mode with the touch of the remote control. The description below describes an incident of a stranger entering the café.

> A Hispanic male entered the café. Immediately after the individual entered the café, the patrons quickly notified the owner by yelling out the owner's name. The owner immediately grabbed a remote control from behind the counter and placed it in his hands and walked up to the stranger and nicely asked him, "Can I help you?" The stranger replied, "Do you have some matches?" The owner then stated, "Yes," and walked to the counter, grabbed some matches, and brought them to the stranger, all the while blocking the stranger from further entrance into the café where the gambling machines were in operation.

Although it is illegal to limit any person from entering the café based on race, creed, or color, the owners of the business can be wary of such individuals without raising any racial issues. Generally, only individuals of Vietnamese descent with the ability to speak Vietnamese enter Vietnamese cafés. As such, individuals not of Vietnamese descent would immediately raise suspicion, resulting in measures aimed at protecting the business.

Gambling Procedures

Owner/Gambling Operator

There is only one owner of the café shop. He has family members who frequent the café and help him run the business. Generally, the owner is the only individual running the business. At times when he is the one running the business, he plays the role of owner and gambling operator (an individual responsible for taking wagers, controlling the machines, cashing out, etc.). However, when family members are at the café, they may help out by operating the gambling machines. When this occurs, the owner and family members may switch roles based on convenience as to who is watching the store and who is controlling the gambling machines. Only family members have been observed helping out the owner as the gambling operator.

Gambling Machines

Gambling machines are all tabletop machines. Cafés can have both gambling machines and video game machines, which are also tabletop machines. The exterior appearance of the gambling and video game machines is similar. The only difference is the software inside. If an individual entered the café, he or she would visually see machines that all look as though they are video game machines, even though some may be gambling machines. In the café observed, there were a total of eight machines, five gambling machines and three video game machines.

Gambling machines have the ability to switch from a gambling machine to a video game machine using a remote control. Only the owner or the gambling operator has access to the remote control, which is usually kept behind the counter. Once the machine is in gambling mode, an individual may gamble on it with the controls present on the machine. During gambling, the owner may switch the machine to video game mode (usually done when a suspicious individual enters the café) and with the same buttons that the gambler was using to gamble, he or she can now play video games. Once the suspicious individual leaves, the owner can switch the machine back to gambling mode and let the gambler continue exactly where he or she left off. The video games that the gambling machine switches to include games such as Columns, Pac Man, and Tetris (Yi 2000). All machines are in video game mode when there are no individuals gambling in the café. At the touch of a remote control, an individual may control all aspects of the game including switching the display screen, resetting the credits (tilting), and inserting credits.

Initiating Gambling

Gambling on video poker machines in Vietnamese cafés is not available to anyone who wishes to play. There is a high level of cautiousness within the café community in regards to unknown individuals. This is because the café is operating an illegitimate gambling business that if discovered by law enforcement, would be detrimental to the business as well as the patrons. As such, anyone wishing to gamble in Vietnamese cafés must first be introduced to a regular or the owner of the café by an individual who is already a member of the social environment of the café (i.e., a regular, gambler, or family or friend member).

Individuals who would like to gamble initiate a gambling game in the following ways. They may sit at one of the gambling tables and alert the owner that they want to play by calling out his name or raising a hand when the owner sees them. They also may initiate a gambling game by first socializing with the owner and patrons of the café and then ask to play. Once the owner has been notified, the gamblers must sit at one of the gambling tables and wait for the gambling operator to approach the gambling machine. The description below is an example of an observation of a gambler initiating a gambling game. All the names have been changed to protect the identity of the individuals described.

> Ng came into the café and walked over to Hu [the owner of the café], who was sitting at the chess table, shook his hands, and sat down with him. Ng sat with Hu and conversed with him for about 25–30 minutes. Then, Ng walked over to the gambling machine near the entrance of the café. Hu immediately walked over to Ng with a remote control in hand.

Prior to gambling, many gamblers will socialize with the owner and patrons of the café. A description below is an example of the transition from socializing to gambling that a gambler would make once he or she enters the café.

> Soon after Yap entered the café, he walked over to the chess table where Hu was sitting with two other regulars. Yap shook all of their hands and sat down with them. After conversing for about 15 minutes, Yap walked over to the gambling table in the left corner of the café and sat down. Immediately after, Hu walked over to the gambling table.

Taking Wagers

Gambling within Vietnamese cafés is a cash only business. As such, only cash is accepted as a form of deposit. Cash makes transactions much easier and straightforward both for the gambler and the gambling operator. Accepting other forms of payment, such as jewelry, electronics, cars, and so forth, which are accepted methods of payment within many underground Vietnamese communities, is seen by the owner as more troublesome since he or she must, in turn, sell the items in order to retrieve his or her money. Tabs are also not accepted in the café. In order to gamble, a player must make a cash deposit.

Once a player has seated himself or herself at a table and is ready to gamble, he or she gives the gambling operator a certain amount of cash. In the majority of the cases, gamblers make cash deposits at the gambling table. However, an initial deposit also may occur away from the gambling table. This occurs in cases when the gambler is away from the table and opts to hand the cash to the gambling operator at the moment that he or she informs the gambling operator of the intention to gamble. A description below is a typical example of how gamblers make cash deposits prior to gambling.

> After speaking with Hu at the counter of the café, Jn walked over to the gambling table and sat down. Hu immediately walked out from behind the counter and over to the table where Jn was sitting. Once Hu got to the table, Jn retrieved an unspecified amount

of cash from his pocket and put it on the table. Hu picked up the money and used a remote control which he was holding in his hands and inserted the credits into the gambling machine. Hu then walked away and Jn began playing.

After a player has handed the deposit to the gambling operator, the gambling
operator inserts the credits, equivalent to the amount deposited, into the machine, using a remote control. At that time, the video game mode is switched over
to gambling mode. After the gambling operator deposits the credits, the gambler
may begin playing.

Once the gambler has lost all of the credits in the game, he or she may continue
playing by handing an additional deposit of a specified amount of cash to the
gambling operator. After this, the gambling process begins again from the start.

Cashing Out

After the gambler has completed the gambling and has accumulated a certain
amount of credits and decides to cash out, he or she notifies the gambling operator. The gambling operator will then approach the gambling table and determine
how much money is due to the player. The gambler must pay attention to the
amount of credits accumulated in order to verify that the amount paid out is
correct.

After the gambling operator has observed the amount the player has won, the
gambling operator resets the machine using the remote control so that the credits
are at 0. After the credits are reset, the gambling operator compensates the gambler for the winnings. Compensation for gamblers' winnings is almost always
completed at the gambling machine. The following description is an example of
an incident of the process of cashing out that the researcher observed. Every incident of cashing out occurred in a similar manner.

Once Sj finished gambling, he called Hu by yelling out Hu's first name. Hu looked over
at Sj from the chess table and Sj said, "I'm done." Hu then got up from the chess table,
walked over to Sj, and looked at the gambling machine to determine how much Sj had
won. Hu then pulled out a remote control from his pocket and used it to "tilt" the machine or reset the points back to 0. Hu then walked back to the counter and retrieved an
amount of cash, walked back to the gambling table where Sj is sitting, and handed the
cash directly to Sj. After which, Sj got up and left the gambling table.

The gambling operator rarely carries with him or her the money that is set
aside for paying off winning gamblers. Rather, the cash is kept behind the counter
or in the back room. After the gambling operator determines the amount a player
has won, the gambling operator retrieves the money and pays off the winner.
Usually, this is completed in a 5-minute timeframe in order to complete the gambling transaction and clear the gambling table for other gamblers.

Throughout the research, the researcher observed six cash outs by winning
gamblers. In comparison to the amount of gambling observed, approximately 30

gambling observations, the winning rate seemed to be stacked highly against the player. Although the payoff rate of the machines in the cafés are unavailable and were not provided by the owner, from the observations, 6 winners out of 30 observations seems one sided. Whereas, according to the Nevada Gaming Commission and State Gaming Control Board (2003), the payout rate of Nevada casinos must be at a minimum of 75% of the total amount wagered.

Discussion

The phenomenon of video poker machines in cafés, bars, or taverns is a growing concern. McSkimming (1996: 177) stated that "the most popular form of gambling in taverns today is not betting on pool or dart games. Rather, there are strong indications that systematic gambling in taverns is largely, limited to establishments with video poker machines." Nevertheless, gambling of this sort within Vietnamese cafés seems to be a difficult business to maintain, especially in southern California. A discussion with the owner of the café indicated that the business of gambling with these poker machines is a dying one and for good reasons.

First, the availability of legitimate casinos in southern California has made it difficult to maintain the illegal gambling business in Vietnamese cafés due to the competition for gamblers. Presently, there are four legitimate casinos in Los Angeles County (i.e., Bicycle Club, Hawaiian Gardens Casino, Commerce Casino, Crystal Park Casino) that are less than an hour's drive from Orange County, California. Many Vietnamese gamblers are now frequenting these casinos and, as a result, illegitimate gambling dens are losing clientele.

Another factor that has contributed to the lower demand for gambling on these illegal poker machines is the difficulty of attracting new clientele, especially since individuals who wish to gamble must be introduced to the owner by another individual who is already a known patron of the café. As such, the majority of gamblers that cafés now accommodate are those who are long-time gamblers. However, even the number of long-time gamblers is dwindling as these gamblers are also finding it much more advantageous to gamble at legitimate casinos.

Finally, the introduction of legitimate casinos in southern California has resulted in gambling that is regulated and controlled and, as such, individuals who engage in gambling do not have to be concerned about unfair gaming odds. Individuals who gamble in Vietnamese cafés may question the odds because video poker machines are not regulated and appear to overwhelmingly favor the house. Although it is unclear exactly how much the odds are in favor of the house in the café, one can speculate that it is much higher than gambling machines offered at casinos. For example, Nevada casinos generally give a payout rate of 90% to even 98% of the total amount wagered (Nevada Gaming Commission and State Gaming Control Board 2003).

Due to the factors presented above, gambling using video poker machines in southern California appears to be disappearing. It is difficult for illegitimate gambling businesses to compete with legitimate casinos, which offer better odds and a safer atmosphere in which to play. Even the café in this study is having a difficult time attracting new players. But this is not to say that gambling of this sort may end elsewhere. In the majority of cities across the United States, legitimate casinos are much less available to the public and, even if available, are not within driving distance. As a result, illegitimate gambling businesses similar to the one in this study may have no problem attracting a clientele of gamblers who have no other place to gamble.

References

Abt, V., J. F. Smith, and E. M. Christiansen. 1985. *The Business of Risk: Commercial Gambling in Mainstream America.* Lawrence, KA: University Press of Kansas.

Devereaux, E. C., Jr. 1949. *"Gambling and Social Structure: A Sociological Study of Lotteries and Horse Racing in Contemporary America."* Unpublished Doctoral Dissertation, Harvard University.

Katovich, M. A. and W. A. Reese, 11. 1987. "The Regular: Full-Time Identities and Memberships in an Urban Bar." *Journal of Contemporary Ethnography* 16:308–43.

McSkimming, M. 1996. "Deviance and Tavern Culture in Rural Pennsylvania: Gaming vs. Gambling." Unpublished Doctoral Dissertation, Indiana University of Pennsylvania.

Minnesota State Lottery. 1998. "Gambling in Minnesota: Gambling Participation Rates of Minnesota Adults." Report 1997–1.

Nevada Gaming Commission and State Gaming Control Board. 2003. Retrieved from http://gaming.state.nv.us/stats_regs.htm#regs

Nguyen, Tomson H. 2004. The business of illegal gambling: An examination of the gambling business of Vietnamese cafés. *Deviant Behavior,* 25, (5), 451–464.

North American Association of State and Provincial Lotteries. 2004. Retrieved from http://www.naspl.org/faq.html

Rosecrance, J. 1988. *Gambling Without Guilt: The Legitimation of an American Pastime.* Pacific Grove, CA: Brooks/Cole.

Spradley, J. P. and Mann, B. J. 1975. *The Cocktail Waitress: Work in a Man's World.* New York: John Wiley.

Yi, D. 2000. "Latest Game: Pacman with a Poker Face." *Los Angeles Times.* May 5, p. 7.

Zola, I. K. 1963. "Observations on Gambling in Lower-Class Setting." *Social Problems* 10:353–61.

6. Graduating from the Field

Richard Tewksbury

Learning how to conduct a high-quality research project is one of the core skills that social scientists are expected to acquire throughout their education. From high school sciences classes, to undergraduate research methods classes, through graduate level seminars in specific methodological techniques, the ways to conduct a research project are central to the social scientist's career. The specifics of how we carry out our research, and how we experience the process of conducting research, however, vary quite widely. Some methodologies (i.e., surveys and analyses of secondary data sets) are clearly more frequently employed than others. Other methodological approaches, such as documentary analysis and field research, are less frequently employed, although they provided the historical foundation for the social sciences.

Field research, most closely associated with the work of anthropologists and the Chicago School sociologists, today yields only a very small portion of published social science literature. The reason for this is not as important as the simple fact that few of us engage in the time-honored, traditional approach of studying social groups, processes, and settings by immersing ourselves in them and struggling to understand (and then explain to others) how a social setting is structured, how it operates, and what the rules, roles and experiences are within that setting.

To conduct high-quality, valuable (i.e., truly informative) field research, it is necessary to immerse oneself in a setting/community/context for extended periods of time and to interact with the individuals found there on a personal level. This means that the field researcher has to be willing to give a significant amount of time and personal emotional investment to the work. Fieldwork can drain a researcher's time, energy, emotions and put major strains on social and professional life while also drawing into question long-held moral, ethical, and value-laden stances.

Fieldwork, however, is not a never-ending activity. The stresses and strains of conducting field research have been well established and detailed by numerous others. However, one aspect of the fieldwork process that is typically addressed only as a postscript to discussions of "how-to" or cautionary tales regarding the conduct of such endeavors is the process and experience of terminating a field research project. The neglect of this important stage of the research process has been recognized for decades. Snow pointed out a quarter-century ago, "the disengagement process has received scant attention in published discussions. . . . a number of works allude to dis-engagement as one of the 'phases' or 'stages' . . . but with few exceptions . . . it is typically glossed over" (Snow 1980:101). Or, as Jorgensen says, the process of leaving the field "commonly is a routine process. As you move from concentrating on the collection of data and making notes to establishing files, analyzing findings, and theorizing, the amount of time spent in the field generally decreases" (1989: 117). Clearly, not even all guides to conducting fieldwork believe that there is much to be concerned with in the process of leaving the field. Even the major sociological instructional texts on the conduct of fieldwork essentially ignore the issue (see Berg 2001; Jorgensen 1989; Lofland and Lofland 1995). And, when the issue of leaving the field does arise, advice typically "is not unlike the advice one might give or receive in everyday life" (Lofland and Lofland 1995: 63). The neglect of this aspect of the research process is a clear weakness in the literature and in the training of new field researchers.

When the fieldworker anticipates the end, actually ends, and then moves back to a life void of daily fieldwork experiences, there are stresses, strains, and losses that the researcher must find ways to manage. It is this stage of the fieldwork endeavor that I wish to discuss and assess, hopefully assisting neophyte social scientists embarking on a fieldwork journey manage. The present discussion builds on, and adds to, that provided more than two decades ago by David Snow (1980). At that time Snow focused on three questions:

> One, when should the fieldwork or data-collection stage of the research enterprise be brought to a close? Two, are closure and disengagement primarily a function of informational sufficiency, or are they precipitated by various extraneous factors that pressure the researcher to bring the study to a close? And three, what are the various factors that often pressure the ethnographer to stay in the field and which work against closure and disengagement? (1980: 101).

I propose to elaborate on the same three questions as posed by Snow, but to do so in more depth while approaching them from a different view. Whereas Snow drew heavily from the anthropological literature (including traditional primitive society fieldwork) and other now-dated research studies, I propose a discussion that is both more sociologically centered and contemporary. While the processes, concepts, and emotions are largely the same, I draw only on my own experiences, offering both a more reflexive approach and examples with which sociologists, criminologists, and criminal justice scholars are more likely to relate.

I have found it most beneficial (both professionally and personally/emotionally) to view the process of approaching and working through the last stages of actual fieldwork as similar to a graduation. The emotions (anticipation, excitement, pride, apprehension, sadness) are the same as those I have found during my graduation experiences, and the effects on my life (again, personally and professionally) have been very similar to those accompanying my graduations. Both graduation and the termination of the field researcher's time in the field site are marks of having finished an educational process. Both are also times that mark one's readiness to move away from a group of others and activities that have occupied a central place in one's life. And, both graduation and the conclusion of active fieldwork are (most often) times that bring a change in one's social contacts and activities. Using this perspective, the experience of concluding one's active involvement with a field research setting may allow one to more easily manage the emotional and professional stresses and strains of the experience, as well as providing a familiar framework within which to reflexively see the experience.

My Fieldwork Experiences

The observations offered in this article are based on my own fieldwork experiences. Each of these projects has been very different in terms of the form and intensity of the fieldwork. From my completed fieldwork projects three are used as the basis for the content of this article. These three projects include over eight months of intensive, several days a week work with an urban police undercover unit, more than two years worth of semi-regular work with a traveling troupe of male strippers, and a briefer, multisite exploration of the structure and dynamics of gay bathhouses.

My work with the urban, undercover police unit is my most recently completed fieldwork. As I write this manuscript, I have not yet completed a substantive manuscript from this project. However, this fieldwork is clearly the impetus for the present manuscript; the idea for this article was generated as I drove home from my very last day of work in the field with the police. I worked 481 hours over an eight-month period actively engaged in data collection; this calculates to more than 60 hours a month, on average. However, for most of the period I worked three or four days a week (several weeks I was able to work only one day a week due to other professional responsibilities), with one or two days per week reserved for completing fieldnotes and other personal/professional responsibilities. During my time in the field I was integrated into a five-person undercover unit specializing in narcotics and prostitution enforcement. I worked with every member of the unit, often filling in as someone's partner when one officer was on vacation, in court, in training, or for some other reason not working. I was treated as a member of the unit, expected to do what the others did and received no special treatment. I worked all shifts, as the unit did not have a set work schedule but determined it by the needs of their cases. This included working day shifts, evenings, weekends, and overnight. The only restrictions on my participation were that I did not carry a firearm, nor did I have official authority to arrest, detain, or otherwise restrict any individual. However, to the civilians that we encountered, and to officers from other districts and departments, I was almost always identified as a unit member. Because of my open status as a researcher, I was able to openly take notes throughout our days (or nights).

My work with the male strippers involved my working with a traveling troupe of male dancers over a two and one-half year period (Tewksbury 1993, 1994). During the time I was with the troupe more than three dozen others passed through the troupe (only one other dancer was there when I started and still there when I left). Throughout my time with the troupe I was open, always identifying myself to new dancers as a researcher. Again, I was integrated into the day-to-day work of the troupe, but in this instance had no restrictions on what I did. The intensity of this project was less than that of the police work, in that we never worked more than two or three nights per week (although our shows very rarely began before 11:00 P.M., and we often did not finish before 3:00 A.M.). However, throughout the week we would put in hours rehearsing, working on costumes, and planning our travels (we traveled to approximately a dozen states while I was with the company). My role as a researcher was known to all insiders, but not to any outsiders (audiences, nightclub managers, men in competing troupes, etc.). I openly recorded notes while working, and several of my fellow dancers assisted me with interpretations and making sure I recorded "special" events and occurrences.

The third fieldwork project upon which this article is based is the most unique. My work in gay bathhouses is a strictly observational study (Tewksbury 2002). Because of the social structure and norms of these settings, men basically do not interact socially or verbally. The interactions that occur are of two varieties: those leading up to sexual activity and sexual activity. Interactions leading up to sexual activity are almost all based on body language, facial expressions, movements, and subtle gestures. This was only one of the special methodological challenges posed by the setting, however. A second challenge was that I was unable to openly take notes (no one knew who I was or what I was doing and to openly take notes would have been a major disruption to the setting), and I had no way to carry paper and pen with me. The norm in the setting is that men are nude, except for a bath towel that is either worn around the waist or carried. Consequently, I had nowhere to stash a notebook or pen! The time in the field for this project, however, was probably the most intense of all three projects. Whereas with the police and the strippers there were clearly "down times" when I could relax or concentrate on my job tasks, in the bathhouses it was necessary to constantly be watching (but not appear to be watching) the actions of others, including their obvious and subtle actions. In attempting to decode the communication methods and social structure/hierarchy of these settings there was not time to let my guard down or to fail to pay attention to my surroundings. Consequently, although I only completed 50 hours of formal observations in bathhouses, these were an especially intense 50 hours.

The discussion that follows focuses on identifying and assessing the experiences of a field researcher from the point of approaching the end of the data collection stage of the fieldwork through the time of actually leaving the field and moving to the process of formally analyzing field notes and writing the findings of the project. Within this context I discuss three issues that are at the core of the transition from active data collection in the field to former fieldworker: knowing when it is time to leave, the actual process of leaving, and the stresses of separation. Throughout the accounting of these issues my comments focus on how a field researcher can approach the issue in a healthy and productive way. And, while presenting this discussion, I frame the experiences in the context of a graduation, the transition marking the conclusion of one stage of life/work/research and the commencement of a new status and activities.

Knowing When It's Time to Leave the Field

Knowing when to actually terminate fieldwork is an important, yet also complex, issue. Snow (1980) suggested that fieldworkers know it may be time to leave when what is being experienced comes to be "taken for granted" and nothing new is being seen/noted, when no new data are being discovered to illuminate the researcher's interests/theories, and when the researcher has developed a high degree of confidence that what he or she sees and knows about the work being studied is accurate. These are difficult points to recognize, however. More than anything, the decision of when to leave the field is either a "gut-level" decision or something that may be decided for you.

Not only are there benefits to knowing when is the "right" time to leave the field, but so too are there some definite costs to staying too long and myriad issues that need to inform the decision. The benefits of being able to recognize when it is time to leave, and having the fortitude and preparation for leaving, include both professional and personal issues. Professionally, if you leave at the right time, you leave on positive terms with your field contacts, and you leave with your field contacts holding you in positive regard. This means that after you have returned to your "normal" life and settings, you are more likely to be welcomed back when the need arises to ask for clarification of issues or to get input from those in the field about whether your interpretations are accurate. Leaving when the time is right also means that you are more likely to be welcomed back for future research (or other professional activity), as are your colleagues who may wish to come to this field site in the future. In my own experience, when I left the police site, I felt that it was time, in part because in order to carry out other professional tasks (other research endeavors and my role as an advisor to the department) required that I not become too closely affiliated with the individuals with whom I was spending my time. So as to be able to return to the role of departmental advisor and "objective" researcher, I felt I had to leave. But, the timing was also (to some degree) contingent on my looking to the future and seeing that a change in administration was about to occur in the department. With the local government changing (due to elections), there would soon be a new police chief appointed, and in all likelihood an entirely new administration would come to the police department. If I hoped to maintain my position in the department, I needed to move back to my "objective" role, not remain in a role that could be perceived as advocacy or "too close" to the current administration. In my work with the male strippers, one issue that led me to conclude that it was time to leave the field was my repeatedly encountering students at our shows and students at the start of a new academic term recognizing me from a show they had previously attended. In order to maintain my status as a respected classroom instructor, I felt I had to leave the field; to have stayed in the field would have risked more recognitions by students. Rumors were already starting on campus, and some students were referring to me as "that stripper teacher."

Personal benefits of knowing when it is time to leave include the idea of leaving before your field contacts with whom you have started to develop a personal relationship get tired of having you around and leaving before you (as the researcher) become too immersed in the field to be able to effectively continue with the next stages of the research process. All too many of us know of colleagues who spent years and years on their dissertation (or other major) research, only to get the point of writing up the project and saying "I just can't stand to look at that data any longer!" The personal costs of this are obvious. You have spent immense amounts of time and energy in the field and end up feeling so overwhelmed that you need a break from the topic. All too often, however, this extends into a "permanent break." In my work, I had intended to develop the male stripper fieldwork into a book-length manuscript. However, the saturation I felt after the extended time in the field coupled with my completion of graduate school (i.e., graduation) and move to a new city/university/social life all contributed to my struggles to produce even a few articles from the data. To this day, I will occasionally pull the files of field notes out and think, "you know, I really could do something with these." However, it is now more than a decade later, my ambition and memories have faded and my time is sufficiently occupied that I do not feel I could do the project justice at this time. Consequently, I never have followed through on my original intent. In some ways, I feel that I did not really do justice to that project. This is not uncommon, however, as fieldworkers often report collecting significantly more data than they use (see Wax 1971).

The costs of staying too long include that the field contacts you have developed may simply become tired of your presence and either begin to avoid you or change their behavior in your presence. This really is not surprising, though, as such changes occur in many/most social situations. As a researcher, it is important to be aware that it is possible that a delayed Hawthorne Effect (Roethlisberger and Dickson 1939) can occur, in which your presence becomes noticeable—and field contacts alter their behavior—after your presence becomes normalized. This may be the consequence of rumors about what you are really doing in the site or simply a means for field contacts to try to distance themselves from someone who is not so interesting once the novelty has worn off. The important point is, if you stay too long, your data collection will suffer. After about seven months of my police research, several officers in my district began asking, "so, what are you really going to say in that book? You aren't going to talk about things like the X incident, are you?" Once officers realized that they had become comfortable enough with me being around that their behavior was the same as if I was not present, they then started to think about the implications of my presence. Some officers began to avoid me, or say to me very early in the day "now, this isn't for your book, but. . . ." When these instances began to occur, I started to realize that the time to end my fieldwork was drawing near.

Staying too long can also lead to the cost of, as so many anthropologists have documented, going native. Perhaps the most obvious way to see this occurring is in a researcher's everyday language. After several months with the strippers I found that some of my friends and acquaintances away from the field began to react differently to me in everyday situations. Whether it was my fellow graduate students in class or in our offices, or friends or family members in social situations, people began to noticeably react to my "different" language. When I reflected on these situations I realized I was having "stripper lingo" infiltrate my everyday conversation. This included unprovoked comments about other men's bodies, hypotheses about men's sexual escapades, and simply a lot more cursing and sexual references in my conversation. Even more obvious were the changes noted in my behavior during the police research. Both officers and my friends away from the field started to make comments that I was "becoming just like a real cop." It was at this time that I started to think it might be time to leave the field, or at least take an extended break from the fieldwork. When told that I was becoming "just like a real cop," I assessed my attitudes, language, behavior, dress, and general outlook on the community and I realized that I was taking on a large number of traits I saw in my field contacts. The cost here is not that it is bad to be "just like a cop," but as a researcher, if I was becoming my subject, how could I be a keen observer and interpreter of that world? In all likelihood, I could not. When this realization came to me, I was fortunate that other professional responsibilities arose that took me away from the fieldwork for three weeks' time. I used this time to reassess my views and literally take some time to not think about the fieldwork. This helped, but in short order after returning to the fieldwork, my "cop-like" ways began to return. At this time, I knew it was time to leave.

So, how can a fieldworker decide when to actually leave the fieldwork site? There are several ways this can be handled. According to Snow (1980), there are the feelings of readiness based on realizations that one's work is complete, and there are "extraneous precipitants" (p. 106) that can be institutional, interpersonal, or intrapersonal in nature. For some, especially those who are experienced and can somewhat accurately (or so we assume) predict when the costs will get too great, a preset date can be established at the outset (or more likely during the course) of the fieldwork. This should be merely a general target though, with recognition of a need to be flexible so as to be attuned to the actual dynamics of the experience. Or, as I attempted to do, a preestablished number of hours/days of fieldwork can be established and used as a goal.

In both my police and gay bathhouse research I established for myself a goal of total hours to complete in the field. For the bathhouse project I sought to complete 50 hours of intensive observations, while for the police research my goal was 500 hours of actual observation. (The large difference in number of hours was based on my anticipated final products—an article or two on the bathhouses and a book on the police—and practicality. The police research was close to home while I was on sabbatical, the bathhouse project required that I travel several hours to the research sites.) I did reach my goal in the bathhouse research, but not in the police research. Rather than complete the full 500 hours, I ended up concluding my fieldwork with a total of 481 hours of data collection.

The fact that I missed my target (by only 3 days of full-time observation/work) was due to three factors. First, I knew in my heart it was time to leave—this "feel" for when it is time is the third main way to decide when it is time. Based on what I perceived as the increasing self-consciousness of others when I was present and my own diminishing enthusiasm for the project (I was no longer looking forward to a day in the field, but rather beginning to think "it wouldn't hurt to skip today"), I knew that I was at a point of saturation. Yes, I had set a goal for myself, and I wanted to reach that goal. In fact, I probably would have stayed on for three more days, except for the fact that a natural break arose. The unit was going to be off for several days over the Thanksgiving holiday, and immediately after that I was leaving town for two weeks of consulting in other cities. So, the time was right: I felt it was time to leave and there was a natural break in my access/availability. I missed my target number of hours, but still remain confident that it mattered little, if at all. And, finally, the reality is that for most fieldworkers, the decision of when to leave will be based on some combination of factors, as was the case with my work.

The Process of Leaving the Field

Once you have decided to leave the field, it is time to make some decisions about how to actually handle the act of leaving. Decisions that are both professional and social need to be made, although how you plan to handle the situation and how it actually transpires may be quite different. Again, the similarities to a graduation are clear. When you actually stop going to the field site, it is like when you stop going to class (or actually finish the last revisions on a thesis or dissertation!) and are told you are now ready to go forth and be productive in a new stage of life. Your education (or at least this particular stage of it) is complete, and you have been provided with the information and tools necessary to succeed in your next endeavors. For the field researcher, this means you have learned what you can from the field site and your field contacts, and you are now equipped to write the definitive statement about how the field site functions. Graduations also mean leaving your friendships and day-to-day support systems and moving away from current friends and sources of support. When graduating from school, one typically moves on to find new friends; when graduating from the field, one will typically move back to spending (more) time with pre-fieldwork friends.

Leaving the field and graduating are both times to reflect back on what you have experienced and learned and to look forward to what your new goals are and how you will achieve them. The emotions a field researcher experiences when leaving the field, as the graduate experiences at a commencement, are a mixture of joy, sadness, pride, apprehension, and confusion (also see Jorgensen 1989). Also like a graduation, leaving the field is an event that researchers need to anticipate and plan for, just as the student should be thinking about a job or the next level of school. What this means in practical terms is that both the graduate and the concluding field researcher should be preparing for the end of their current repertoire of activities, beginning to think about what they will do next, and considering how the process of saying goodbye will be handled.

The consideration of how to handle the goodbyes, like just about everything involved in the graduation/termination-of-fieldwork experience, has both personal and professional implications. Therefore, it is important to plan for the event and prepare for the inevitable questions. When you have determined that you are going to leave, do you give your field contacts advance "warning" or this fact, or do you just leave? If you give your notice, how far in advance do you do it? Since doing fieldwork is really a job, do you give the standard two weeks' notice? If you decide to just leave, do you tell your contacts that you are leaving? Do you tell all of them or just some of them? When do you tell them? What do you tell them? How a fieldworker decides to answer these questions will be primarily guided by specifics of the circumstances of the field site, the culture of the field site and how the fieldworker and the field site contacts have interacted in the past. Sadly, there is little guidance offered by the texts on field research. Jorgensen (1989) suggests slowly disengaging from field contacts and gradually spending less time in one's field sites. However, this may not be possible, or it may draw attention to the fieldworker doing something "different" than he or she had previously done. Berg (2001: 172-173) is less specific, yet more realistic, in his advice. "(T)here are different nuances to exiting. . . . Perhaps a quick exit will work in some cases, whereas a more gradual drifting off may be required in other circumstances. Unfortunately, these research-related decisions are not easily made." The advice I would offer is also less specific than some might desire. There is no universal "best" way to leave a field site. Each site, each researcher, and each relationship is different. Consequently, each researcher needs to make these decisions based on his or her knowledge of the field contacts, the impact of leaving on the daily activities in the field, and how he or she feels about him- or herself. The important point here is to be aware of these issues and to plan ahead with these in mind.

In addition to these difficult decisions, once it becomes known that the researcher is going to be leaving, or has left, the issue of how the inevitable questions asked by field contacts should be handled arises. "Why are you leaving?" "We didn't expect this. Did something happen?" "Is there something we can do to change your mind?" (Actually, this is a nice one to hear, it means (if sincere) that your field contacts were not truly tired of you being around.) Of course, the best way to answer these questions is to be honest (unless being honest will bring significant costs to you or the research endeavor/product).

The questions that may be more difficult to answer are those about your personal feelings regarding the fieldwork experience, your intentions for how you will use the information you have learned, what you will be doing next, and how the field contacts can see what you end up producing. Answering the first two of these issues should be done honestly, although you might need to give less than complete answers. The third issue is also fairly easy to answer. You will probably be working on analyzing and thinking through what you have learned in the field and then working on doing some writing. Or, you might be returning to other professional responsibilities (such as teaching at your university).

The potentially problematic issue here is the last one. In every one of my field-work projects, most of my contacts have asked if they will be able to see my final product(s) and if I will provide them with copies. When I planned for the project to lead to a book, I always told them they would certainly be welcome to read the book, and I would let them know when it was available. I made the decision to never tell anyone that I would provide him or her with copies of the book, ex-plaining that I really could not afford to buy as many copies as this would re-quire. In the vast majority of instances, however, and as I fully expected, by the time I finished with my data analysis and writing, and something came out in print (either journal articles, book chapters or a book), my field contacts had lost interest. In some ways this is an instance where the "speed" of academic publish-ing works to our benefit. If my work had appeared within a month or two after leaving the field, I am sure some of my contacts would have read the work. But, when it has been a year or two since I left the field, interest wanes and memories fade. In all honesty, I am glad that some of my contacts never did read what I wrote about them and their worlds. Although I never intended to say mean or unflattering things about these people, in the end some of my analyses and con-clusions are not what my contacts would have liked.

Another issue that needs to be contended with when leaving the field centers on how you will handle the "secrets" that you learn while in the field. This issue is especially salient in two types of situations: when you have developed true personal relationships with field contacts and when you have been working in a setting that relies on the production and use of "secret" information.

Personal secrets are those issues that come up in any friendship; secret infor-mation is the knowledge that insiders have in truly closed environments (such as an undercover police unit). The best advice that I can offer for how to handle ei-ther type of secret information is to handle it as it deserves to be handled. If you believed that this information was worthy of keeping secret while you were in the field, then there is no reason to violate the confidence of your field contacts once you leave the field. However, do you use "secret" information in your analyses and do you write about it? This is where the matter becomes a bit more complicated. If you are seeking to truly and completely explain the workings of a setting/context/community, it is likely that at least some of the secrets you learned while in the field are critical to this explanation. However, if secrets are shared, it may be possible that some harm may come for some of your contacts. So, do you use this information? There are three ways to respond to this. The re-searcher can go ahead and use the information and share it, justifying doing so on the basis that field contacts knew the fieldworker's purpose. If the contact did not want a particular piece of information to be made public, it should not have been shared with the researcher. Second, the secret can be maintained, and the re-searcher can try his or her best to achieve a full explanation and understanding of the field site without this important information. Or, third, and what I suspect is the most common approach that has been used by field researchers, the specific facts of the secret (and the individuals to whom they apply) can be modified in an effort to hide the identities of the "guilty." This may or may not be successful, however. Secret information is dangerous to have, and in the hands of a field researcher, it may never be able to be handled in a way that both fully protects field contacts *and* informs the research endeavor.

The best examples of issues that may arise around secret information learned in the field arose in my work with the police. While in the field I learned the identities of numerous drug dealers, prostitutes, and police informants. I spent time with snitches and worked side by side with many of them. I learned where the police hide to observe drug deals and prostitutes carrying out their work. I learned who was selling high-quality drugs and which dealers were selling "shit." Much of this information could be very valuable on the streets and potentially dangerous in the wrong hands. Should this information be addressed with my police colleagues before leaving the field? Or, should I simply assume that they trusted me at one time, and this trust would remain in effect, unless they indicated otherwise? If I raised the issue about whether they trusted me, would this make it look like I should not be trusted? Secrets arise in all types of fieldwork settings, however. In both the stripper and bathhouse fieldwork I encountered people I knew from other areas of my life. There I was, wearing my towel around my waist and walking through the halls of the bathhouse when I run into, well, let me simply say an acquaintance (this happened more than once, too). Similarly, while working the crowd with the strippers, on more than one occasion I came across someone I knew, and sometimes they were with someone other than their significant other. There probably is no universally "right" answer for these questions and situations; different researchers, in different contexts, will reach different decisions. Not every field researcher will face this issue, but every field researcher needs to be ready for it. Knowing this ahead of time, and making careful, informed decisions is the best we can do.

Another way of looking at this issue is to consider whether and what apprehensions field contacts may have about the fieldworker's trustworthiness regarding secrets shared. As with a friendship that ends, field contacts may wonder if their previously shared secrets are safe, or whether the fieldworker will violate their trust. The most significant way that a field contact may worry about a fieldworker violating their trust is to actually share his or her secret in print, in the research product. While in the field, the fieldworker is likely to come to be viewed as a "friend" or "colleague" or at least someone that after time is "always around, and knows how it really is." When viewed this way, even though field contacts know the researcher is a researcher, sharing of personal information is normative. However, once it is learned that the researcher will soon, or has already, left the field site, concerns may arise as the role attributed to the fieldworker may drastically change. My police contacts became concerned when I started hinting that my time in the field was getting short. I was called aside several times by commanding officers who reminded me that "while I don't mind you being here, you have to remember that some things you've seen could really hurt some of these guys. I hope you'll remember that and not put any of that in your book. Okay?"

Or, in the case of the male strippers with whom I worked, several often retold stories of "crazy shit" that happened during or after our shows began to be discounted by the guys as "exaggerations" that "didn't really go down that way at all. Yeah, that's what we tell people, but we all know it's not really true." Yes, in both of these projects I witnessed a number of events that my field contacts would not want to become public knowledge. Knowing this in itself can be stress-inducing. What do you do when people with whom you've spent long hours and with whom you've done some "crazy shit" obviously begin to question whether they can trust you? These are issues a fieldworker needs to be ready and able to handle, in interactions and emotionally.

The Stresses of Separation

Making the decision and then actually leaving the field can be a stressful experience. As with any significant change in life—such as a graduation—altering what we do, where we do it, and with whom we do it can bring stresses to our lives. This simple social fact, however, is almost never acknowledged in the literature, although a few observers do mention that when a fieldworker leaves a field site, some field contacts may experience stress (see Shaffir, Stebbins, and Turowetz 1980). Fieldworkers who have worked intensely in their field sites will find themselves postgraduation with radically altered daily behaviors and social contacts. Psychologists tell us that the most stressful events in our lives center on issues of changes in social contacts, health, and our work (Holmes and Rahe 1967). Leaving one's fieldwork site encompasses two of these three major types of stress-inducing factors.

Whereas previously the field researcher had spent his or her time interacting in the field and carefully observing and noting what occurred around them, once leaving the field, those contacts are gone and the need to carefully watch and document activities around one are not necessary. This may mean that the researcher finds him- or herself with a large amount of "free" time, or it may mean being faced with taking on the daunting task of working through field notes and embarking on the formal data analysis stage of the research. Taking on a new, large task can be stressful, as can searching for how to fill one's time. Yes, many of us may believe that there would be nothing better than having nothing to do and large chunks of free time. However, for most of us, those of us who are driven by our work and find challenges such as field research rewarding, extended periods of "free" time can be stressful.

It can also be stressful to find yourself without your field contacts that have served as your primary source of social contacts for an extended period of time. For some field researchers their field contacts may serve as their primary, if not only, social contacts during the course of the field research. In my work with the male strippers, our primary work hours were on weekend nights. I spent the majority of my Friday and Saturday nights traveling and working. When I ended the data collection, I was left to find others with whom to spend my weekends and others with whom to converse about the daily events in my life.

When I terminated the data collection stage of my work with the police, I was happy to know that I would have more time to be home with my family, but my days were now unscheduled, and I faced the possibility of having an empty calendar for several weeks. This was a new experience for me, and one that induced a fair amount of concern and worry for me. I resolved the issue by finding other endeavors to dive into and immediately began traveling and working on other projects (such as this manuscript).

Field contacts may come to be friends while the researcher is in the field. However, once graduated from the field, will these friendships remain? Questions are likely to arise for the fieldworker concerning the strength and reality of these "friendships." Were these truly friendships in the first place? Should they be expected to survive the change in roles and activities that accompany the researcher leaving the field? Should these relationships be maintained? Typically fieldworkers and the field contacts with whom they have developed personal relationships will commit to maintaining their relationship. When I left the male strippers, we all pledged to stay in contact and still be involved in each other's lives. However, this never transpired. Similarly, I made this same pledge when I graduated from high school, and from college, and from graduate school. Today, I have annual contact with one friend from high school, occasional email from one friend from college, and regular interactions with two people from graduate school. I do not know what became of my male stripper friends. My field contacts in the police department are rapidly fading away. These have not been intentional separations, but natural developments as we have all moved on with our busy lives. So, were my friendships with field contacts real? I believe they were, although perhaps not the deepest or strongest of my life.

So, why is it stressful to leave the field? It is for the same reasons that it is stressful to graduate. This is a time you look forward to, work toward, and then when it comes you realize that you must find some other ways to fill your time and provide yourself with social contacts and daily stimulation. You are leaving something familiar and moving to what may well be an unknown. This is a very simple recipe for stress, and all of the accompanying maladies.

Conclusion

Graduating from the field marks a turning point in the field researcher's life and career. No longer a data collector, he or she moves to the status of a fully knowledgeable researcher with the challenge of demonstrating his or her understanding of the field site to others. The graduate has been educated and now must decide how to go about putting to use the knowledge gained in a productive and beneficial way.

At the point of graduation the field researcher is likely to be conflicted with a range of emotions, including anticipation, apprehension, perhaps a bit of fear, and a mix of excitement and sadness. No longer spending his or her days (or nights, as the case may be) seeking knowledge and interacting with others in the educational process, now the fieldwork researcher has moved into the status of knowledge user and producer. No longer interacting with the same people that consumed so much of the time while in the field, the fieldwork graduate must now search out new (or attempt to return to old, i.e., pre-fieldwork) social relationships and interactions. The graduate has left one set of friends behind, probably with promises to stay in touch (although knowing deep down "things will never be the same") and now faces the necessity of creating yet another social circle. In all likelihood, this leads to feelings of stress for the fieldwork graduate. This should not come as a surprise, however, for "relationships are the stock and trade of a good ethnographer, care must be taken when leaving the field" (Berg 2001: 171). And, although these feelings may not be able to be avoided, knowing that they are likely to beset the fieldwork graduate can help prepare both the researcher and those that provide his or her support systems to manage these emotions in a productive, or at least minimally harmful, manner.

There is a plethora of literature that provides guides for how to conduct fieldwork and confessionals from graduated fieldworkers about their experiences *while in the field*. However, the literature essentially ignores the postgraduate experiences of researchers. This is likely to leave the neophyte field researcher with the impression that the process of preparing for and following through on graduating from the field is a simple, stress-free, unproblematic phase of the research process; graduating is something to be celebrated. This, clearly though, is not the full story.

One of the primary goals of this article is to provide readers with a sense of what the issues are at this phase of the fieldwork process that can be problematic and disturbing (both professionally and personally) for the fieldworker. These are issues that are important to address so as to enhance the emotional health and well-being of researchers engaged in fieldwork. Sadly, few social scientists have addressed these issues (however, see Snow 1980). One of the issues that has been brought to the fore by feminist researchers is that it is important that we not only view our work reflexively, but so too should we be aware of our own impact on our field sites and contacts and how we and our work affect our selves. While this has a reflexive value that can be important to understanding our work, so too is it important in that if we are not aware of how our work and our role in our work affect us, we are likely to suffer unnecessarily. Our suffering may come in the form of emotional, psychological, physical, and/or social harms, or it may come in the form of a lack of productivity.

If we are not aware of how our experiences in the field have affected us as persons, we may simply suffer from our losses and thereby avoid actually moving on with our work. This means we may find reasons (sometimes creative) to avoid moving forward into the analysis/writing stages of our work. Again, the analogy to graduation is pertinent. How many students find themselves either approaching or having just completed their graduations and avoiding moving forward with the next steps of their lives? How many high school graduates "forget" to get their college applications submitted, because they are grieving the loss of high school? Or, how many scholars get their dissertations drafted, but never "done," thereby minimizing the changes in their lives, allowing them to maintain their known/comfortable lifestyles and place of residence? Similar is the field researcher who (perhaps after prolonging his or her time in the field) leaves the field but cannot bring him- or herself to write about the experience and new-found knowledge, thereby failing to be productive.

Just like college freshmen, new masters-level students, or even new assistant professors may need support groups, so too can this be the case for newly graduated field researchers. However, there is no structure for this group. Therefore, it is important that all of us—both those of us who have graduated from the field and those of us who know a graduate—recognize this need and do what we can to provide that necessary support to the new graduate. In the end, graduation is not just a time to mark the completion of a stage of life, but as every graduation speech I have ever heard has emphasized, a graduation is a beginning, not an end.

References

Berg, Bruce. 2001. *Qualitative Research Methods for the Social Sciences* (4th edition). Boston: Allyn and Bacon.

Holmes, Thomas H., and Richard H. Rahe. 1967. "The Social Readjustment Rating Scale." *Journal of Psychosomatic Research, 11:* 213-218.

Jorgensen, Danny L. 1989. *Participant Observation: A Methodology for Human Studies.* Newbury Park, CA: Sage.

Lofland, John, and Lyn H. Lofland. 1995. *Analyzing Social Settings* (3rd edition). Belmont, CA: Wadsworth.

Roethlisberger, F.J., and William J. Dickson. 1939. *Management and the Worker.* Cambridge, MA: Harvard University Press.

Shaffir, W.B., R.A. Stebbins, and A. Turowetz. 1980. *Fieldwork Experience: Qualitative Approaches to Social Research.* New York: St. Martin's Press.

Snow, David A. 1980. "The Disengagement Process: A Neglected Problem in Participant Observation Research." *Qualitative Sociology,* 3(2): 100-122.

Tewksbury, Richard. 2002. "Bathhouse Intercourse: Structural and Behavioral Aspects of an Erotic Oasis." *Deviant Behavior,* 23(1): 75-112.

Tewksbury, Richard. 1994. "A Dramaturgical Analysis of Male Strippers." *Journal of Men's Studies,* 2(4): 325-342.

Tewksbury, Richard. 1993. "Male Strippers: Men Objectifying Men." In *Doing Women's Work': Men in Nontraditional Occupations,* edited by Christine L. Williams. Newbury Park, CA: Sage Publications.

Wax, Rosalie. 1971. *Doing Fieldwork: Warnings and Advice.* Chicago: The University of Chicago Press.

Part 3: Danger and Stigma in Crime and Deviance Fieldwork

Researchers who use qualitative methods often face a number of difficulties and obstacles that researchers using quantitative approaches usually do not encounter. Many of the topics that are studied with qualitative methods are activities and types of people/communities that some no doubt find distasteful, irritating, embarrassing, or simply something that brings a negative light to those associated with the topic. Hence, when a researcher devotes time, energy, resources, and/or his or her career to advancing understandings and explanations for such types of activities, the research may come to be viewed as unsavory or disreputable. In other cases, when a researcher is working with (or inside of) communities that are rife with danger or that do not necessarily want to be studied and exposed, there is the chance that such persons may react to a researcher's presence with anger and/or violence. Or, sometimes the communities into which a qualitative researcher must venture can be dangerous in their own right. Simply being present in some situations can be dangerous, if not physically dangerous, then certainly dangerous for one's reputation and standing in the community. Or, for many (if not most) qualitative researchers, there are likely to be situations in which the course of appropriate action may be less than crystal clear. When faced with a situation where what is right might not be what one is being pressured to do, the stress can be immense. However, in all these types of situations, as we will see in the six articles in this section, knowing that trouble might be encountered and having at least some idea of how to handle a troublesome situation can be the best for which one can hope.

The themes of ethical questions and dangers to researchers is common throughout much of the research that qualitative methodologists pursue. As clearly outlined in the article by Williams, Dunlap, Johnson, and Hamid, qualitative researchers may encounter physical dangers and frightening and intimidating situations. This article shares personal insight to the stresses that many qualitative researchers should be anticipating. However, even more important is the practical advice these authors give about how to handle such situations. Although they argue that some personal concessions and compromises may be necessary to ensure that a project can be completed, the most important thing to keep in mind is how to protect oneself. Although the research is certainly (usually) important, keeping oneself safe is always more important.

The question of what is an ethical way to handle the information that a researcher learns and how those that are being studied may fear what will be done with the data collected is at the center of Bostock's article in this section. In this piece she discusses how researchers interested the lives of poverty-level mothers who have been targeted by child protection workers can negotiate the interview process successfully. What this article clearly shows is that the "dangers" that may be present in qualitative research extend beyond those confronting the researcher. To be successful and ethical, qualitative researchers need to think about how the research endeavor may be experienced by those we are studying.

Israel's article on researchers who study sexuality highlights the possible professional risks that may confront qualitative researchers. Some research topics, such as human sexuality, are often viewed as "dirty" by some observers. When researchers are interested in marginal or "dirty" topics, there may be others (both professionals and lay persons) who grant stigmas to such researchers. While this is not to say that some topics are best left untouched, it is important to consider that engaging in some types of qualitative research may mean that questions could be raised about the researcher as a person. However, as Israel argues, these stigmas can be managed and should not be seen as insurmountable or reasons to avoid important research topics and questions.

The fourth article in this section also looks at stigmatization of researchers, and raises questions about what constitutes ethical behavior on the part of researchers. Goode's confessional tale about engaging in sexual relations with research subjects should raise questions for the reader about both what is and is not appropriate researcher behavior and questions about if and where a line should be drawn between our personal and professional activities. Goode argues that engaging in sex with those we study is not unethical, and in some situations may actually benefit the research endeavor. This position is not without its critics, and many have argued that this is an unethical and wholly inappropriate thing for a qualitative researcher to do. The questions that are raised in this article are very relevant, and sometimes not necessarily easy to answer. Think carefully about the full range of consequences for the researcher, for those being studied, and for the research endeavor as you read Goode's article.

The last two articles in this section focus on the consequences, political and psychological, that are encountered by some qualitative researchers. Sonenschein's article about his experiences having his qualitative data seized and having authorities demand that he provide information to law enforcement officials raises questions about the responsibilities researchers have to those they study. While the situation he reports on is far from the norm, it also points out that while some observers may argue that qualitative data is "less scientific," it clearly can be seen as informative and valuable to many persons.

Finally, in the last article Johnson and Clarke discuss the psychological toll that can be experienced by learning and experiencing some of the things to which qualitative researchers may be exposed. Whereas quantitative researchers deal with numbers and "impersonal" forms of data, qualitative researchers usually get to know the people they study and can easily become personally invested in their topics and participants. To truly "know" a situation and the people involved is likely to affect us (as researchers) on a very personal level. In large part, this is at the heart of the qualitative approach. Qualitative researchers study "real people, in real places" and as a result may find themselves having "real costs."

What all of this means is that qualitative field work is important, useful, sometimes exciting, and sometimes stigmatizing, dangerous, or (by some people's standards) an ethically questionable approach to social science. These articles will probably raise more questions than they provide answers for readers. But, if you think about these issues and consider why you feel the way you do about these issues, you are well on your way to more fully understanding why those of us who use qualitative methods choose to do so. Qualitative research is not easy to do and not always easy to experience. However, at least for those of us who engage in qualitative fieldwork (especially in topics related to crime and deviance), we believe the rewards outweigh the potential costs.

Questions to Consider

1. Why would a qualitative researcher put him or herself at risk in a research role?

2. Do the benefits outweigh the risks/costs? Why or why not?

3. What advice would you have for a beginning researcher who wants to pursue qualitative research in issues of crime/deviance?

1. Personal Safety in Dangerous Places

Terry Williams, Eloise Dunlap, Bruce D. Johnson, and Ansley Hamid

Personal safety during fieldwork is seldom addressed directly in the literature. Drawing from many prior years of ethnographic research and from field experience while studying crack distributors in New York City, the authors provide a variety of strategies by which ethnographic research can be safely conducted in dangerous settings. By projecting an appropriate demeanor, ethnographers can seek others for protector and locator roles, routinely create a safety zone in the field, and establish compatible field roles with potential subjects. The article also provides strategies on avoiding or handling sexual approaches, common law crimes, fights, drive-by shootings, and contacts with the police. When integrated with other standard qualitative methods, ethnographic strategies help to ensure that no physical harm comes to the field-worker and other staff members. Moreover, the presence of researchers may actually reduce (and not increase) potential and actual violence among crack distributors/abusers or others present in the field setting.

A serious problem confronting many social scientists is assuring the physical safety of ethnographers and other staff conducting research among potentially violent persons who are active in dangerous settings. Of equal concern is attempting to assure the personal safety of potential research subjects. Even when extensive ethnographic experience shows that physical violence against ethnographers has rarely occurred, researchers may have considerable difficulty convincing others (including colleagues and family members) that they can safely conduct fieldwork.

Some ethnographic research may be a dangerous enterprise. Howell's (1990) discussion of safety offered an extensive discussion of common law crimes (robbery, theft, rape) in the field. Fieldworkers have encountered illness, injury, or death in the course of fieldwork due to natural and criminal causes. It is often unclear whether the fieldworkers were harmed by research subjects and other members of the social networks or whether they were merely victimized like any other citizen (Howell 1990).

The question of personal safety is rarely addressed as a methodological issue in its own right (Howell 1990; Sluka 1990), particularly in regard to the social milieu in which ethnographers carry out their work. There is relatively little discussion about how to minimize risks and dangers that ethnographers may face in the

Terry Williams et al. *Journal of Contemporary Ethnography*, Vol. 21 No. 3, October 1992 343–374. © 1992 Sage Publications, Inc. Reprinted by permission of Sage Publications, Inc.

field, with suggestions to help ensure their personal safety. Some hints about safety may be gleaned from the extensive methodological literature in ethnography (Agar 1980; Fetterman 1989) that deals with such topics as gaining access and recruiting subjects (Johnson 1990), striking a research bargain (Carey 1972), entering the field, making observations (Broadhead and Fox 1990), selecting roles to pursue in the field (Adler and Adler 1987), building and maintaining rapport (Dunlap et al. 1990; Rose 1990), conducting interviews (McCracken 1988), and writing field notes (Fetterman 1989). In practice, paying attention to the personal safety of ethnographers goes hand in hand with learning and applying skills in these areas.

The lack of good guidelines and methodological strategies for conducting safe ethnographic fieldwork in potentially violent social settings is especially noteworthy. In one of the few articles addressing safety issues, Sluka (1990) provided a systematic discussion of the risks and dangers facing ethnographers in a politically charged potentially violent setting by studying supporters of the Irish Republican Army in Belfast. His suggestions are strikingly relevant for ethnographers in the substance abuse field and for those who study street- and upper-level crack dealers. Sluka called for "foresight, planning, skillful maneuver, and a conscious effort at impression management" (p. 115) to minimize personal risk and danger in potentially violent settings. He further suggested that field-workers become well acquainted in the community, cultivate well-respected persons who vouch for them, avoid contact with police, be truthful about the purpose of the research, identify potentially dangerous locales and topics, and be flexible concerning research objectives. He proposed that successful fieldwork in dangerous settings "can be done by recognizing how people are likely to define you, avoiding acting in ways that might reinforce these suspicions, and being as honest and straightforward as possible about who you really are and what you are really doing" (p. 121).

. . . In this article we will conceptually extend and apply his and others' (e.g. Adler and Adler 1987; Denzin 1970; Douglas 1972) ideas to ethnographic research in inner-city settings. We focus on issues of personal safety while conducting fieldwork in potentially dangerous settings. Closely related ethnographic issues—rapport, recruiting subjects, ethnographer roles, reciprocity, personal experiences with contacts, and so on—are briefly included in the discussion. While recognizing that ours is but one approach to doing ethnographic research, we contribute to the literature on ethnographic methods by underscoring themes and practices for personal safety that may be of interest to all ethnographers and staff conducting research in dangerous settings—or even in "safe" settings.

Method

This article emerges from the authors' many years of experience in conducting both quantitative (Johnson 1973; Johnson, Elmoghazy, and Dunlap 1990; Johnson et al. 1985, 1988) and qualitative (Carpenter et al. 1988; Dunlap 1988; Dunlap et al. 1990; Hamid 1979, 1990, 1992; Johnson, Hamid, and Sanabria 1991; Williams 1978,

1989, 1991; Williams and Kornblum 1985) research among abusers and sellers of marijuana, heroin, cocaine, and crack. All of the authors have done much of their work among low-income and minority populations (Dunlap et al. 1990; Hamid 1990; Johnson et al. 1985; Johnson, Williams, et al. 1990; Williams 1989, 1991; Williams and Kornblum 1985). These professional ethnographers (Dunlap, Hamid, Sanabria, and Williams) have extensive experience in qualitative field research on drug-related issues and other topics in New York City, Latin America, and the Caribbean. Four staff members (Arnold, Beddoe, Randolf, and Miller) are ex-drug users and/or ex-dealers who developed wide networks among upper-level dealers. Collectively, the staff has many years of experience working in or researching various aspects of drug use and dealing. The authors are professional researchers and ethnographers whose primary careers are built around research funded by grants. . . .

Building on this experience, we systematically trained staff members on issues of personal safety during an ongoing study called "Natural History of Crack Distribution." This was a qualitative study about the structure and functioning of crack distribution, including the careers of dealers in New York City (Johnson, Williams, et al. 1990; Johnson et al. 1991). During the fieldwork phase of this study, November 1989–March 1991, the ethnographic staff spent an average of 15–20 hours per week in several of New York City's most dangerous locales interacting with numerous street people. Staff members conducted intensive fieldwork in four New York City neighborhoods (Harlem, Washington Heights, Brownsville, and Williamsburg). They wrote field notes that contain observations and references to over 300 different crack distributors. They also conducted openended life history interviews (5–15 hours long) with 80 distributors. Fifteen of these were upper-level dealers buying and selling kilograms of cocaine; the remainder were independent sellers. To obtain this information, they conducted three or more sessions with most dealers. All interviews were recorded and transcribed. Our data and analyses rely on the strategies and experiences of ourselves and our ethnographic staff for maintaining their own personal safety as well as on specific experiences reported by other ethnographers in the drug abuse field.

Laypeople and ethnographers anticipate and are fearful about several potential sources of physical danger associated with the use and sale of crack (Brownstein and Goldstein 1990a, 1990b; Goldstein 1985; Goldstein et al. 1990, 1991a, 1991b; *New York Newsday* 1990; *New York Times* 1990a, 1990b; *Washington Post* 1990): Crack abusers may be paranoid and behave "irrationally"; dealers routinely use violence and may threaten subjects who talk to ethnographers; use of guns leads to "random" shootings; researchers may be robbed or have articles stolen. The mass media typically feature the most violent and extreme activities of crack distributors (Reinarman and Levine 1989), so laypersons are led to believe that severe violence occurs all the time in this business. Despite these fears, ethnographic research in dangerous settings has been safely conducted for years. Our staff and many other researchers (Adler 1985; Biernacki 1988; Feldman 1974; Goldstein et al. 1990; Hanson et al. 1985; Spunt 1988; Morales 1989; Smith and Kornblum 1991) have met, talked with, and interviewed many potentially violent persons over long periods and have never been physically assaulted.

Styles of Safety

Researchers can create "safety zones" in which to conduct research in dangerous settings so as to protect themselves and the persons with whom they are interacting from physical harm or violence during the research endeavor. The following sections are organized according to conceptual themes regarding styles of safety that emphasize demeanor, protector roles, safety zones, neutrality, and common sense during fieldwork.

Style and Demeanor

Style and demeanor are central to safety. First impressions are very important. Wearing clothes appropriate to the setting prevents drawing undue attention and exhibits a sense of belonging in the setting. Researchers' attire can be viewed as an extension and manifestation of their personalities as well as a willingness to fit into the social setting. As ethnographers enter and attempt to establish a presence in the field, they explain the purpose of research, exhibit personal interest in others, and avoid drug use or sales (Adler and Adler 1987; Agar 1980; Horowitz 1986; Johnson 1990). Failure to establish this presence, and especially being perceived as a victim, by those in the drug business for instance, may greatly increase personal dangers of theft/robbery and difficulty in establishing rapport with potential subjects. Although various roles have been employed by ethnographers in a variety of settings (Becker 1960; Adler and Adler 1987), those conducting field research among drug abusers generally employ a variation of friendly stranger (Agar 1980) or friendly outsider. This role is partially mandated by a professional code of ethics forbidding illegal behavior and institutional requirements to obtain informed consent from research subjects.

Purpose and Access.   Once accepted as an ordinary person in the area, initial conversations are the first step in seeking persons with whom to develop rapport. Williams has been conducting research among cocaine users since 1974. During a 17-year career, he has visited hundreds of after-hours clubs, base houses, crack houses (Williams 1978, 1989, 1991), number holes, and other settings where illegal and legal activities occur. Williams explained several strategies for gaining entry into such locales:

> Initially I prefer to be taken into a crack house or dealing location by someone who is known there. They vouch that I'm OK and no cop. When initially approaching a crack house without someone to introduce me, I'll claim to be sent by someone they may know, like Robby, KeeKay, or someone else with a common street name. When I get inside, I may explain that I'm writing a book on crack houses (or another topic). I usually have a copy of a book I've written to show people. This approach goes a long way toward convincing skeptical persons that I'm an author and serious about my intentions.

After gaining initial entry and some rapport with one or more persons in the setting, Dunlap found it necessary to arrange a meeting with one or more drug dealers to explain herself, to seek their permission and informed consent to conduct long life history interviews, and to strike the research bargain (see Carey 1972). The dealers can also examine the project's Certificate of Confidentiality. Dunlap explained:

> I begin by telling them about myself, my life, and why I'm interested in them. I spend much time explaining how their identity will be concealed and how our interviews will be protected and never be available to police or law enforcement agencies. I explain the risks and benefits of the research to them in terms of their participation and obtain their informed consent. Even after these lengthy explanations, most subjects tend to remain tense and somewhat terse in their answers. Only during and after the first session of the in-depth interview do they begin to relax and talk openly about themselves. Such conversations would not even begin, however, without the assurances of confidentiality and the promise of benefits.

The end result is that ethnographers have built substantial rapport with one or more persons, carefully explained the purpose of the research, provided assurances of protection and safety, and obtained informed consent from persons who will become potential research subjects. Of course, the ethnographer must continue to meet with and show a genuine personal interest and friendliness to such persons. Such further conversations and interactions help build strong rapport with subjects.

The "Victim" Role.

As ethnographers, we need a "mindset" that assumes safety and does not lead to fearful behavior. Street people act on their intuitions and are experts in reading behavior. Dunlap expressed the critical importance of not being perceived as a victim ("vic"):

> The ethnographer's state of mind on entering the field must not include fear about studying violent people; at least such fears must not be at the front of one's mind. Overconcern about violence may cause ethnographers to appear afraid or react inappropriately to common street situations and dangers that do not involve themselves. Fearful behavior is easily inferred by violent persons from the way one walks and the way one interacts with others. Fearful behavior may place an ethnographer in the "vic" category to be targeted by others as a true victim of crimes like robbery and assault.

Not exhibiting fearful behavior does not mean abandoning choices about a sensible course of action. Rather, the mindset we have found appropriate is cautious, friendly, understanding, and open. This mindset emphasizes a degree of determination and self-confidence that does not leave room for ethnographers to be labeled as "vics." Likewise, *not* using or selling drugs is also important for avoiding the "vic" role. If potential subjects observe ethnographers buying or selling illicit drugs, they may be suspected of being undercover agents, or expect them to be potential customers, or people who will share or provide drugs. Further decisions about whether to enter specific locales or meet certain persons must be made deliberately and based on the other themes discussed below.

Locator and Protector Roles

Two roles are especially important in conducting research among upper-level and in many instances among lower-level drug sellers. The roles of *locator* and *protector* are vital to the safety of persons working within the illicit drug industry. Locating individuals who can perform these roles can be critical to ethnographers' safety with and access to upper-level dealers. The ethnographic literature (Agar 1980; Johnson 1990; Liebow 1967; Whyte 1955, 1984) provides advice about finding one or more key informants who can provide access to others in the setting and who give much information about the phenomena being studied. . . .

Crack sellers and upper-level dealers, however, have very good reasons to insulate their identities, locales, and illegal activities from everyone (excepting their trusted co-workers). They are concerned with avoiding detection and arrest and with preventing robbery or injury by other street persons. They systematically evade conversations that may build close relationships (Adler 1985). Yet to conduct their business safely, they must rely on others who perform a variety of roles such as steerers, touts, guards, lookouts, connections, runners, and muscle men (Johnson, Williams, et al. 1990; Johnson et al. 1991). Approaching a crack dealer directly (without an intermediary) threatens the dealer, as it proves his identity is known or suspected. Ethnographers will always be suspected initially of being a "cop" or an "informer," thus elevating the probability of personal risk and possible harm from the dealer or his associates.

Ethnographers can seek access to drug dealers through someone performing a *locator role* and rely on others to play a *protector role* as access is gained. Experience has indicated that access to crack dealers was most successful when ethnographers worked with a highly trusted former associate of the dealer who performed both the locator and the protector roles. The same person, however, need not perform both roles.

Critical in studies with drug dealers is someone who will perform the locator role of introducing the ethnographers into a setting where dealers are present. Recovered substance abusers who have had management roles in drug-selling organizations or have been incarcerated for several years for drug distribution crimes are particularly valuable in such roles. These ex-dealers typically have a large network of current sellers and dealers, know how to negotiate with active dealers, and can be trained to assist with fieldwork. They can locate and introduce ethnographers to several dealers (the locator role), provide protection in dangerous settings (the protector role), become systematic observers and interviewers (field-worker or interviewer role), and explain many of the informally understood norms to a professional ethnographer (the "expert" role).

Proper Introductions.   At the early stages of fieldwork among crack sellers, ethnographers generally do not attempt to enter a setting alone. Someone familiar with the locale is recruited or hired to assist in arranging "proper introductions" of the ethnographers to dealers as well as to provide protection. As a paraprofessional staff member, Arnold contacted several dealers and helped arrange interviews with our ethnographers. He stated that "the contact person has a major affect for the ethnographer upon people in the setting." From his network of acquaintances, he had initial contacts and helped persuade dealers to talk with the ethnographer.

Another paraprofessional, Beddoe, explained why and how proper introductions occur among street dealers:

> They [good contact persons] tend to have contact across time in the given area. Most street dealers are middle men. They will continue to work together and routinely rely on each other. Introductions by one dealer who vouches to other dealers that someone is "right" and "not a cop" is a vital part of street life and everyday dealing hustles. If an ethnographer gets a positive reference from a dealer, another dealer will still be a little suspicious. They study how you handle yourself in the field and then decide whether to talk more.

Having the appropriate person provide an introduction to a dealer is vital. Group members respond according to the reputation of the individual who provides the introduction. If that person is not trusted, the ethnographer will not be trusted. Dunlap's field notes recorded why she was unable to gain access to several dealers in one Harlem block:

> My early contact on this block was Chief, a female who worked for several dealers, mainly as a "fill-in seller" at the street level. Chief had committed some act which had deemed her untrustworthy to most of her suppliers. She was only trusted to sell small portions of drugs at a time, never large amounts. When she attempted to introduce me to one of her bosses, it was disastrous. The dealer refused to even meet me. Seeing this, other street sellers whom I had informally met at the same time ceased interacting with me. From this and other experiences, I learned that lower-level crack users/dealers can seldom provide good introductions to their bosses or suppliers.

When a respected and trusted former dealer provided the introduction to other dealers only a few blocks away, several meetings and interviews were the outcome. Amold reported:

> I contacted several dealers who trusted me because we had done prison time for drug sales. After explaining the study to them, they were willing to attend a meeting. I set up the meetings and got them there, so that she [Dunlap] could explain it in more detail and build some relationship with them. This resulted in several interviews.

The Protector.   Ethnographers usually assume that they do not need protection from persons in a social setting. In the context of the drug business, this usual assumption is false; everyone must arrange protection to assure their personal safety. Once ethnographers are properly introduced into a setting, finding someone to perform the protector role is usually not difficult. Everyone in a drug dealer's network is expected to "watch backs" (i.e., help each other avoid possible dangers). Even freelance sellers competing for customers on the same block quickly reach agreement to "divide up" the territory and to "watch backs" for each other in case of physical danger (Johnson et al. 1991). Williams reported:

> In every field setting, some person always appears to perform a protector role and "watches the back" of the ethnographer; he discourages violence among others in the setting "because the Man [ethnographer] is here." If I leave the street for a month, it feels like a year. I need to maintain regular visits. Because I rely on them for protection, my best protectors in the street are enemies of the police: drug dealers, con men, robbers.

After gaining experience in similar settings, ethnographers can enter another site and expect to rapidly encounter someone who will perform the protector role. Usually, the protector will be among the first to speak to the ethnographer. In the event that a protector does not emerge or cannot be found (see "safety zone" next), or if a feeling of safety is lacking (see "sixth sense" below), researchers are encouraged to leave that setting.

Field Roles.
Ethnographers have an anomalous position that potential contacts may find unfamiliar or unclear. While conducting field research, they occupy roles that are "betwixt and between" (Jackson 1990) their own professional roles and the roles enacted by potential subjects in the field setting. The dual role of observer and participant (Adler and Adler 1987) played by the friendly outsider (Agar 1980) is unfamiliar to most subjects. Rather, subjects tend to project familiar roles onto ethnographers.

In fact, field roles are fluid and changing during a typical day and during the course of the field research (Denzin 1970; Spradley 1980). In conversation and interaction with individual subjects and with groups, ethnographers can listen closely for the roles that others assign to them. This is helpful in designing one or more field roles that are compatible with the research, yet understood by subjects and protectors. During this study, several subjects referred to Dunlap as "auntie," "mom," "sister," or other fictive kin; Williams was perceived as a "book author" and a "sharp dude"; Hamid and Curtis (1990) were "voyeurs" when conducting research in a "freak-house" (where crack use and sexual activity occur). These subject-assigned roles were effective because they permitted access to the setting, were used by the protector to briefly explain the ethnographer's presence, and permitted informal conversation, questioning, and direct observations to occur—without suspicion that the ethnographer was a cop or a police informer.

As a single female living in a crack dealing neighborhood, Dunlap did not want research subjects to know where she lived, but she had to return home during early morning hours when only drug dealers and street people were awake. Dunlap described how she created and maintained a "right citizen" role with five regular crack dealers who helped assure her safety when she returned home very late:

> I first observed who had the most respect from others and who appeared to have control over various situations—this was usually crack dealers. Then I walked by and said,

"How you doing?" and engaged in "nonsensical" conversations about such things as the music on the street, street language, the drunk leaning against a fire hydrant. We avoided conversations about what they were doing or about what I did. I also avoided talking to the drug users. By being friendly with the drug dealers, they quickly accepted me as someone who would do them no harm. In return, they protected me in little ways. For example, one night after speaking briefly to my local dealer, a crack user began to approach me for some money; the dealer told her to "move on" and not to bother me. If some threatening situation were to arise, I feel certain they would act to protect me or intervene if necessary.

Dunlap also practiced this role in other research settings when interacting with persons who were not to be approached as research subjects.

During the past 6 years, many ethnographers and paraprofessionals have assumed the role of health worker doing outreach on AIDS prevention projects (e.g., Broadhead and Fox 1990). The "AIDS outreach worker" is an effective street role for ethnographers; it has become well known and respected among street people in several communities. The AIDS outreach worker role clearly "sides" with subjects and potential subjects and provides a basis for interaction with a variety of persons. Such persons express concern about subjects' health, facilitate referrals to other health service agencies, and help ethnographers to avoid being seen in a law enforcement role.

Safety Zones.

When conducting research in settings that may be dangerous, or among persons who may be suspicious or hostile toward researchers, a first order of business is to create and maintain a physical and social environment in which ethnographers and potential subjects accept each other's presence.

In settings where many persons are present, effort should be made to include several persons as protectors in a safety zone. This is conceptualized as a physical area extending a few feet around the researcher, in which researchers and other persons within this area feel comfortable. The safety zone has three major components. First, researchers must have a feeling of a "psychological safety"; that is, they must not feel endangered, they must experience some degree of acceptance by others, and they must be willing to stay in the location (see "sixth sense"). Second, other persons in this zone should accept ethnographers' presence, trusting that they are "right" and "not a cop." Third, the physical environment must not be hazardous (e.g., the floors should not be likely to collapse; the ceiling should not be likely to fall).

When entering a locale, ethnographers can quickly scan the physical environment for obvious signs of danger. They should test steps and flooring, especially in abandoned buildings, and be cognizant of all exits. By introducing ethnographers to others at the site, the protector can facilitate social acceptance. Ethnographers must then establish their own right to be present in the locale during subsequent conversation with others. Such interaction typically brings about an implicit (and sometimes explicit) agreement, thus creating a shared sense of psychological acceptance or a "safety zone."

During the initial visit to a setting, ethnographers can state plans to return in the future and attempt to judge how others in the locale feel about this. If a good relationship has been developed with a key person at the site (apartment resident, owner/manager of crack house, street dealer), ethnographers can return to the location without the initial contact and rely on people in the setting to provide protection and to help maintain the safety zone. Beddoe suggested,

> Look how they talk with each other, and how they deal with each other, and try to copy their style. This will help you get to other people in the social circle. Any conversation is generally better than none.

When entering a new setting, Dunlap generally located potential exits and figured out who was in charge:

> This is accomplished in a subtle and gradual way in order not to cause suspicion or make anyone feel they are being watched. I call this getting the feeling of the place, people, and conditions. Try to fit in by taking a comfortable stance, giving the impression of familiarity with various situations or scenarios.

Williams usually created the safety zone by paying careful attention to the setting and people's activities:

> Use your own style and smooth approach. Usually don't be aggressive. Try to figure who is available for a conversation and talk to them when [they're] ready; otherwise wait. They communicate with each other via certain physical gestures which can be learned, especially when "thirsty" for smoke [crack]. Let them know that you really want to talk to other people and meet others.
>
> You don't want to create enemies out in the field. You have to be constantly improvisational in the setting. Don't overstay your welcome. Three to 4 hours in one place is too long, so move on. You have to be aware of who you are [a researcher] and where you are at. This is not a recreational place; it is a place where you are conducting research but others are buying and selling illegal cocaine. One should follow the rules of the street—which is surviving.

As rapport with persons in such settings is increased, a safety zone is created among those present. Norms usually include strong expectations of reciprocity. Dunlap described how she responded to these, expectations:

> Be counted on to "do the right thing" for them personally, even though [you're] not taking part in what is happening (you do not sell or smoke crack). I was always prepared to participate in ethically appropriate exchanges. I would accept a cigarette but more frequently provided them to those present. I would provide food or coffee that was shared by all or help a person read something. On the other hand, I avoided sharing drugs and declined to chip in to buy drugs.

This safety zone is a short-term agreement among persons in a concrete locale about the right of other persons to be present. Such temporary agreements do not imply that the potential subjects present have provided ethnographers with informed consent, acceptance, rapport, or a willingness to be interviewed. The safety zone only provides a locale and time during which ethnographers can begin to obtain further co-operation from some of those present.

Humor and Neutrality

Even when ethnographers function within a safety zone, a variety of tense interactions and situations may arise in specific locales. The effective use of humor and neutrality in these settings by ethnographers may also have important benefits for persons in these settings.

Ethnographers' neutrality in tense social situations is well described (Fetterman 1989; Agar 1980; Adler and Adler 1987), but it is sometimes a source of tension between their subjects and themselves (Broadhead and Fox 1990). Humor can defuse such tense situations and build solidarity among group members (Seckman and Couch 1989). Less well documented is the way in which humor and neutrality may help in dangerous situations (Carpenter et al. 1988).

Crack houses and drug-dealing locales are characterized by high levels of mistrust, paranoia, and potential violence. At the same time, these locales are at least partially organized to reduce violence and informally control persons (*New York Times* 1991) who act aggressively. Hamid described the dangers:

> In crack houses, users constantly argue and accuse others of using too much or hiding or stealing crack or money. Street sellers face frequent arguments about money, the quality of crack or other drugs, threats of robbery, and other topics. Usually these arguments are resolved by the disputants reaching some kind of agreement, but other persons (guards, boss, owner) may occasionally intervene if the argument begins to escalate to physical violence.

After establishing a safety zone and acquiring protectors, ethnographers in a crack house or crack sale location may introduce an element of stability and safety. Ethnographers are not under the influence of drugs or alcohol and can think swiftly and clearly. They do not want to buy crack or sell drugs or to be used for such purposes. They are neutral in the various disputes between persons and attempt to maintain communication with all. They have requested and generally been granted protection and safety while in the location. Moreover, ethnographers are sophisticated in interpersonal relationships and can deal with tense situations. Hamid described how he sometimes intervenes:

> When two crackheads are arguing about who got the most crack or stole it [the truth is, they've both used it up], and the dispute is heading toward a physical fight, I begin telling an outrageously funny story that has nothing to do with the conflict. The disputants are distracted from their conflict, they laugh and separate; usually the dispute

is forgotten. Humor is a major way that tense arguments between crackheads or distributors may be resolved without blows and without any loss of face by either party.

Williams also noted that

a humorous remark, well-timed comment, or casual-appearing interruption by the
ethnographer may distract persons who are headed toward violent confrontations. Bring
humor into a very tense situation; get them laughing with the ethnographer and with
each other. The gift of gab will get you [and them] out of all kinds of difficult situations.

Dunlap explained how she has deliberate conversations with crack users while
they are "straight" to reduce the potential for subsequent violence:

Many crack users try to convince themselves and others that the drug does not affect
them. They claim their behavior remains the same after they smoke crack as it is before
they smoke crack. I always bring this discussion up when the individual is sober, before
he of she has ingested any drug. When their behavior begins to change after smoking, I
can usually bring them back to normal behavior by remarking that they are acting differently by smoking crack. Persons will try to prove that the drug does not affect them
in various ways, and that they can handle the drug. While restating these claims, they
generally abandon various kinds of behavior associated with crack intoxication. Also, I
never take sides in any disagreement. Let the situation work itself out. If I feel the situation is becoming too dangerous, I leave.

Williams also noted,

In crack houses or similar settings, the ethnographers' presence can help reduce the risk
of violence among people who argue and fight over drugs. People respect ethnographers and choose not to express overt violence in their presence. Local norms that are
tolerant of threats and violence are set aside, and temporary norms prohibiting such
threats are accepted.

By remaining neutral but interested parties, ethnographers gain respect from
people in these settings. In many potentially violent situations, ethnographers
may be the only "neutral" person who is not high and may become a mediator
between individuals and groups. Such neutrality involves not engaging in personal (especially sexual) relationships with subjects during the study as well as
avoiding alignment with only one group. Ethnographers' personal "safety zone"
is frequently extended to protect subjects and potential subjects from the possible
dangers that their own behavior and willingness to use violence may bring about.
Thus the presence of ethnographers probably reduces the risk of violence among
crack users and sellers in crack houses and dealing locations rather than increasing the potential for violence.

"Sixth Sense" and Common Sense

Not all conflicts and issues in dangerous settings can be resolved by neutrality and humor. Ethnographers need to be prepared to respond effectively in a variety of potentially dangerous circumstances (paranoia, sexual approaches, robbery, theft, shootings, police raids, and arrests) that actually occur infrequently but are a major fear among nonethnographers. Reliance on prudence, common sense, and a "sixth sense" can help reduce physical violence to a minimum. Different kinds of potentially dangerous situations can be handled by evasion and movement away from the danger, controlled confrontation, or rapid departure from the setting. The ability to handle a variety of situations requires both a "sixth sense" for danger and skill in moving away from and evading physical harm. Dunlap provided an illustration:

> Acting from the "sixth sense" is relatively easy. We use it all the time in everyday life when we walk into new situations. There is an uneasiness, an inability to verbalize what is wrong. You may be able to explain everything that is taking place, do not see anything out of the ordinary, but still feel uncomfortable. This is a warning that something may go wrong. When such discomfort occurs, leave as soon as possible. For example, I had planned to hang around Ross and his family on a particular weekend. Each time I made preparations to leave, this uneasy feeling arose—I did not want to go and could not explain it, so I did not see him until the following week. Upon arrival, Ross reported that one of his partners had been shot and killed. If I had gone that weekend, I might have been next to Ross, who was sitting beside his drug-selling partner when the latter was shot by the father of a crack customer.

When and if ethnographers get a feeling of discomfort without reason, they will be safer by leaving the setting and returning another time—even though they may fail to gather some data and violence may not actually occur. But if their "sixth sense" has extracted them from the locale, they will not be harmed during those rare occasions when serious violence does occur.

Crack-Related Paranoia.   Cocaine and crack induce a short-term paranoia in which users are very suspicious of others around them. They may believe others are enemies out to arrest or harm them. If challenged, pushed, or threatened, they may become unreasonably aggressive or violent. Yet crack users opt for avoidance and non-confrontation to handle such short-term paranoia exhibited by other crack users. Williams has dealt with crack-induced paranoia in many settings:

> When people are smoking crack, they go through different stages, one of which is paranoia. The crackhead may comment, "I don't like to be around people who don't get high" or "Why are you watching me?" This person may even be your sponsor or protector but is no longer the rational person you came with. The easy solution is to move away and not watch. Above all else, don't confront or challenge them. Usually you can

find another person who is in a talkative stage where they want to talk. After a while, the first person's paranoia will subside and the person is open to conversation again—with no or little recollection of his comments or implicit threats while high.

Sexual Approaches.   While using crack, a person may express a desire for physical closeness or sexual intimacy and approach others (including the ethnographer) for satisfaction. Williams explained how he responded to various levels of physical closeness:

> There are touchers; persons who seek affection while they ingest drugs and smoke crack. They seek such affection and closeness when they get high, just before the effect wears off. Usually, I just move away or shift to conversation with someone else. What do you do when sexually approached? Be forceful and let them know that your aren't available for sex play; they usually will not pursue it further.

Several female ethnographers have had their fieldwork severely constrained or have had to terminate it completely (Horowitz 1986; Adler and Adler 1987; Howell 1990; Warren 1989) due to the sexual expectations and demands of subjects or other males in the research setting. The threat of sexual assault or rape is a real concern for most female ethnographers and staff members. As a woman, Dunlap followed several strategies to reduce vulnerability to sexual approaches:

> Smoking crack causes many individuals to be stimulated sexually. Yet when first developing rapport, potential subjects frequently assign a fictive-kin role. I may seem like a sister, cousin, mother, or aunt to them. Assuming such roles leads individuals to become "close friends" and share many behaviors they would not otherwise exhibit. When projecting such roles to me, they place me "off limits" for sexual approaches and affairs. Enough crack-using women are available for sexual affairs; neither male nor female subjects need me for sex and usually agree to protect me from advances by others. The crack-sex link focuses on the sexual act, not personal relationships. Even women who routinely exchange sex for crack or money will refuse sexual foreplay and intimacy for short periods during their crack consumption cycles; both men and women leave them alone at those times.

The value of the protector role was evident one evening while Dunlap was observing several prostitutes with whom she had established good rapport:

> I was standing on the sidewalk talking with Lisa (a prostitute who used crack), when a John (customer) drove up and starting talking dirty to us. Lisa talked back to him while I listened. When Lisa said she wants $20 for a blowjob, the man replied, "I don't want you. How much is she [referring to me]?" Lisa exploded: "She ain't one of us. You leave her alone and keep your fuck'n hands off her." She started kicking and pounding the car. The man looked surprised and drove off quickly.

Abandoned Buildings and Other Dangerous Locales.   Most ethnographic research is conducted where the physical environment is structurally safe. Assuming such safety can be dangerous when researchers are studying crack dealers. Crack dealers may set booby traps to slow police or potential robbers. The sale and use of crack often occurs in abandoned buildings, run-down tenements, and hidden locations (e.g., under bridges or tunnels). Such locations are best approached only with a protector who knows it well. Even then, visits should occur only when the ethnographer feels comfortable. Dunlap recalled her trepidations:

> A street contact said, "Let's go to a place where a friend lives. I'm doing this as a favor to you." She took me into an abandoned building where her friend gave us a back room. I could have been robbed. But nothing happened. The interview went well but the place was unheated and filthy. On other occasions, I have rented apartments or hotel rooms for interviews because I didn't want to go into particularly bad abandoned buildings where subjects lived. If I enter an abandoned building (most have serious structural defects like broken steps or holes in floor), I do so only with people who know their way around defects that could cause serious harm.

The presence of a protector who can vouch for the safety of the premises and serves as a guide around several obstacles is critical in deciding whether to go into abandoned buildings or outdoor locales that researchers perceive as dangerous. Typically, ethnographers and subjects prefer more neutral settings like a coffee shop, restaurant, storefront, or apartment of a friend (which usually have comfortable chairs, heat, and some privacy).

Crimes and Threats Involving Money.

Robbery, burglary, and theft from field staff are uncommon but do occur (Spunt 1988). In fact, many crack distributors are frequent and proficient robbers, burglars, and thieves (Johnson, Elmoghazy, and Dunlap 1990). Furthermore, crack users are constantly broke and in need of money. Thus we have developed strategies to minimize criminal victimization and monetary losses. Ethnographers and field staff can expect to be constantly approached for money, "loans," and "advances" (Johnson et al. 1985, 205–6). When these are not provided, implicit threats may be made. Dunlap defused threats by trying to provide balanced reciprocation:

> While declining to provide cash to the "kitty" towards the next purchase of drugs, providing cigarettes, candy, food, drinks, and refreshments will usually satisfy one's social obligation to contribute to shared group activities in a crack house or among drug sellers.

Usually, persons in protector roles will prevent threats from becoming robbery attempts. Johnson described one simple precaution that may reduce the magnitude of monetary losses if a robbery or theft occurs:

> While in the field, wear clothing with a lot of pockets. Distribute the money into different pockets and keep $10 in a shoe for emergencies. While in the field, only take money from one pocket—conveying the impression that all my money is in that pocket. If someone observes and actually attempts a hold-up [which has not happened yet], give the contents from only that one pocket. When money in that pocket gets low, go to a private place (e.g., a bathroom) and transfer money to the spending pocket.

In prior or concurrent research projects (Johnson 1990; Johnson et al. 1985; Goldstein et al. 1990), some staff members have been robbed, and in one case, a physical assault without serious injury (Spunt 1988) occurred. When crimes occur, staff members usually report them to police to indicate that such violations will have consequences. Several thefts of tape recorders and minor personal possessions were not reported, due mainly to lack of police interest.

Fights.   A physical fight or show of weapons may break out without warning so that ethnographers have little chance to use humor and neutrality to prevent it. Almost always, such weapons and fights have nothing to do with the ethnographers' presence. Rather, they are linked to disputes with other crack abusers in the locale. Williams followed several strategies for dealing with such occurrences:

> Sometimes knives or guns appear, more frequently as a display of possessions (like gold chains or sneakers) than as a means of threatening persons. If they seek approval for their new possession, I may comment about how nice it is, but add "Guns aren't my favorite thing. Could you put it away?" I've been in hundreds of crack houses and dealing locations where weapons were widely evident, but I've never been present when guns were used in a threatening manner. If such an event were to occur, I'd leave as soon as possible, and not get involved as an intermediary.

Stickup Men and Drive-by Shooting.   Perhaps the most dangerous situation is a "rip off." This occurs when robbers surprise the occupants at a crack-dealing locale with the clear intention of taking all cash and drugs present. Likewise, when two or more drug dealer groups are competing for a good selling location, they may try to "warn" others by street shootouts. These are not situations for mediation or humor, only for getting out of the way or following orders. Beddoe noted:

> Stickup men have usually cased the location and are quite certain who is present before coming in. They want money and drugs. Keep quiet and provide what they want.

Williams noted that ethnographers who have good rapport with dealers may be relatively safe:

> How do you know a territorial dispute is going on? Generally, someone will let you know so you can stay out of the way 'til some order has been reestablished. You have more warning of trouble than ordinary citizens in the contested area. Your contacts can provide information later—without your being present.

Violence and shooting in the drug culture/business is unpredictable and without warning because surprise is frequently a major element in its use. But most violence by crack dealers is intentionally directed at specific persons and occurs in a concealed setting (so no witnesses are present). Drive-by shooting/machine-gunning of people on street corners and "stray bullets" that kill children remain the exception in drug-related violence, even though they are a major feature of sensationalizing mass media coverage (*Daily News* 1990; *New York Newsday* 1990; *New York Times* 1990a, 1990b).

Contacts with the Police.

Since 1983, police task forces directed against dealers have frequently engaged in surprise raids against dealers and crack houses. Despite concerns about police action and fear of arrest, ethnographers who avoid using and selling drugs themselves are rarely involved with the police. The police are authorized to use force only when a person resists physically, so ethnographers contacted by police are rarely arrested (Bourgois 1990). Particularly in street settings, ethnographers must be careful in dealings with police. Informal conversations with police should be avoided so that subjects and potential subjects do not have a basis for believing that the ethnographer is talking to or "informing" the police. When the police behave unprofessionally toward subjects, ethnographers who are observed to "stand up" to police gain respect in the eyes of potential subjects. Williams reported one such incident:

> One night I was on the streets with a white ethnographer in a copping area. One police officer came up and asked, "Say, white boy, why don't you buy drugs in your own neighborhood?" and pushed him against the squad car to search him. After producing identification showing that he lived within a couple of blocks, he got off with no further hassle. People in the community saw this as harassment by police and concluded that the ethnographer was not a police officer.

Dunlap's field notes recorded the following incident:

> One afternoon I was with two female subjects who were going to cop some drugs inside an abandoned building. While they copped, I went to the store to buy sodas. When I came out, two male cops had the two subjects against the wall and were patting them down. One of the cops was verbally degrading a subject. I inquired what happened and observed the police action. Not finding any drugs (only a crack stem), they let the subjects go. The women believed that my inquiry had saved them from arrest and that the cops were trying to "shake them down" for money. They felt that my presence had deterred the police from carrying out any adverse actions.

Despite many hours and days spent with crack dealers in crack sales locations where police were observed several times a day, our research staff have never been present when "busts" occurred. During a parallel study of sex-for-crack in Miami in 1989, however, Inciardi (personal communication) walked through the back door of a crack house as a police raid came through the front door. He and others present were taken to detention where he was held for 5 hours; he was released at booking without formal arrest following the procedures outline below. He did not, however, return to that crack house or others in its general vicinity.

On a parallel research project evaluating the impact of Tactical Narcotics Teams (TNT), ethnographers at Vera Institute (in cooperation with the New York City police) have been instructed about appropriate procedures to follow in the event of being caught in a police sweep or raid. The ethnographers are not to resist arrest nor attempt to talk to police officers at the arrest location. Rather, they are to follow instructions, let police gain control, and allow themselves to be hand-cuffed and taken to the station house. At the point of booking, ethnographers should present identification as a researcher working for a nonprofit organization and ask the booking sergeant to call the principal investigator or let the re-searcher make such a call. If possible, staff members try to arrange the re-searchers' release at booking, without formal arrest charges. Otherwise, senior staff or a lawyer will be present at arraignment and will attempt to persuade the judge to drop charges or provide bail money. Subsequent efforts will be made to have charges dismissed or the conviction overturned. To date, researchers at Vera Institute or Narcotic and Drug Research, Inc. have not been arrested while con-ducting research during the 1980s. Narcotic and Drug Research, Inc. now retains a lawyer to act quickly to represent staff, both ethnographers and paraprofession-als, arrested during fieldwork or AIDS outreach activities.

Conclusion

In this article, we have drawn on concrete experiences with a wide range of dan-gerous situations and subjects we encountered in conducting field research. The approaches described here have evolved over more than 25 years of ethnographic research successfully conducted by ourselves and others among users and sellers of heroin and crack in some of America's most dangerous social settings (see Broadhead and Fox 1990; Feldman 1974; Goldstein et al. 1990; Johnson et al. 1985; Preble and Casey 1969). Yet after spending 2 years involved in direct research among crack distributors and many other years of research with robbers, bur-glars, murderers, and heroin sellers, none of our professional ethnographers or paraprofessional staff (ex-dealers, ex-drug users) has ever been physically in-jured; few, in fact, have been robbed or burglarized while performing their re-search roles. If violence in the drug culture truly occurred on a random basis then several ethnographers should have been harmed. This is not to suggest that the participation and activities of ethnographers is inherently less dangerous than those employing survey or archival methods. Yet recognizing the potential dan-gers, it is still possible for ethnographers to choose their field of study with a clear awareness, preparation for, and avoidance of the risks involved.

References

Adler, P. A. 1985. *Wheeling and dealing*. New York: Columbia University Press.

Adler, P. A., and P. Adler. 1987. *Membership roles in field research*. Newbury Park, CA: Sage.

Agar, M. H. 1980. *The professional stranger*. New York: Academic Press.

Becker, H. 1960. Participant observation: The analysis of qualitative field data. In *Human Organization research: Field relations and techniques*, edited by R. N. Adams and J. J. Preiss, 267–89. Homewood, IL: Dorsey.

Biernacki, R 1988. *Pathways heroin addiction.* Philadelphia, PA: Temple University Press.

Bourgois, P. 1990. In search of Horatio Alger: Culture and ideology in the crack economy. *Contemporary Drug Problems* 16:619–50.

Broadhead, R. S., and K. J. Fox. 1990. Takin' it to the streets: AIDS outreach as ethnography. *Journal of Contemporary Ethnography,* 19:322–48.

Brownstein, H. H., and P. J. Goldstein. 1990a. A typology of drug related homicides. In *Drugs. crime and the criminal justice system,* edited by Ralph Weisheit, 171–92. Cincinnati, OH: Anderson.

———. 1990b. Research and the development of public policy. The case of drugs and violent crime. *Journal of Applied Sociology,* 7:77–92.

Carey, J. T. 1972. Problems of access and risk in observing drug scenes. *In Research on deviance,* edited by Jack D. Douglas, 71–92. New York: Random House.

Carpenter, C., B. Glassner, B. D. Johnson, and J. Loughlin. 1988. *Kids, drugs, and crime.* Lexington, MA: Lexington Books.

Daily News. 1990. Slaughter of the innocents. October 19:1.

Denzin, N. K. 1970. *The research act.* Chicago, IL: Aldine.

Douglas, J. D., ed. 1972. *Research on deviance.* New York: Random House.

Dunlap, E. 1988. Male-female relations and the black family. Ph.D. diss., University of California, Berkeley.

Dunlap, E., B. D. Johnson, H. Sanabria, et al. 1990. Studying crack users and their criminal careers: The scientific and artistic aspects of locating hard-to-reach subjects and interviewing them about sensitive topics. *Contemporary Drug Problems.* 17:121–44.

Feldman, H. 1974. *Street status and the drug researcher: Issues in participant observation.* Washington, DC: Drug Abuse Council.

Fetterman, D. M. 1989. *Ethnography: Step by step.* Newbury Park, CA: Sage.

Goldstein, P. J. 1985. The drugs/violence nexus: A tripartite conceptual model. *Journal of Drug Issues* 15:493–506.

Goldstein, P. J., B. Spunt, T. Miller, and P. A. Bellucci. 1990. Ethnographic field stations. In *The collection and interpretation of data from hidden populations,* edited by Elizabeth Lambert, 80–95, Research Monograph 98. Rockville, MD: National Institute on Drug Abuse.

Goldstein, P. J., P. A. Bellucci, B. Spunt, and T. Miller. 1991a. Volume of cocaine use and violence: A comparison between men and women. *Journal of Drug Issues.* 21:345–68.

————. 1991b. *Frequency of cocaine use and violence: A comparison between men and women.* Rockville, MD: National Institute on Drug Abuse.

Hamid, A. 1979. *Ganja in Granada.* Ph.D. diss. Teachers College, New York.

————. 1990. The political economy of crack-related violence. *Contemporary Drug Problems* 17:31–78.

————. 1992. *The political economy of drugs.* New York: Plenum.

Hamid, A., and R. Curtis. 1990. Beaming up: Contexts for smoking cocaine and sex-for-drugs in the inner-city and what they mean. Manuscript, John Jay College, New York.

Hanson, B., G. Beschner, J. Walters, and E. Bovelle, eds. 1985. *Life with heroin: Voices from the inner city.* Lexington, MA: Lexington Books.

Horowitz, R. 1986. Remaining an outsider: Membership as a threat to research rapport. *Urban Life* 14:409–30.

Howell, N., ed. 1990. *Surviving fieldwork. A report of the Advisory Panel on Health and Safety in Fieldwork.* Washington, DC: American Anthropological Association.

Jackson, J. E. 1990. Deja entendu: The criminal qualities of anthropological field-notes. *Journal of Contemporary Ethnography* 19:8–43.

Johnson, B. D. 1973. *Marihuana users and drug subcultures.* New York: Wiley.

Johnson, B. D., E. Elmoghazy, and E. Dunlap. 1990. *Crack abusers and noncrack drug abusers: A comparison of drug use, drug sales, and nondrug criminality.* New York: Narcotic and Drug Research. Inc.

Johnson, B. D., B. Frank, J. Schmeidler, R. Morel, M. Maranda, and C. Gillman. 1988. Illicit substance use among adults in New York State's transient population. *Statewide Household Survey of Substance Abuse, 1986.* New York: Division of Substance Abuse Services.

Johnson, B. D., P. J. Goldstein, E. Preble, J. Schmeidler, D. S. Lipton, B. Spunt, and T. Miller. 1985. *Taking care of business: The economics of crime by heroin abusers.* Lexington, MA: Lexington Books.

Johnson, B. D., A. Hamid, and H. Sanabria. 1991. Emerging models of crack distribution. *In Drugs and crime: A reader,* edited by Tom Mieczkowski, 56–78. Boston, MA: Allyn & Bacon.

Johnson, B. D., T. Williams, K. Dei, and H. Sanabria. 1990. Drug abuse in the inner city: Impact on hard drug users and the community. *In Drugs and crime,* edited by Michael Tonry and James Q. Wilson, 9–67. Chicago, IL: University of Chicago Press.

Johnson, J. C. 1990. *Selecting ethnographic informants.* Newbury Park, CA: Sage.

Liebow, E. 1967. *Tally's Corner: A study of Negro streetcorner men.* Boston, MA: Little, Brown.

McCracken, G. 1988. *The long interview.* Newbury Park, CA: Sage.

Morales, E. 1989. *Cocaine: White gold rush in Peru.* Tucson, AZ: University of Arizona Press.

New York Newsday. 1990. Stray bullets kill 7 in New York in 1990. December 28:4.

New York Times. 1989. Drug wars don't pause to spare the innocent. January 22:25.

———. 1990a. Woman is killed in Bronx drive-by shooting. October 7:40.

———. 1990b. Record year for killings jolts officials in New York. December 31:25.

———. 1991. In a crack house: Dinner and drugs on the stove. April 6:1. 24.

Preble. E. J., and J. J. Casey. 1969. Taking care of business: The heroin user's life an the street. *International Journal of Addictions,* 4(1):1–24.

Reinarman, C., and H. G. Levine. 1989. Crack in context: Politics and media in the making of a drug scare. *Contemporary Drug Problems.* 16:535–78.

Rose. D. 1990. *Living the ethnographic life.* Newbury Park, CA: Sage.

Seckman, M. A., and C. J. Couch. 1989. Jocularity, sarcasm, and relationships. *Journal of Contemporary Ethnography,* 18:327–34.

Sluka, J. A. 1990. Participant observation in violent social contexts. *Human Organization.* 49(2):114–26.

Smith, C., and W. Kornblum, eds. 1991. *In the field: Readings on the field research experience.* Westport, CT: Praeger.

Spradley, J. P. 1980. *Participant observation.* New York: Holt, Rinehart & Winston.

Spunt, B. 1988. Backstage at an ethnographic field station. Paper presented at the annual meeting of the American Society of Criminology, Chicago.

Washington Post. 1990. Violence in the '90s: Drugs deadly residue. October 14:A1, A12.

Warren, C. 1989. *Gender issues in field research.* Newbury Park, CA: Sage.

Whyte, W. P. 1955. *Street corner society.* 2d ed. Chicago, IL: University of Chicago Press.

———. 1984. *Learning from the field: A guide from experience.* Beverly Hills, CA: Sage.

Williams, T. 1978. The cocaine culture in after hours clubs. Ph.D. diss., City University of New York.

———. 1989. *The cocaine kids.* New York: Addison-Wesley.

———. 1991. *The crack house.* New York: Addison-Wesley.

Williams. T. and W. Kornblum. 1985. *Growing up poor.* Lexington. MA: Lexington Books.

2. "God, She's Gonna Report Me":

The Ethics of Child Protection in Poverty Research

Lisa Bostock

The ethics of social research with children has been the source of considerable debate. In particular, issues of how to address potential disclosures of child abuse have been highlighted. What ethical implications are raised, however, when children are the indirect focus of the research? This paper explores the ethical dilemmas of conducting research with mothers about their experiences of caring for children. It is based on qualitative research with 30 mothers on low incomes. The paper concludes that strategies to tackle structural disadvantage as well as those that take account of individual risk are key features of future child welfare.

The ethics of researching the experiences of children has been the subject of considerable debate among social scientists from a range of disciplines. These disciplines include anthropology (Davis, 1998), geography (e.g. McDowell, 2001; Young and Barrett, 2001; Valentine and others, 2001), sociology (e.g. Alderson, 1995; Alderson and Goodey, 1996; Morrow and Richards, 1996), social policy (Mahon and others, 1996) and social work (Thomas and O'Kane, 1998). Negotiating power relations between adults and children, and in particular the positioning of children as 'vulnerable', appears to be a key theme running through these debates. This theme is woven around a desire to 'do right' by respondents thereby ensuring that children come to no harm emotionally, physically or spiritually. What ethical implications are raised, however, when children are the indirect focus of social scientific research?

This paper explores the ethical dilemmas of conducting research with mothers about their experiences of caring for young children. It is based on qualitative research that involved interviewing 30 mothers on low incomes. . . .

The paper addresses three aims. First, it describes the development of a child protection protocol designed to protect the rights of children within the research process. Second, it explores the experiences of mothers who agreed to take part in an interview explicitly framed by a child protection protocol. Third, the paper reveals that child protection is integral to mothers' caring routines. Their accounts showed that it is caring in conditions of poverty that posed the greatest threat to their children's well-being.

Children & Society Volume 16 (2002) pp. 273–283 Published online 10 May 2002 in Wiley InterScience (www.interscience.wiley.com). DOI: 10.1002/CHI.712

The Study Of Mothers On Low Income

The study was designed to update previous research on motherhood and provide a comprehensive picture of caring for children in poverty during a period of increasing income inequality (Bostock, 1998, 2001). Thirty mothers on social security benefits were interviewed and all were caring for at least one pre-school child. Mothers were living in the Midlands, England at the time of the interviews and were selected to reflect differences in ethnic identity and household forms. Over 50 per cent of mothers identified themselves as lone mothers. While just over 60 per cent (19) of mothers in the study were white, the remaining mothers identified themselves as black, Pakistani, Indian and Gujarati Muslim.

. . . The majority (85 per cent) were in receipt of income support. Most (90 per cent) were living in rented accommodation and only 14 per cent owned a car or van. This contrasts sharply with the majority (70 per cent) of UK families with children who live in owner-occupied accommodation and have access to a car or van (OPCS, 2000). Two-thirds of mothers in the current study assessed that their health was either fair or poor. This again contrasts with surveys of self-assessed health, which indicate that most (75 per cent) British women enjoy excellent or good health, with only a minority assessing their health as fair or poor (Blaxter, 1990).

Mothers were invited to reflect on their experiences of caring in disadvantaged circumstances. This involved taking part in a semi-structured interview designed to capture the complexities of women's day-to-day lives. . . .

Developing data collection methods that encourage mothers to talk at length about their experiences of caring for children poses some serious ethical dilemmas. Research conducted during the early 1980s, before child abuse was widely recognised as a public health and children's right issues (Campbell, 1997), suggests that the combination of fatigue, stress and sense of isolation often fills mothers of new born babies with feelings of anger and aggression toward their children (Graham, 1980).

Given that the mothers in the current study were caring for children in what were often very trying circumstances (e.g. in the face of interlocking layers of disadvantage: low income, little social support, poor housing and lack of transport), it seemed reasonable to anticipate that some mothers might reveal similar feelings of anger and agression. Stress and poverty go hand-in-hand (Dill and Greywolf, 1982; Wilkinson, 1996), while feelings of irritability and tiredness are common side-effects of motherhood (Popay, 1992). This means that contemporary research on the experiences of caring for children on low income runs the risk both of inviting respondents to 'incriminate' themselves (i.e. share stories of stress and feelings of aggression toward their children) and of silencing children whose 'voices' may be lost in an approach in which the mother is the primary respondent. The following section examines one means of addressing this dilemma, the development of a child protection protocol that frames the interview from its inception in terms of a concern for the safety of the children.

From Ethical Principles to Child Protection Protocols

The development of the child protection protocol used in the current study was born from a wider concern about the nature of ethics in social research. In recent times, the concept of a feminist ethics of care has been the closely debated, and has highlighted the importance of reciprocity, inter-dependency and the role of affective relationships (Held, 1995; Larrabee, 1993; Sevenhuijsen, 1998). To the layperson, ethics is often reduced to questions of 'who one cares more or less about' or 'what makes an action the right, rather than the wrong thing to do?' (Singer, 1994). In the same way, questions of research ethics are guided by questions of what is morally right or wrong. What will be the consequences of adopting a particular research topic or pursuing a particular research question? How can confidentiality and anonymity of respondents be guaranteed? What steps can be taken to ensure the well-being of those who take part in the research? These are just some of the questions that pervade the minds of those about to embark on empirical research.

These questions come into particularly sharp focus in the context of researching mothers' experiences of caring for young children. How does one balance the desire to both 'do right' by respondents, in this case mothers, while at the same time recognising ones' responsibilities toward children? There has been considerable debate among researchers working with children and young people about how to address disclosures of child abuse. On the one hand, there appears to an emerging consensus among researchers that complete confidentiality can never be guaranteed to children as research respondents (Mahon and others, 1996; National Children's Bureau, 1993). This is because it is thought that if a child reveals that he/she is being abused, then it is the researchers' duty to report such a disclosure to the relevant child protection agencies. On the other hand, this approach is believed to damage the integrity of the research relationship and reduce the credibility of the research (Boyden and Ennew, 1997; Thomas and O'Kane, 1998). What happens, however, when the respondent is a mother who reveals that a child is at risk of harm, rather than the child itself? What is the researchers' responsibility in this situation? Is it simply to report the mother, or other third party, to the appropriate authorities?

One means of addressing this dilemma is through the development of a code of ethics. The development of the current research project was guided by two sets of ethical standards: the British Sociological Associations' (BSA) Statement of Ethical Practice (n.d.) and Child Protection Procedures produced by Barnardos (1994). The BSA statement was designed, primarily, 'to inform members' ethical judgements rather than impose on them an external set of rules' (BSA, n.d.: 1). Barnardos' child protection procedures, on the other hand, were produced in order to prescribe how a staff member should respond in cases where 'a child is [suffering], or is likely to suffer significant harm' (Barnardos, 1994: 3).

While the BSA guidelines were never designed to be exhaustive or indeed prescriptive, they do not take account of the dilemmas of conducting research with adult carers which, at the same time, is sensitive to its potential impact on children. This is because a view has tended to predominate within sociological circles that rigid, inflexible sets of ethical rules for research could leave us with undesirable consequences (Burgess, 1984; May, 1993). Indeed, it has been argued that in the most extreme case this would mean that the 'only safe way to avoid violating principles of professional ethics is to refrain from doing social research altogether' (Bronfenbreener in Barnes 1979, quoted in May, 1993: 56). Even sociologists researching the experiences of children have recognised that in using ethical guidance one should leave room for choice by the researcher in response to particular situations (Morrow and Richards, 1996).

All staff at Barnardos, however, including research staff, are bound by the organisations' child protection procedures which define the welfare of children as paramount to its work. These state that if child abuse is suspected by anyone connected with Barnardos' work then the 'protection of the child is the primary focus and any other organisational principles . . . are secondary considerations' (Barnardos, 1994: ii). In order to resolve, if only in part, the dilemmas of undertaking research with adult carers while considering the potential to silence the voices of children, a child protection protocol was developed to provide guidelines in the event that it was observed, or a mother disclosed, information that indicated that a child might be at risk of significant harm.

The child protection protocol was designed to be used by myself and another research student . . . (see Dearlove, 1999). It was developed over several months of discussions with colleagues at Barnardos and was based, with her permission, on a similar approach adopted by Marjorie Smith (see Smith, 1999 for review of methodologies used to investigate parenting). The protocol was intended to cover situations where we were provided with, or became aware of, information which raised concerns about a child's safety or welfare.

While it was recognised that it was unlikely that child protection concerns would be raised within the context of a relatively short encounter with mothers (in a one-off semi-structured interview) the child's safety was of paramount importance to the design of each research study. The child protection protocol involved the following three steps:

- First, if information was disclosed or a situation was observed that suggested a child was at risk of harm, we were to discuss our concerns with the mother at the end of the interview (unless this was thought to put the child at risk) and tell her that we would have to inform colleagues linked to the project.

- Second, a consultant paediatrician based at the University, agreed to discuss any child protection concerns raised by myself or my colleague and consented to contact Social Services if further child protection action was deemed necessary. This action was to be taken within 24 hours of the interview. It is important to note that this person was highly experienced in child protection issues, and agreed to make the final judgement, rather than the doctoral student on whether contacting Social Services was necessary.

- Finally, if action was going to be taken, we would contact the mother, preferably by visiting, but by phone, where available, if visiting would delay contact with her.[1]

All mothers in the current study were informed of the existence of the child protection protocol. At the beginning of each interview, I would start by telling the mothers that everything that they said to me would be confidential unless they made it clear to me that a child was at risk of harm. All the mothers accepted this level of information without comment and all continued their participation in the research.

The development of the child protection protocol was of both practical as well as symbolic importance. There was something profoundly unsettling, however, about having to suggest to the women that they might be putting their children at risk. There was something particularly disturbing about this when hoping to capture the experience of caring for children in what were often very difficult circumstances. This raised the question for me, as a (hopefully ethical) researcher, was I just simply another outsider out to survey the parenting skills of poorer mothers? In order to allay my own fears and insecurities that framing the interview in this way had damaged my relationship with the women (and hence affected the quality of the data), I asked all respondents at the end of the interview to reflect on how they felt at being confronted with the child protection protocol. Their responses are explored in the section below.

'It Puts the Frighteners On You': Framing Interviews With A Child Protection Protocol

The BSA statement on ethical practical (BSA, n.d.) states that although sociologists, like other researchers, are committed to the advancement of knowledge, that goal does not, of itself, provide an entitlement to override the rights of others. It suggests that sociologists have a responsibility to ensure that the physical, social and psychological well-being of research participants is not adversely affected by the research. However, the current study, by interviewing only mothers, created the potential to override the child protection rights of children who are in a more vulnerable position than that of their carers, the primary respondents of the research. This is why the child protection protocol was developed in the event that a mother disclosed, or I observed instances suggesting that a child might be at risk from significant harm.

While mothers consented to participate in an interview framed by such considerations, it was not an unproblematic issue. Many mothers expressed ambivalence about the suggestion that their child might be at risk and questioned me about whether they had any cause for concern about the interview with them. Although these mothers felt that the child protection protocol was understandable

---

[1]The child protection protocol was never called upon during the course of the research.

and that the rights of children should come above the rights of respondents, it had made them initially wary of my intentions.

> LB: At the beginning of the interview, I am aware that we discussed the possibilities of having to report anything if you made it clear to me that a child might be at risk. Can you tell me how you feel about that?

> Well, I think that's right really. I think it's for the sake of the child that you have to do that, don't you? But it does put the frighteners on you, yes, I thought 'God, she's going to report me'. But I do believe in that, if a child's at risk, you should say something because a child can't say it himself (white lone mother, on income support, caring for one child aged 19 months).

Other mothers also expressed an ambivalence concerning the child protection protocol. Although these mothers appeared less concerned about whether I considered their child to be at risk, they were at pains to point out that their children were not at risk and therefore had no qualms about participating in the interview. This suggested that mothers felt that had they refused to take part, even though they were offered informed consent on issues of confidentiality, it would have been an admission of guilt when no suspicion of child abuse was justified.

> Well, it's fair enough you know, but it's, you know, it's a horrible feeling as well that you have to be asked that question. Not that you had to ask, maybe some people you do, some children are at risk and it feels bad for me when I think other people's children are at risk, you know, but mine are okay (Pakistani mother, with partner, on income support, caring for four children aged twelve, ten, seven and three years).

Many of the mothers, however, commended the development of a child protection protocol and described how they felt it could help mothers experiencing difficulties with their children. These mothers also alluded to the high quality of care that they provided for their children, but recognised that if they themselves, or someone else, had put a child at risk then the child protection protocol afforded an opportunity to get help. As with the accounts provided by all mothers, it is clear that the welfare of their children is a paramount concern and integral to the development of caring routines and strategies.

> I think that it is good to say it and if someone is in a situation and they wanted to tell you that their child was at risk because they were so stressed. And you ask so many questions about coping and maybe they might feel that they could tell you. But others may not feel so right about saying it, they might find it unnerving. Obviously if my kids were at risk, I wouldn't be blasé about it and tell everyone, but maybe in an interview like this, then someone might give a hint. If I was looking after someone's child and I thought that they were at risk, I would tell someone (Gujarati Muslim mother, with partner, on family credit, caring for two children aged seven and four years).

'Child Protection? Ain't That What I Do Already?': Mothers' Caring Routines

The mothers' largely supportive reactions to the development and use of the child protection protocol are gratifying but also troubling. On the one hand, I felt that these reactions affirmed the quality of the research relationships. They also indicated that the trust that had been established between myself and the mothers had not been unduly damaged by my (implicit) suggestion that they might be putting their children at risk. On the other hand, I was concerned that their acceptance of the need for the protocol indicated that they were used to having their child care skills surveyed.

This point has been made by Parton (1985) who argues that poorer people are often very aware that their performance in child care is being monitored. It is true to say that all the mothers in the current study had had contact with their local health services. . . .

Perhaps what lay at the heart of mothers' essentially positive reactions, however, is that child protection was already integral to their caring routines. Protecting their children was central to the mothers' sense of self and so they had little reason to worry about the suggestion that they might be placing their child at risk of harm. As one mother exclaimed 'Child protection? Ain't that what I do already?'. The mothers in the current study devoted their days to carrying out caring routines designed to protect and promote the health and safety of children. These routines provided both a structure to their day and the space in which to exert agency in the most unpromising conditions of poverty. The following account of one mother's 'typical day' may appear unusual in the respect that this mother was caring for six children. She was caring for two children from her relationship with her current partner and four children from his previous marriage. Her account, however, is typical of many mothers in the study who described how their whole day, bar a few glimpses of space, was spent meeting the health-care needs of others. This mother was 22 years old.

LB: Can you take me through a typical day?

. . . . A typical day or a nightmare, you mean? Well, I get up in the morning, get the kids ready for school. Dean [her partner] takes them to school. Then I will get the younger three ready. Then I tidy my house and then I take them to nursery at one o'clock. Then I go round to my mate's house for a cup of tea, and that, and then I pick them up from school. Come home, make their dinner, make our dinner and then play for a bit and I tidy up again, and then like get them ready for bed one by one. I eventually I get to sit down and rest about 9.30. That's every day, the same routine apart from when I go shopping. My whole day is routine. I have got set times for everything. I do the same things every day at the same time, so my whole day is routine (white mother, with partner, on income support, caring for six children aged ten, eight and six years, two four year olds and a two year old).

It must be remembered that mothers on low income are charged with the responsibilities of protecting and promoting the health and safety of their children within circumstances of chronic disadvantage. They are faced with a series of multiple and reinforcing conflicts within and between the different dimensions which shape caring on benefit, such as low income, poorer housing and lack of transport (Bostock, 1998). This means that, however hard mothers try to protect their children from the worst effects of poverty, low income conspires to work against them.

Kempson (1996: 68) argues that 'people who live on state benefits generally cannot overcome their [financial] problems no matter which approach to managing their money they adopt'. She states that social security benefits are simply inadequate to cover the costs of caring. Attempting to make ends meet while meeting the care needs of their children is intrinsic to the lives of the mothers in the current study.

> I cope with it, my routines help me cope, I just need more money. More money would make things a lot easier (black lone mother, on income support, caring for one child aged two years).

Coping, exerting agency, resisting poverty, however one wishes to describe how mothers survive all come at a price: that price is poorer health (Popay and Bartley, 1989). Stress alongside chronic tiredness were part and parcel of lives characterised by little or no respite from the many emotional and financial crises thrown up by caring with fewer resources than needed to provide children with quality care. It was in these circumstances that mothers were most likely to talk of feeling 'worn out', 'ground down', 'at the end of their tether'. At the same time they were wary to point out that their children were not at risk of harm.

> LB: So, when you are feeling tired does it get more difficult to look after him?

> I suppose it is part of motherhood, really, I suppose, I could be feeling a little tired and he keeps going on and on and on and he starts doing something naughty, and you are trying to teach them right from wrong, and you say 'now stop, stop it, naughty'. But yes, you know, you just have to be on your toes all the time and you want the best for them you want to teach them right from wrong, you don't want to lose your rag, but sometimes you have to sort of shout but I would never, you know, harm him in any way or anything like that (white lone mother, on income support, caring for one child aged two years).

Keeping children safe required mothers to be constantly inventive as they sought to develop a host of strategies that coped with the conflicts of caring on low income. Some of these strategies, and smoking in particular, is closely associated with poorer health. Smoking is also associated with being a poor mother. . . . Smoking is an expensive strategy. Indeed, Graham (1993: 179) argues that smoking 'tends to be seen as an irresponsible indulgence, a pattern of behaviour which suggests that mothers are neither as caring nor as poor as they claim'.

Graham (1993) suggests that smoking forms part of mothers' daily routines. Along with a cup of tea or coffee, it marks the (typically short) spaces of time snatched from a tight schedule of caring. It is also part of the way women cope with breakdowns in their routines of caring. Smoking is a contradictory, but appears to be, a key child protection strategy. It is a means of maintaining sanity and staying in control of emotions: emotions that can spiral out of control through the pressures of caring in poverty.

> I go out in the garden or the kitchen normally to smoke, because when they start they start and you can pull your hair out, put your hands round their throat quite easily and strangle them but it's like, 'I have got to get out of here' and it's like the first thing that I do. Basically you blank everything out. I try looking out, if I go into the kitchen, I try looking out the kitchen window. If I go upstairs I will just lie on the bed and it's like 'yes, that's it', and then I come down and it's 'shall we start again, shall we?'. And I am quite calm then, it does yes, it calms my nerves. Stops me shaking as well, especially if I am angry (white lone mother, on income support, caring for three children aged five, three years and 17 months).

Child protection is at the core of mothers' caring routines. Working to protect children within limited resources, however, is a source of constant stress and strain. The mothers did describe the joys as well as the pitfalls of looking after their children in conditions of poverty, but poverty constrained their child protection strategies. Strategies that often came to rely on leaving the room while lighting up a calming (albeit potentially cancer inducing) cigarette.

Conclusions: Anti-Poverty Strategies: A Truly Ethical Response?

This paper has examined the ethics of using of a child protection protocol designed to take account of the rights of children when researching the experiences of their mothers. It has explored the dilemmas of asking women to take part in an interview that begins with an implicit suggestion that they might be putting their child at risk. This process led to a fear on behalf of the researcher that relationships with the respondents had been harmed. In order to alleviate anxieties that the quality of the data had been damaged by such concerns, mothers were asked to reflect on their feelings about participating in the research.

Mothers' responses showed that they were supportive but uncomfortable about taking part in an interview framed by child protection concerns. As one woman described it, it served to 'put the frighteners on you'. Responses from mothers also revealed, however, considerable understanding about children's rights in the research process. They agreed that the child protection protocol represented both a practical as well as symbolic means with which to address the potential to uncover stories of child abuse. A number of mothers also pointed out that some women might use the child protection protocol as an opportunity to seek support if they were struggling to keep themselves going.

More importantly, mothers' positive reactions may reflect their lack of concern at the suggestion that they might be putting their children at risk. This is because mothers' accounts reveal that child protection was already integral to their caring routines. Their accounts recast an understanding of child protection in terms of structural rather than individual issues. From their perspective, it was caring in conditions of poverty that posed the greatest challenge to child protection and served to undermine their coping strategies. . . .

While the mothers in the current study worked to protect the safety of their children, research demonstrates that poverty in childhood can leave a long term legacy. Children who grow up in conditions of poverty are, as adults, more likely to be unemployed, experience poor health, be in trouble with the police, live in social housing and have drug and alcohol problems (Fimister, 2001). This paper has highlighted the importance of considering the research ethics of uncovering uncomfortable truths such as child abuse. Child poverty figures such as these, however, show that tackling structural inequality through systematic anti-poverty strategies will ultimately be the most effective as well as ethical child protection protocol.

References

Alderson P. 1995. *Listening to Children: Children, Ethics and Social Research*. Barnardos: Barkingside.

Alderson P, Goodey C. 1996. Research with disabled children: how useful is child-centred ethics? *Children & Society* **10**: 106–116.

Barnardos. 1994. *Barnardo's is a Child Protection Agency*. Barnardos: Barkingside.

Blaxter M. 1990. *Health and Lifestyles*. Routledge: London.

British Sociological Association (n.d.). *Statement of Ethical Practice* [online]. Available: http://www.britsoc.org.uk/about/ethic.htm [1 August 2001].

Bostock L. 1998. *'It's Catch-22 All the Time': Mothers' Experiences of Caring on Low Income in the 1990s*. Unpublished Ph.D. thesis. Lancaster University: Lancaster.

Bostock L. 2001. Pathways of disadvantage?: walking as a mode of transport among low-income mothers. *Health and Social Care in the Community* **9**: 11–18.

Boyden J, Ennew J. 1997. *Children in Focus: A Manual for Participatory Research with Children*. Radda Barnen: Stockholme.

Burgess R. 1984. *In The Field*. Allen and Unwin: London.

Campbell B. 1997. *Unofficial Secrets: Child Sexual Abuse: The Cleveland Case*. Virago: London.

Davis JM. 1998. Understanding the meanings of children: a reflexive process. *Children & Society* **12**: 325–335.

Dearlove J. 1999. *Lone or Alone?: A Qualitative Study of Lone Mothers on Low Income with Reference to Support in Their Everyday Lives.* Unpublished PhD thesis. University of Warwick: Coventry.

Dill D, Greywolf E. 1982. Daily lives. In *Lives in Stress: Women and Depression*, Belle D (ed.). Sage: London.

Fimister G. 2001. *An End in Sight: Tackling Child Poverty in the UK.* Child Poverty Action Group: London.

Graham H. 1980. Mothers' accounts of anger and aggression towards their babies. In *Psychological Approaches to Child Abuse*, Frude N (ed.). Batsford: London.

Graham H. 1993. *Hardship and Health in Women's Lives.* Harvester Wheatsheaf: London.

Held V (ed.). 1995. *Justice and Care: Essential Readings in Feminist Ethics.* Westview: Oxford.

Kempson E. 1996. *Life on Low Income.* Policy Studies Institute: London.

Larrabee MJ. 1993. *An Ethic of Care: Feminist and Interdisciplinary Perspectives.* Routledge: London.

Mahon A, Glendinning C, Clarke K, Craig G. 1996. Researching children: methods and ethics. *Children & Society* **10:** 145–154.

May T. 1993. *Social Research: Issues, Methods and Processes.* Open University Press: Milton Keynes.

McDowell L. 2001. It's that Linda again: ethical, practical and political issues involved in longitudinal research with young men. *Ethics, Place and Environment* **2:** 87–100.

Morrow V, Richards M. 1996. The ethics of social research with children: an overview. *Children & Society* **10:** 28–40.

National Children's Bureau. 1993. *Guidelines for Research.* NCB: London.

Office of Population Censuses Surveys (OPCS). 2000. *1998 General Household Survey.* HMSO: London.

Parton N. 1985. *The Politics of Child Abuse.* Macmillan Education Ltd: London.

Popay J. 1992. My health is alright, but I'm tired all the time: women's experiences of ill health. In *Women's Health Matters*, Roberts H (ed.). Routledge: London.

Popay J, Bartley M. 1989. Conditions of labour and women's health. In *Readings in the New Public Health*, Markin C, McQueen D (eds). Edinburgh University Press: Edinburgh.

Sevenhuijsen S. 1998. *Citizenship and the Ethics of Care: Feminist Considerations on Justice, Morality and Politics.* Routledge: London.

Singer P. 1994. *Ethics.* Oxford University Press: Oxford.

Smith M. 1999. Sample plan of action in case of disclosures. In *Exploring Infant Health,* Conroy S, Smith M (eds). Foundation for the Study of Infant Deaths: London.

Thomas N, O'Kane C. 1998. The ethics of participatory research with children. *Children & Society* **12:** 336–348.

Valentine G, Butler R, Skelton T. 2001. The ethical and methodological complexities of doing research with "vulnerable" young people. *Ethics, Place and Environment* **2:** 119–125.

Wilkinson R. 1996. *Unhealthy Societies: The Afflictions of Inequality.* Routledge: London.

Young L, Barrett H. 2001. Ethics and participation: reflections on research with street children. *Ethics, Place and Environment* **2:** 130–134.

3. Studying Sexuality:

Strategies for Surviving Stigma

Tania Israel

Feminist researchers have highlighted challenges encountered when studying sexuality, particularly in terms of other people's reactions to their work. Sexuality research is often viewed as lacking rigor, illegitimate (Tiefer, 1995), suspect (Reavey, 1997) and embarrassing (Braun, 1999). I experienced some of these responses first hand when I chose to study female strippers for a graduate course on qualitative research. This study was my attempt to reconcile the contradictory feminist perspectives on women's sexuality. As I learned that the dancers' experiences were neither completely liberating nor completely oppressive, I found that my experience of researching sexuality embodied both emancipatory and oppressive potentials. Here I explore these potentials through the narrative of my own experience, and suggest approaches that researchers can use to manage the stigma associated with sexuality research, based largely on strategies I saw the dancers themselves use.

Attention and Stigma

Conducting sexuality research is similar to sex work, in that one of the most difficult aspects is coping with other people's reactions. The stigma for the academic is, however, far less severe because conducting research on sexuality is considered more legitimate than participating in the experiences that we study. The dancers felt that they were not taken seriously if people knew what they did for a living, they experienced the stress of hiding their occupation, and they were constantly identified by their status as strippers. I, too, found that my identity became fused with my project. Others were titillated and entertained by my research, and I feared marginalization and discrimination because of the nature of my work.

My identity became fused with the research project as people introduced me socially as if 'she does research on strippers' were my last name. Like the dancers, I felt as if my association with sexuality overshadowed any other aspect of my life. I found it disconcerting when I was introduced at a wedding as 'this is Tania — she has a degree in sex'. This was typical of the way I was introduced at parties and conferences, and it grew tiresome. I felt I lacked control over whether or not to display my identity as a sexuality researcher because so often other people displayed it for me. The dancers frequently expressed concerns about who knew,

Feminism & Psychology © 2002 SAGE (London, Thousand Oaks and New Delhi), Vol. 12(2): 256–260.
[0959-3535(200205)12:2;256–260;023348]

who would find out, and who they would tell about their work. Although the level of stigma I experienced was far less than that of the dancers experienced, I none the less could empathize with the experience of information being shared without my consent.

My stripper study continues to arouse the interest of colleagues and friends, and I have found this notoriety to be a mixed blessing. People remember me and my work, or at least they remember the 'sexiest' of my research. The one study I did on female strippers tends to overshadow more current and extensive lines of research. I have never had a job interview in which I was not asked about my research on strippers. I certainly make an impression, but I grow weary of the titillation others find in discussing my research.

While I was collecting data for the study my friends often asked about my research, but their interest seemed piqued by the fact that I was going to strip clubs more than by the results of my investigation. Although many of my male friends volunteered to assist me with my research, the offers were diminished by their juvenile and joking tone. My involvement with this project also seemed to give my friends licence to engage in frequent discussions of stripping and even hold a birthday celebration at a strip club. Whereas I was interested in the experiences of the dancers, my friends seemed interested only in their own amusement. Their actions and questions seemed voyeuristic, and I felt like they were exploiting and belittling the seriousness of my research.

When I started the project on female strippers, another graduate student warned me to stay away from the subject, based on her negative experiences. She believed that her research on female strippers had damaged her professional credibility and had led to harassment from faculty in her department. Her experience was consistent with Tiefer's observation, 'our motives for specializing in sex are always being scrutinized and snickered at' (1995: 189). Fortunately, the response from my academic affiliations was generally quite positive. I received a great deal of support from the faculty in my department and the Women's Studies Program, I was invited to present my research at colleges and conferences, and I was quoted in the *New York Times*.

In addition to concerns about their professional credibility, the dancers feared that their families would ostracize them because of their work. In contrast, I never feared reproach by my family for my association with stripping; rather, my family has been an unwavering source of support for my sexuality research. For example, my mother and aunt traveled several hours to see me present my stripper research, and my grandmother asked me to do a repeat performance of the presentation in her living room.

Although my sexuality work has been well received, I realize that because it is very clear that I do research on sexuality, I will likely only get jobs where that work is welcomed, or at least tolerated. I can never know which jobs I did not get due to the nature of my research. I am fortunate, however, that there are enough venues for my work that I have been able to secure employment. It seems like being up-front about my work in sexuality has been adaptive for me. Not so for one of the dancers I interviewed, who wanted to get out of the stripping business. She found a clerical job, and in her interview she was honest with her employer about the nature of her work experience. Once she started working, her supervisor harassed her to the point where she quit her job and went back to stripping. Whereas my sexuality research has been a useful screening device to test the support I would receive for my research, finding a work environment in which experience as a stripper is not stigmatized is not a realistic option.

Despite the stigma described here, neither sex work nor sex research is necessarily an entirely negative experience. The dancers described positive aspects of their work in terms of money, autonomy and enjoyment of their work. The rewards of sexuality research have been professional attention and freedom to do work that I find meaningful and interesting. These rewards can be enjoyed more fully if the stigma associated with the work is managed effectively.

Managing Stigma

The dancers had a great deal of experience of managing sexual stigmatization and developed a number of key strategies. Sexuality researchers may benefit from using some of the dancers' strategies.

The dancers found a great deal of support in each other. They complained together, comforted each other about negative interactions with customers, and helped the newer dancers acclimate to the environment. Sexuality researchers may benefit from connections with people doing similar research. Sharing stories about problems encountered during the course of research can validate the in-appropriateness and unpleasantness of the experiences. Such a network can also provide a forum for discussing sexuality research with some seriousness because non-researchers may be comfortable talking about the topic only in jest. Unlike the dancers, who worked together, many sexuality researchers are working alone in hostile academic environments. This professional isolation increases the demand for us to create supportive networks that span geographic and disciplinary fissures. Some possible avenues for increasing such connections are joining a professional organization such as the Society for the Scientific Study of Sexuality or the Association for Women in Psychology, establishing a feminist research collective, or scheduling phone meetings with supportive colleagues at other institutions.

A second strategy that sexuality researchers can use is to protect their identity. The dancers generally described themselves as 'entertainers' or told people they were cocktail waitresses in the strip clubs, rather than expose their true job. Similarly, researchers can vary the way they portray their work depending on the audience. I have described my research as 'diversity issues' or 'gender issues' when I haven't wanted to open myself up to public discussions of sexuality. Although this strategy can save individual researchers from engaging in unwanted conversations, keeping silent about taboo topics also serves to maintain the status quo by suppressing discussion of controversial topics (Braun, 1999). One possible alternative is to share the nature of one's work, but to set limits regarding the length and depth of the discussion. Just as I tell people that I am 'off the clock' as a psychologist in order to curb confessions from virtual strangers, I am learning to say, 'I don't feel like talking about research right now'. This strategy may enable the researcher to discontinue undesirable conversations without keeping the subject of sexuality completely clandestine.

The dancers developed strategies for negotiating their relationships with the customers and setting limits. Official regulations about interactions between the dancers and the customers were defined by the club management and by local governments. In practice, however, each dancer defined her own limits to some extent, and the bouncers knew what each dancer considered permissible behavior. In this way, the dancers exerted some control over their relationships with the customers and felt justified protecting themselves from violations of these rules. Researchers may benefit from developing such clarity about their limits and establishing protection against violation of these limits. Preparation for sexuality research should include anticipating difficult situations that may arise with participants, colleagues, friends and family, and identifying strategies for addressing boundary violations and harassment. A mentor or colleague with experience in sexuality research may provide insights about likely dilemmas and effective solutions. Such consultation may have helped me anticipate some of the problematic situations that arose during my research, and I would recommend that researchers seek such assistance before starting a sexuality research project.

A strategy that might help with such negotiations is to find your voice as a researcher to talk about these experiences. I benefited from keeping a research journal because I was able to express feelings that were coming up about the research. I did not, however, write about the interactions I had with friends and colleagues, and I did not continue the journal after I had completed the data analysis. Taking these additional steps may have helped me to reflect on problematic situations and to seek solutions and support. The focus of my research was to help the dancers' voices to be heard, and it was an after-thought to voice my own experience as a researcher. The process of preparing a commentary on this topic for a conference became an opportunity to recognize the impact of the research on myself and to identify ways of dealing with the negative effects and appreciating the positive ones. This process has helped me to see ways that I can find support in other feminist researchers, protect my identity and clarify and enforce my limits. Furthermore, finding our voices to speak about sexuality research will benefit the field since the more we talk about our work, the less controversial it becomes.

Finally, appreciate the complexity of your work. My study concluded that the dancers' work was neither completely liberating nor completely oppressive, and they seemed to accept these multiple simultaneous realities. It has taken me several years to recognize the full range of positive and negative effects that resulted from this research project. As sexuality researchers, we need to talk about the triumphs as well as the pitfalls. We should be prepared to respond to the stigma, but we should not fear it.

References

Braun, V. (1999) 'Breaking a Taboo? Talking (and Laughing) about the Vagina', *Feminism & Psychology* 9(3): 367–72.

Israel, Tania. 2002. Studying sexuality: Strategies for surviving stigma. *Feminism & Psychology*, 12, (2), 256–260.

Reavey, P. (1997) ' "What Do You Do for a Living Then?" The Political Ramifications of Research Interests within Everyday Interpersonal Contexts', *Feminism & Psychology* 7(4): 553–8.

Tiefer, L. (1995) *Sex is Not a Natural Act: And Other Essays.* Boulder, CO: Westview Press.

4. Sex With Informants as Deviant Behavior:

An Account and Commentary

Erich Goode

Engaging in sex with informants in social research is regarded as deviant; hence, it is rarely admitted in print. The author argues that such behavior is likely to influence what the researcher sees, how conclusions are reached, and what is written about. He summarizes what has been discussed on the issue of sexual self-disclosure and indicates how his own intimate relations with informants on three projects may have shaped his vision and conclusions. Sex with informants both provides benefits and poses risks; some of them are discussed as well. In addition, ethical issues are raised and discussed. Some possible reasons are advanced as to why reticence tends to be the rule in ethnographic sexual experiences.

Unlike the practitioners of most other disciplines, sociologists and anthropologists are in an extremely privileged position with respect to autobiography. That is, not only can they write literal autobiographies in the same sense that, say, mathematicians can—that is, they can narrate their life story—they can also tell the story of the intersection of their lives with their work in ways that mathematicians cannot. However, historically, sociologists and anthropologists were supposed to pretend that they had no biography, no self, no experiences relevant to the subject they studied. This was a pose, of course, but it revealed their insecurity on the question of objectivity. Malinowski's posthumously published journals, *A Diary in the Strict Sense of the Word* (1967), should have annihilated that naive notion once and for all. After reading it, one wonders, how could this sensitive, insightful observer have understood the Kiriwina if he harbored such contempt for them? The uproar the publication of the posthumously published diary generated expressed more about the challenge that personal life and feelings posed to social science than about the issue of our right to privacy. If physicists are disembodied observers, analyzing and explaining the mysteries of the universe, perhaps it is a denial of the self that is the key to being taken seriously as a real science. Or so some social scientists believe. Susan Krieger (1991) has argued, to the contrary, that social scientists ought to view the self not as a "contaminant" but as a "key to what we know. . . . The self is not something that can be disengaged from knowledge or from the research process. Rather we need to understand our participation in what we know" (pp. 29–30).

Deviant Behavior: An Interdisciplinary Journal, 20: 301–324, 1999

To specify the matter a bit, for the most part sociological and anthropological researchers have been remarkably coy about what they do on the job. I do not mean by what they "do" the kinds of experiences that form the basis of their research reports. I mean their personal experiences, what does not get written about in their research reports, what goes on behind closed doors, their unauthorized experiences—experiences they are not permitted, whether by informal social convention or professional decree, to discuss; even more important, experiences that, were they to violate these rules, most of their peers would feel they should not have had in the first place.

Even more specifically, social researchers very rarely discuss the subject of emotional and physical intimacy with their subjects, informants, and interviewees, however important it may be to the conceptualization and results of their research projects. (Usually it is not relevant; often it is.) Do they avoid the subject because it is unimportant, because it does not impinge on how they think about the issue, what they see, what they write about in their books and articles? How can we ever know this if the topic is hidden from view? The fact is, we are not being given the full story on the actual participation of most social science observers in the behaviors they examine and involvements with the people they study. By that I mean that there is almost certainly a great deal more participation and involvement than is admitted; full self-disclosure tends to be the exception rather than the rule.

Self-Disclosures of Sex with Informants

For the most part, sexual practices by researchers tend to be off limits; sociologists hardly ever admit—in print, anyway—that they participated in them while they engaged in their research. Gary Alan Fine (1993) discussed 10 "lies" of ethnography, myths that are widely disseminated in print as true but that insiders know to be false. "Illusions are essential to maintain an occupational reputation," Fine explained (p. 267). Actions that would shatter the illusions "are typically hidden in the backstage regions from which outsiders are excluded" (p. 267). One of these myths is that the researcher is sexually chaste. The reality, Fine asserted, "so secret and so dirty that it is hard to know how much credence to give, is the existence of saucy tales of lurid assignations, couplings, trysts, and other linkages between ethnographers and those they 'observe' " (p. 283). The violent contrast between myth and reality is remarkable, implied Fine. After all, he said, "Humans are attracted to one another in all domains. They look, they leer, they flirt, and they fantasize." And yet, he remarked, the "written record inscribes little of this rough and hot humanity" (p. 284). Although he admitted to no more than "a few looks and thoughts," he said, "others can" (p. 284).

Murray Davis (1983:xxi) claimed that researchers are discouraged from crossing the boundary separating research from participation for fear of "sexual contamination." James Wafer (1996:264), an anthropologist, wrote that one such boundary crosser is Tobias Schneebaum, whose book *Where the Spirits Dwell* (1988) is widely regarded in anthropology "as a dirty joke. As though it were not sufficient provocation to admit that he is gay, Schneebaum breaks the ultimate taboo by being explicit about the fact that he had sex with the natives." One of Wafer's (straight) colleagues went so far as to say that Schneebaum's main motivation for conducting anthropological research "was to get screwed" (p. 264). To this critic, Wafer added, this was "sufficient reason for dismissing the writer and his work" (p. 264). "But why?" he asked. The researcher is supposed to be "a disembodied" and "asexual" being, Wafer answered.

> Ideally, there would not only be no sex in the text, but also no desire. Yet it is hard to imagine that the actual field experience of ethnographers could be so insipid. Surely eros plays as great a role in structuring their relationships in the field as it does in any social context. (p. 265)

There are several major exceptions to the rule of sexual revelation in addition to Schneebaum—nearly all written by anthropologists—and they are extremely instructive.

Paul Rabinow (1977), who conducted field research in Morocco, described a single episode with a Berber woman, a prostitute, in such elliptical terms that the reader does not know for sure whether they even engaged in intercourse. "This woman was not impersonal," Rabinow said, "but she was not that affectionate or open either" (p. 69).

George Lee Stewart, at the time a sociology graduate student and with every intention of writing a book about "the world of the brothel"—apparently it was never published—detailed his first-hand experience with having sex with a prostitute in "On First Being a John" (1972). Stewart described his nervousness, awkwardness, and inexperience and speculated on what his wife would think about the matter.

Charles and Rebecca Palson (1972), two anthropologists, studied comarital "swinging" by exchanging sexual partners themselves. Swingers first, researchers later, for 18 months they engaged in a participant observation study of 136 swinging couples. As they explained, "Most of our important insights into the nature of swinging could only have been found by actually experiencing some of the same things that our informants did" (p. 29). However, aside from informing their readers that they did it, they do not supply any detail about their own experiences.

John Alan Lee (1978, 1979), writing well before the AIDS crisis, studied the social ecology of urban gay sex, that is, the territories, the times, and the social and physical "niches" of homosexual encounters. Sex, Lee claimed, is an "artificially scarce" commodity in Western society; that is, if there were no norms restricting the circumstances under which it takes place, it would be vastly more abundant than it is (p. 175). Gay culture, Lee claimed, subverts the principle of scarcity and provides abundant opportunities "in which individuals may enjoy large number of casual encounters" (p. 177). Having lived "an exclusively heterosexual lifestyle," complete with wife and children, until the age of 32, Lee came out as a homosexual. His participation in the research, he said, was "sometimes as an observer and sometimes for the purpose of personal sexual encounters" (p. 178). The reader gets no more detail than this.

Colin Turnbull (1986) briefly described his sexual relationship with a young Mbuti woman, sent to him by her father, the chief of a tribe. (Apparently, sexual abstinence in young persons is considered abnormal among the Mbuti.) She taught him a great deal about local custom, he explained. Interestingly enough, his relationship with the young woman was not mentioned in his full ethnographic report (1962) but was reported only in a book of readings devoted specifically to the topic of sex, gender, and fieldwork (Whitehead and Conaway 1986).

Joseph Styles (1979) engaged in a study of homosexual bathhouse sexual encounters. Originally, he had resolved to limit himself strictly to observation. "I would go to the baths," he told himself, "see what went on, even talk with the other men—but I wouldn't have sex" (p. 137). In short, initially, Styles said, he would be "a nonparticipating insider" (p. 137). Contact with the action at the baths, however, put an end to that resolve in fairly short order. The first evening "was unremitting chaos," with naked and half-naked men shoving, wandering, crowding, and jamming the hallways; while he stumbled around in the dark, one man tore his towel off his body while a second groped for his genitals (p. 138). He soon realized that his mere presence in the baths made him "a potential sex object"; moreover, his attempt to strike up a conversation, presumably for research purposes, "was one sign of showing sexual interest in another man" (p. 138).

After talking with several bathhouse insiders, Styles "radically changed" the way he conducted his research. On his return to the bathhouse, rather than rejecting the advances of "a good-looking fellow," Styles thought, "to hell with it!" and "had sexual relations with him" (p. 141). Initially, playing the dual role of observer and participant made him uneasy; hence, he began observing in one bathhouse and participating in a different one. Eventually, however, "the asexual observation became more and more tiresome, more tedious, and more frustrating until," he said, he "gave up observing without sexual intent and plunged fully into the sex life of the baths" (p. 142).

Van Lieshout (1995) conducted an observational study of encounters at a rest stop in the Netherlands that had become well-known in the gay community as a locale for homosexual sex. In this locale, by unspoken convention, Monday evenings were reserved for "leather" and S&M (sadism and masochism) activities. The author explained that his role "became a mixed one"; that is, for some of the time during the evening, he said, "I was an observing participant" and for other times, he was "a participating observer" (p. 25). Van Lieshout explained that his prior experience "in leather bars and cruising areas made it possible to feel at ease almost immediately" (p. 25). It made him, he says, an insider from the moment he surveyed the scene (p. 25). Interestingly, however, in his published account, van Lieshout supplied next to nothing about his own personal experiences. He also explained in a footnote (p. 37) that information obtained from sex partners may be tainted in that the two goals—obtaining sex and supplying information—may work at cross-purposes. For instance, someone may be unwilling to state his actual age for fear of discouraging a potential partner.

Bolton (1992, 1995, 1996) came as close as any ethnographer does to an outright endorsement of sex in the field. To study sexual behavior as it takes place, he said, "We must go beyond the narrow concept of participant observation" (p. 132), that is, mere observation without participation. Indeed, he argued, "Some of the very best cross-cultural work on homosexuality has benefited from insights gained through participation" (1992:132). As for engaging in his ethnography of sexual practices among gay males and how they impact on the transmission of AIDS, Bolton said, "I did not merely observe but participated fully in all aspects of gay life. . . . In my casual sexual encounters with men I picked up in gay cruising situations," he informed the reader (pp. 134, 135), "my approach during sex was to allow my partner to take the lead in determining which sexual behaviors to engage in" (high-risk activities—unprotected anal intercourse—excepted). His activities were consonant with the norms of the gay community he investigated and hence, his sexual activity while engaged in research, he felt, was perfectly ethical.

Gendering Self-Disclosures of Sex With Informants

Female ethnographers are by no means strangers to sexual activity with informants in the field; a few who have engaged in the experience have even been willing to discuss it in print. Anthropological disclosures of sexual relationships in the field tend to be densely gendered. One gender difference is that women tend to be more vulnerable to male violence; for heterosexual women, while there is pleasure in intimate experiences with men, there is danger as well. This duality assumes prominence in much of the writing of female social scientists who discuss sex in the field. And, although the descriptions of the sexual liasons that both men and women offer are elliptical, sketchy, more implicit than explicit, this might be a bit more so for women than for men. Still, what is so remarkable here is the similarity rather than the difference.

Dona Davis (1986) studied menopausal women in a small fishing village in Newfoundland. Although the norms of her community condemned sex outside of marriage, in practice couples were expected to pair off sexually before marriage. During her fieldwork, Davis met a hydraulics engineer who lived in a trailer near the village. Far from receiving negative sanctions as a result of her romantic relationship, Davis said, it "seemed to make people a bit friendlier and more at ease around me. . . . I was simply breaking a rule everyone else broke" (p. 254). Note the singular here: one sexual relationship. Note, too, Davis's extremely laconic description of her liason:

> Local matchmakers arranged a meeting and we became close friends. . . . I often went to his trailer for privacy and some peace and quiet in which to work. . . . One night . . . , there was a severe snowstorm and I was not able to get back to the village. (p. 253)

Manda Cesara (a pseudonym) engaged in fieldwork among the Lenda (also a fictitious name). The Lenda are an extremely sexually permissive people, discouraging sexual and emotional dependence on a single partner and encouraging a "relatively frequent change of partners" (1982:146). Among the Lenda, sex is regarded as a joyful experience, typically "nonprocreative" and "rejuvenating" (p. 146). In a letter to her mother, Cesara described a man "stepping into my life." (She is married.) He is westernized, has a PhD, spent many years in Sweden, is "bureaucratic, staid, cautious, correct" (p. 147). How, she asked her mother, does one undress in front of such a man? Rather than robbing her of a clear mind and her freedom, as her husband does, her relationship with this Lenda man gives her "freedom . . ., a kind of power over myself" (p. 147). Given her newfound freedom, her anonymity, the intensely personal nature of her book, and the central place of recreational sex in the lives of the people she is studying, it is surprising that Cesara offered virtually no other details about her sex life among them. The reader walks away feeling that this is a deeply gendered book.

Gearing (1995) said that "sex in the field remains a tabooed topic, addressed metaphorically if at all" (p. 188); at the same time, she said, "If we are serious about examining ourselves as researchers, we must grapple with the impact of our sexuality on our fieldwork" (p. 188). Gearing discussed her love affair and marriage with (and eventual divorce from) "E.C.," her best informant. Although in St. Vincent, Gearing's fieldsite, sex is not shameful for women—indeed, an uninhibited view of sex is encouraged—nonetheless, the island "is not a woman's sexual paradise" (p. 189). Gearing described the sexual double standard, "under which the sexual conquest of multiple partners contributes to a man's prestige" (p. 192), whereas for women, there is the ever-present reality of sexual harassment, as well as the ever-present possibility of sexual violence. E.C., she said, was "different." He "was the only Vincentian man I met," she says, "who had not had any children by any previous partner" (p. 199). Moreover, she said, he was willing to do chores around the house.

Gearing's relationship with E.C., she said, gave her a closer, more comfortable relationship with the community she studied. Her neighbors seemed happy that she had a man about the house. Among other things, it demonstrated that she viewed Vincentians as equals and proved she was not a racist (1995:202).

> Feeling sexually attracted to the people we [ethnographers] live among and study is a much more positive reaction than feeling repulsed by them. As long as we enter relationships honestly and considerately, and are observant of local norms, we should not reject our sexual feelings toward people with whom we work. (p. 203)

Gearing's (1995) account is predictably scanty concerning the physical details of sex. One understands that her partner has a "sterling character" and "a charismatic charm," is talented at performing a "stand-up comedy routine" (p. 197), and is "tall, well built, handsome, intelligent, funny, charming, considerate, and affectionate" (p. 198). Yet, Gearing's reader must pay close attention to her text to know exactly where her sexual relationship with E.C. begins, since she supplied very little in the way of concrete description about the courtship. Her study is on "gender, kinship, and household" in St. Vincent, and sexual seduction plays a major role in the substance of her research. And yet she was almost completely silent concerning her own involvement in this selfsame process.

Few anthropologists have described their fieldwork experience with more sensuality and intensity than Kate Altork. (She is also a published poet and a fiction writer.) Her descriptions of forest firefighters in action (1995) are so vivid that the reader can smell the smoke, see the fire, feel its heat. "My senses were hit with a constant onslaught of sounds and sights, smells and tastes" (p. 123), she wrote, and, when reading her narrative, the reader's senses come alive as well. Altork described her erotic dreams, pointed out the sensual and sexual references in her fieldnotes, quoted men and women firefighters on how sexually arousing fighting fires is, cited approvingly the work of anthropologists who endorse sex in the field, intimated that she may have engaged in sexual activity of a certain sort in the field ("Defining sex in the field: what is it, anyway?"), and told us that "some of the best lovemaking" she has "yet experienced" with her husband took place after her return from "forays into the world of the firefighters" (p. 131).

And yet, nowhere did she get any more sexually explicit than that. The "blind" reading for gender authorship that Callaway (1992) suggested we do for the classic anthropological texts—that is, can we tell from the text itself whether the author is a man or a woman? (pp. 31, 45)—would yield only one conclusion for this piece: The reader never doubts that the author, Kate Altork, is a woman.

> I am not advocating random and meaningless sexual encounters here, nor am I talking about situations where issues of colonialism and power imbalance enter into the discourse, which may be, in fact, most of the time. . . . The point is not to encourage sensationalistic, *National Enquirer*-type confessionals from the field, replete with descriptive close-ups and minute details about how a given anthropologist had sex in the field. But we might at least acknowledge that we "did it" if we did (or that we wanted to "do it," even if we didn't), and be open to the fertile possibilities for dialogue about the ways in which "it" changed, enhanced, or detracted from what we felt, witnessed, and interpreted in the field. . . . So. Where does this leave us? Do we make love in the field or don't we? And, if we do, how far do we go? How can we untangle the web of moral and ethical issues involved and explore, as well, the dissonance between the unspoken rules of the academy and our own personal beliefs and actions? (pp. 121, 131)

Among personal tales of the field, perhaps no greater disparity exists between the efflorescence of emotion and the total absence of raw, concrete sex than in the writing of Esther Newton (1993a), who conducted an ethnographic study of Cherry Grove, a homosexual enclave 45 miles from New York City (1993b). Newton mentioned that "some of the people who were objects of my research were also potential sexual partners, and vice versa" (1993a:10). She emphasized that the "burden of being, and being seen as, an erotic creature" (p. 15) cannot be evaded. She described romantic feelings, erotic yearnings, sexual urges, physical desire. Yet, there are no descriptions of sex because in the one relationship she detailed, there was no sex, no physical sex at any rate. Newton, a lesbian, describes her "love affair" with Kay, who was 85 years old and confined to a wheelchair. It is almost inconceivable that a male anthropologist, whether homosexual or heterosexual, could have had the experiences Newton had or produced writings equivalent to Newton's. Unlike the classic ethnographic texts (Callaway, 1992:35, 41), today's narratives are deeply and unmistakably gendered.

Peter Wade (1993) represents an exception to the rule that few heterosexual men disclose their sexual relations in the field. Investigating "sexuality and masculinity" in a predominantly Black area of Colombia, he admitted to "two quite long-term relationships" with local women (p. 200). The most gendered aspect of Wade's disclosure is his motive, which was largely instrumental. "I actively sought a young, single black woman as a potential partner," he explained, because of the "desire to transcend the separateness that I received as distancing me from the constructed otherness of black culture" (p. 203). In addition, Wade said, among the people he studied, "sexual continence is odd and to be avoided" (p. 205); to abstain from engaging in the sex with women "could cast doubt on one's masculinity." A small number of affairs allowed Wade to adopt a "comfortable gender identity" and "act like a man" (p. 206) and, hence, be accepted in their culture. His relationships with local women, he explained, made him less threatening to informants and gave him greater access to specific sectors of the society, for instance, to single women. It is difficult to imagine a woman being, or admitting to being, as instrumental about sex in the field as this.

While granting that racial and class hierarchies were always part of his relationships (1993:209–210) and acknowledging that much of the profession regards sex with "native" women unprofessional and unethical (p. 211), Wade argued that his affairs were mutually gratifying and located "in the purely personal realm" (p. 212). A sexual relationship between an anthropologist and an informant, he said, implies "the same kinds of ethical and emotional difficulties as any other relationships between these parties" (p. 212).

This brief roster does not exhaust the revelations of researchers who have been forthcoming about having engaged in sexual behavior among the people they studied. Lewin and Leap (1996:3) claimed that revelations of sexual activity (and fantasies) in the field have nearly always been the perogative of heterosexual men. This is most decidedly untrue, for they did not include the revelations in their own volume, *Out in the Field* (1996), as well as those in *Taboo* (Kulick and Willson 1995), published shortly after their own book went to press. No matter. In spite of these remarkable exceptions, the long and short of it is that, of the thousands of ethnographers who have spent uncountable hours in close proximity with the people whose lives they shared and behavior they observed, engaging in almost every imaginable activity with them, only a few dozen have had the courage to step forward and tell the world about their more intimate moments. Informal consensus has it that most ethnographers have remained chaste in the field, and my guess is that assessment is correct. But vastly more sexual behavior has taken place than is reported, and that disparity is worthy of discussion. Clearly, then, extremely strong norms exist within the academic community that govern the construction of self-revelations, and they are, for the most part, obeyed.

Sex with Informants: Benefit and Risk

I decided to defy this taboo on sexual self-revelation by writing an account of my intimate experiences with informants in three research endeavors: marijuana use (research conducted in 1967 and that culminated in a book published in 1970), personals-generated courtship (in which I participated for the purpose of dating between 1979 and 1983, and which I studied more systematically in the 1990s), and the National Association to Aid Fat Americans (NAAFA), a kind of "Love Boat" for fat women and men who were sexually and romantically attracted to fat women (where I conducted field research, and dated, between 1980 and 1983).

Was it necessary to have sex with my informants to learn what I found out? Of course not, although at the times when I did so, it seemed perfectly natural; in fact, to have done otherwise would have felt awkward and out of step with everything that was going on. By doing so, I felt a natural and organic part of the tribes I was studying, much as Cesara, Gearing, and Wade did. Does sharing intimate moments with informants lend an authenticity to the researcher's vision that might otherwise have been less authoritative? Discounting the possible social disruption that such experiences may cause, yes, I believe so. Is it worth the risk? That's a separate issue. Manda Cesara (1982) claimed that a sexual and emotional relationship with an informant permits "laying hold of the culture in its entirety through that particular individual" (p. 60).

Many commentators have argued against becoming too involved in the lives of one's informants because it is likely to lead to a loss of objectivity. "Going native" is the term that is commonly used: adopting the way of life of the people one studies to such an extent that one becomes more an advocate than an ethnographer. In my experience, it's difficult to sentimentalize and romanticize the people you're studying if you are in their face—and they are in yours—all the time. This is especially the case if you engage in intimate relations with them over an extended period of time. The fact is, you are acquainted with details of their lives that range from the spiritual to the mundane, from the way they express their most heartfelt emotions to the way they trim their toenails. For me, unabashed advocacy of my subjects was impossible precisely because I knew too much about them.

In *Gender Issues in Field Research*, sociologist Carol Warren (1988) argued that unless the details of the researcher's sexual experiences in the field are relevant to and illuminate the research experience, they become "gratuitous" (p. 63). In this book, but not in her published account of the research she summarized (1982), Warren cited her own flirtatious behavior toward a judge as a means of gaining rapport and maximizing information gathering (p. 45). In contrast, she said, in

that report, she did write about sexual "hustling" of her by male courtroom workers (p. 64). The difference between the sexually toned experiences she revealed in
her monograph and those she didn't report, she said, lay mainly in the writing
conventions that prevailed when she wrote up her study in the early 1980s. With
respect to those incidents she did not write about, she said, "I never thought of it"
(p. 64). However, she argued, with most research projects there is no point in
bringing the details of the researcher's sexual activities out into the open.

I do not question her assertion that an examination of one's sexual relationship
with informants might be irrelevant to some sociological research projects. My
guess is, Warren is correct for most research projects, possibly even most participant observation studies. However, it is inconceivable to me that in research contexts in which the field worker lives among informants 24 hours a day the issue
of sex between researcher and informant never at least arises, never needs to be
resolved. Certainly the issue of my intimate relations were central to the work I
conducted. Permit me to spell out how.

First of all, in all three of my investigations, sex was a centrally relevant topic.
In the marijuana research, the conjunction between sex and marijuana use was a
major component, and in the personals ad and the NAAFA studies, sex and ro-
mance were more or less what they were all about. Ignoring my own sexual experiences during the course of these studies now seems inconceivable to me.

Second, as I've stated above, intimacy generates access to information and
usually more information and better information. Sex has a way of riveting one's
attention to the matter at hand; what one learns in bed is not likely to be forgotten. At the very least, establishing an intimate liason with an insider does influence access and rapport, for better or for worse. Moreover, this is likely to be
gender related.

Third, having romantic and sexual relations with informants is likely to influence one's view of the reality of the scene or behavior under discussion. One's vision of how things are and how they work cannot but be shaped by sharing one's
most intimate moments with an insider, who is likely to see things a certain way.

Fourth, the fact that one has shared an informant's bed necessarily alters how
the researcher—author writes up the report. In my case, not only did I change in-
consequential details to protect the identity of my sexual partners, I also left out
certain details for fear those partners would feel that I had betrayed them, even
though their identities were disguised. The very intimacy that grants access to information often results in inhibiting public revelations.

Fifth, sex represented my unconditional entry into NAAFA, and it was sex that
proved to be my undoing in it. Only by dating was I seen as a full-fledged member of the organization, and as a result of dating (admittedly, recklessly and
promiscuously), I found it impossible to continue my research. Sex was the central fact of my investigation in that setting, and any honest account had to take
note of it.

Sixth—and here we come to the issue at hand—sexual intimacy with informants raises a host of ethical questions that demand discussion. At the very least,

admissions of sexual liasons will force researchers to account for their actions as, in the academic environments in which we move, such behavior tends to be frowned on. More on this momentarily.

And seventh: Sexual liasons present risk, especially for women. For all researchers, they may make a research enterprise less viable, close off avenues of information, and upset and anger participants in a given scene. My own, extremely poorly thought-out involvements in NAAFA made it impossible for me to continue with my research. I have no doubt that for most researchers, sex on the job traverses much of the same landmined territory offered by sex off the job. The wrong partner or partners, too many partners, partners under inappropriate times or circumstances, too much time with one partner or not enough time with another—or, for that matter, spurning someone who wants to be a partner: We all know the perils that lie in wait for us when we make the wrong decision.

For women, these risks are far more perilous, manifold, and painful; in fact, are omnipresent whether they engage in sex or not. In one study, 7 percent of the female anthropologists who responded reported rape or attempted rape against them in the field (Howell 1990); it's possible that was an underestimation. In all likelihood, most of the women in this study were completely celibate. At the same time, it is highly likely that sex with a number of men increases the odds of sexual violence. If a woman becomes known in the community as someone who is sexually accessible to more than a small number of men, she may become a target for unwanted attention, including violence. But again, even if she is celibate, she could become a victim of sexual violence.

In addition, I suspect that most members in most of the communities ethnographers might study would treat a woman who is having sex with one or more of her male informants in a fashion that is likely to be counterproductive, detrimental to the process of gathering information. This is not true of all communities. As we've seen, female researchers studying more than a handful of communities have found informants more relaxed and accessible after their affair with a local became known (e.g., Cesara 1982; Davis 1986; Gearing 1995). Unfortunately, this is atypical.

More common is the experience of Ruth Horowitz (1986), who found that her initial, nonsexual research relationship with male gang members began to slide into one where her informants increasingly regarded her as a "chick," that is, a sexually desirable and available woman. She soon realized that the only role available to her that would permit her to remain on the scene was that of a sexual partner, which was unacceptable to her for both tactical and ethical reasons. As the teasing and flirting escalated, she decided to move her fieldwork into a different social sector—girl gang members. Horowitz did not have the freedom to decide her research role, she argued; her options were extremely limited, constrained by the expectations of her informants. In my opinion, she made the right decision.

Far from endorsing sex between researchers and informants, I am arguing that, under certain circumstances, it is likely to be a terrible thing to do. But under others, it may yield insight. Moreover, I am not arguing that discussing it is a relevant issue in every research project; again, this depends on the study under investigation.

The Ethics of Sex with Informants

To be frank, during none of the three research efforts in which I engaged did I give the matter of the ethics of sex with informants a great deal of thought. In fact, it never occurred to me that sex with informants was ethically improper or methodologically questionable.

In 1967, when I conducted the marijuana interviews, I didn't even know about the existence of "human subjects committees." (In 1967, neither New York University, where I taught during the spring semester, nor the State University of New York at Stony Brook, where I began teaching in the fall, even had a human subjects committee.) Even if I had, I would have regarded them as yet another hurdle in a gauntlet of bureaucratic restrictions. I had never been told by an academic advisor or older colleague that researchers were required to treat their subjects in specified ways—and must not treat them in specific other ways—as spelled out in a clearly articulated code of ethics. Did the American Sociological Association promulgate a code of ethics before 1967? At the time, I simply had no idea. In fact, the possibility of the very existence of an ethics code never entered my mind. (A little checking reveals that the American Sociological Association did not formulate one until 1968.) Kai Erikson's famous essay on "disguised observation" was published the same year I conducted my marijuana interviews, 1967, but I was not engaged in deception of any kind, I was just smoking dope and sleeping with some of my female interviewees. Truth to tell, I did not read Erikson's classic piece until years later; when I did, I strongly disagreed with its argument (Goode 1996).

It is true that some of the women in these three sites with whom I had relations expressed their disappointment—or anger—after we stopped seeing one another. But I took this as the normal aftermath of relationships gone sour. I never conceptualized my sexual behavior during the entire course of my research as anything other than a freely chosen activity between two equal partners. Did they see things in that way? Today, looking back, it seems clear to me that many did not; at the time, subjectively constructed disparities in power simply did not occur to me.

To me, in interactions with my marijuana informants in 1967, the relationship seemed completely nonhierarchical. In my interviews, it was I who was invading the users' turf, begging them for their time and words. If anything, I reasoned, I was the subordinate party in this transaction, not the other way around. Any intimate relations that fortuitously transpired seemed to me to have nothing to do with my status as a researcher or a university instructor, I figured. It is true that some of the marijuana interviews took place in my apartment (about a quarter), but half were conducted in the interviewee's domicile and the rest were either in the respondent's workplace or in a neutral territory, such as a public place. In the social settings in which I moved, I assumed I was as free as a bird, and so were my informants. In 1967, I gave little or no thought to the ethical, moral, or ideological implications of what I was doing.

The 1960s was a time of love, broadly interpreted anyway, the expression of sensuousness, a garden of earthly delights, party time, each participant celebrating in his or her own personal fashion. Events were washing over us so abundantly and luxuriously that there seemed to be neither the time nor the need to calculate the possible consequences. Music seemed to gush out of nowhere and explode fireworks in our brain, and the right music, at the right moment, with the right partner, under the influence of a drug of choice, was bedazzling, a vortex of ecstasy.

In short, to me it seemed absolutely inconceivable that any single, under-30 researcher—male or female—who was undertaking a naturalistic or an interview study of marijuana use in 1967 would have abstained from either marijuana use or sex with informants. As I saw things at the time, I was simply doing what came naturally, what seemed most comfortable. In fact, it would have been prudish, unseemly, and out of place to have abstained from joining the party, much like refusing to take off one's clothes at a nudist camp. (Adler [1985:24] said something similar in a somewhat different context.) Having conducted fieldwork among an extremely sexually permissive people, Cesara (1982:59) stated categorically that it is inevitable that certain anthropologists would experience sexual relations with informants. I agree. None of this justifies or excuses my behavior, but it does help explain it.

What about the issue of my dating women by using the personal ads (1979–83)? Under "Ethical Standards," subsection 7, "Harassment," the American Sociological Association (1997) stated that sociologists are not to engage in "harassment of any person." Sexual harassment, the ASA stated, "may include sexual solicitation, physical advance, or verbal or non-verbal conduct that is sexual in nature" (p. 4). (Or it may not. From the wording of this declaration, it's not clear that such actions are by their very nature or by definition sexual harassment.) My behavior could represent a violation of this principle.

Or could it? In answering personal ads, perhaps 90 percent of my motive was for the purpose of dating, and only 10 percent was to gather information. In fact, for all three of these projects, personal and research motives intertwined; I found it impossible to separate them. (I still do.) The politically engaged social scientist informs us that all of us express our ideology in our research, that pure objectivity is a myth, that all science is personal. I'm sure that no one who espouses that position has in mind anything like the sort of behavior I'm detailing here, but drawing a line in the sand between acceptable and unacceptable personal involvements cannot be an easy task.

The fact is, when I answered and placed personal ads, I wasn't certain that I would ever study such behavior more systematically or publish anything from it. In writing about dating via the personals in the 1990s, I was simply drawing on my own biographical experiences to enrich my vision of a given social phenomenon, much the same way an ex-convict (Irwin 1970, 1980), a pool player (Polsky 1969), or a jazz musician (Becker 1963) would have. I'll be blunt about this: I don't see the difference. Riemer (1977) referred to such studies as "opportunistic" research. C. Wright Mills (1959:196) urged us to use our life experiences in our intellectual work. Along with other social scientists, I have taken his advice.

My feelings about my personal and intimate involvements in NAAFA (1980–83) are a great deal more complex and ambivalent than they were for the other two studies. In fact, it is difficult for me even now to put them down on paper, in part because they are too painful and in part because they are partly hidden from my conscious mind. I feel vastly more ambivalent about my efforts in NAAFA than I do about the other two projects because my motives were more mixed; I never clarified for myself or for others exactly what it was I was doing there, what my primary role was. Eventually, I fell off the tightrope because I simply couldn't maintain the dual role I was attempting to play. I do not think that such a role is inherently impossible to maintain. However, I do know that I played it extremely badly. Looking back from the perspective of the better part of two decades, it seems almost redundant for me to admit that I should have handled things quite differently.

Are there sexual actions in the field and revelations of them about which I would be horrified? Of course. Force and sex with minors and those who are mentally incompetent are crimes, crimes of violence, crimes that truly horrify me. Whenever gross disparities in power exist between the researcher and the subject, my sense of ethical disapproval would begin kicking in, sex between faculty and student being the most salient example; in addition, sex between a researcher and welfare moms, heroin or crack addicts, or residents of a battered women's shelter; in short, weak and vulnerable parties. Because the scenes I looked at were inhabited by nonindigent, fairly middle-class informants, to me, none of this seemed to enter into the picture.

Conclusions

In the first volume of Michel Foucault's *The History of Sexuality*, the reader is told that in Western society, sex is *the* secret. To most of us, sex remains a private sanctuary, a sphere of life over which a veil of secrecy must be drawn. Its enactment is special to us. The rules that govern everyday life seem somehow to be recast when sex is involved. When this veil is ripped away and the doings of one of us is forced into the public consciousness—as we've seen with the sexual doings of U.S. President Bill Clinton, under investigation as I write—the attention of a large portion of the public is simultaneously embarrassed by and riveted on the details.

Sex has played a unique and distinctive role in the study of social life; we have thrown a veil of secrecy around not merely sex but its possible role in social research. "Throughout all the decades of concern with the sex lives of others, anthropologists [and, I would add, other social scientists as well] have remained very tightlipped about their own sexuality" (Kulick 1995:3). Even researchers who have been trailblazers in the systematic study of sexual behavior—Sigmund Freud, Alfred Kinsey, and Masters and Johnson come to mind—have remained extremely reticent about their own sexual behavior. Recent revelations about the sex life of Alfred Kinsey (Jones 1997) argue that this topic is hardly an irrelevancy. Derek Freeman (1991) claimed both that Margaret Mead had affairs with at least one of her male Samoan informants and that this was why her teenage female interviewees lied to her. Commenting on what the researcher is expected—and expected not—to do with subjects, Dubisch (1995:31) pointed out,

> We do almost everything else with our "informants": share their lives, eat with them, attend their rituals, become part of their families, even become close friends, and sometimes establish life-long relationships. At the same time, we "use" them to further our goals, writing and speaking about personal and even intimate aspects of their lives, appropriating these lives for our own professional purposes. Could a sexual relationship be any more intimate, committing, or exploitative than our normal relations with the "natives"? (In some societies, it might even be less so.)

Why? one wonders. Does sex play the same "special" and enshrouded role in the professional lives of social researchers that it plays in the everyday lives of all of us? Is it only sex—that is, this Foucaudian "secret" realm—to them? Or is there something more to it than that?

Is it possible that this veil over the sex life of the researcher is even more crucial for the social scientist than it is for the ordinary man and woman? Might this "secret" to which Foucault referred function to maintain an even deeper secret, the secret of research intersubjectivity? What better means of maintaining the traditional social science fiction of objectivity than to pretend that all ethnographers remain completely celibate when they conduct their research? And what more effective means of emphasizing the fact that sociology and anthropology are deeply social, deeply human, and therefore deeply flawed enterprises than to report, explore, and discuss the subject of sex with the people whose behavior we study?

It is perhaps remarkable that the majority of the ethnographers who have written about the subject of erotic subjectivity in social research through the lens of their own personal experience have been either women (heterosexual or lesbian) or gay men. Kulick and Willson (1995:xiii) found that heterosexual men were not only the most "elusive" about their own sexual activities in the field but were also the ones who discouraged them most emphatically about doing their book *Taboo*, which focuses on that selfsame topic. Why? they ask.

Is it possible, Kulick and Willson (1995) suggested, that such discussion would reveal that not only is sex between male researchers and female informants vastly more common than that between female researchers and male informants, but that it would also cast a bright beam of light on the sexism and racism inherent in such practices and, more generally, that is woven into the very fabric of anthropology (Newton 1993a:xiv)? The "disciplinary silence about desire in the field is a way for anthropologists to avoid confronting the issues of positionality, hierarchy, exploitation, and racism" (Kulick 1995:19).

Once the secret is revealed, the social science pose of objectivity will be more difficult to sustain. How long can we validate the "on stage" pose of ourselves as disembodied, disinterested, and uninvolved social scientists acting out the dictates of a methodology textbook? Is the topic of the researcher's entanglements in the lives of their subjects of study not worthy of discussion? Is a simple admonition "Don't do it!" enough? Contrarily, is the fact that most of us are not entangled in their lives as revealing—and as damning—as the fact that some of us are? Are the implications of erotic subjectivity so obvious and banal as to merit no discussion whatsoever?

I do not see intersubjectivity as inherently poisonous to the task of unlocking the secrets of social life. Like almost everything else in life, intimacy between researcher and subject poses a host of dilemmas. Carefully cultivated, it can be a resource; if permitted to run rampant, it makes the researcher's mission impossible. I fear a too-detached relationship with informants because that means I will remain so utterly out of touch with their lives that anything they say, however fanciful, will seem plausible to me. At the same time, I fear a too-cozy relationship with informants because I want to be free to tell the truth about them. The closer we come to the lives of the people we study, the more we touch them, physically and emotionally, the more we will know about them, yet the greater the likelihood that resentments will be stirred up. There is no way out of this dilemma.

References

Adler, Patricia A. 1985. *Wheeling and Dealing: An Ethnography of an Upper Level Drug-Dealing and Smuggling Community.* New York: Columbia University Press.

Altork, Kate. 1995. "Walking the Fire Line: The Erotic Dimension of the Fieldwork Experience." Pp. 107–39 in *Taboo: Sex, Identity, and Erotic Subjectivity in Anthropological Fieldwork,* edited by Don Kulick and Margaret Willson. London: Routledge.

American Sociological Association. 1968. Toward a Code of Ethics for Sociologists. *The American Sociologist* 3 (November):316–18.

American Sociological Association. 1997. "Code of Ethics" (pamphlet). Washington, DC: American Sociological Association.

Becker, Howard S. 1963. *Outsiders: Studies in the Sociology of Deviance.* New York: Free Press.

Bolton, Ralph. 1992. "Mapping Terra Incognita: Sex Research for AIDS Prevention—An Urgent Agenda for the 1990s." Pp. 124–58 in *The Time of AIDS: Social Analysis, Theory, and Method,* edited by Cilbert Herdt and Shirley Lindenbaum. Thousand Oaks, CA: Sage.

———. 1995. "Tricks, Friends, and Lovers: Erotic Encounters in the Field." Pp. 140–67 in *Taboo: Sex, Identity and Erotic Subjectivity in Anthropological Fieldwork,* edited by Don Kulick and Margaret Willson. London: Routledge.

———. 1996. "Coming Home: The Journey of a Gay Ethnographer in the Years of the Plague." Pp. 147–68 in *Out in the Field: Reflections of Lesbian and Gay An-*

thropologists, edited by Ellen Lewin and William L. Leap. Urbana: University of Illinois Press.

Callaway, Helen. 1992. "Ethnography and Experience: Gender Implications in Fieldwork and Texts." Pp. 29–59 in *Anthropology and Autobiography*, edited by Judith Okley and Helen Callaway. London: Routledge.

Cesara, Manda. 1982. *Reflections of a Woman Anthropologist: No Hiding Place*. New York: Academic Press.

Davis, Dona. 1986. "Changing Self-Image: Studying Menopausal Women in a Newfoundland Fishing Village." Pp. 240–62 in *Self, Sex, and Gender in Cross-Cultural Fieldwork*, edited by Tony Larry Whitehead and Mary Ellen Conaway. Urbana: University of Illinois Press.

Davis, Murray S. 1983. *Smut: Erotic Reality/Obscene Ideology*. Chicago: University of Chicago Press.

Dubisch, Jill. 1995. "Lovers in the Field: Sex, Dominance, and the Female Anthropologist." Pp. 29–50 in *Taboo: Sex, Identity and Erotic Subjectivity in Anthropological Fieldwork*, edited by Don Kulick and Margaret Willson. London: Routledge.

Erikson, Kai T. 1967. "Disguised Observation in Sociology." *Social Problems* 14 (Spring): 366–73.

Fine, Gary Alan. 1993. "Ten Lies of Ethnography: Moral Dilemmas of Field Research." *Journal of Contemporary Ethnography* 22 (October):267–94.

Freeman, Derek. 1991. "There's Tricks i'th' World: An Historical Analysis of the Samoan Researches of Margaret Mead." *Visual Anthropology Review* 7(1):103–28.

Gearing, Jean. 1995. "Fear and Loving in the West Indies: Research from the Heart (As Well as the Head)." Pp. 186–218 in *Taboo: Sex, Identity and Erotic Subjectivity in Anthropological Fieldwork*, edited by Don Kulick and Margaret Willson. London: Routledge.

Goode, Erich. 1996. "The Ethics of Deception in Social Research: A Case Study." *Qualitative Sociology* 19(1):11–33.

Goode, Erich. 1999. Sex with informants as deviant behavior: An account and commentary. *Deviant Behavior*, 20, (3), 301–324.

Horowitz, Ruth. 1986. "Remaining an Outsider: Membership as a Threat to Research Rapport." *Urban Life* 14 (January):409–30.

Howell, Nancy. 1990. *Surviving Fieldwork: A Report of the Advisory Panel on Health and Safety in Fieldwork*. Washington, DC: American Anthropological Association.

Irwin, John. 1970. *The Felon*. Englewood, NJ: Prentice Hall.

————. 1980. *Prisons in Turmoil*. Boston: Little, Brown.

Jones, James H. 1997. *Alfred C. Kinsey: A Public/Private Life*. New York:W.W. Norton.

Krieger, Susan. 1991. *Social Science and the Self*. New Brunswick, NJ: Rutgers University Press.

Kulick, Don. 1995. "Introduction: The Sexual Life of Anthropologists: Erotic Subjectivity and Ethnographic Work." Pp. 1–28 in *Identity and Erotic Subjectivity in Anthropological Fieldwork*, edited by Don Kulick and Margaret Willson. London: Routledge.

Kulick, Don and Margaret Willson, Eds. 1995. *Taboo: Sex, Identity and Erotic Subjectivity in Anthropological Fieldwork*. London: Routledge.

Lee, John Alan. 1978. *Getting Sex*. Toronto: General.

————. 1979. "The Gay Connection." *Urban Life* 8 (July):175–98.

Lewin, Ellen and William L. Leap, Eds. 1996. *Out in the Field: Reflections of Lesbian and Gay Anthropologists*. Urbana: University of Illinois Press.

Malinowski, Bronislaw. 1967. *A Diary in the Strict Sense of the Term*. Translated by Norbert Guterman. London: Routledge & Kegan Paul.

Mills, C. Wright. 1959. *The Sociological Imagination*. New York: Oxford University Press.

Newton, Esther. 1993a, "My Best Informant's Dress: The Erotic Equation in Fieldwork." *Cultural Anthropology* 8 (February):3–23.

————. 1993b. *Cherry Grove, Fire Island: Sixty Years in America's First Gay and Lesbian Town*. Boston: Beacon Press.

Palson, Charles and Rebecca Palson. 1972. "Swinging in Wedlock." *Society* 9 (February):28–37.

Polsky, Ned. 1969. *Hustlers, Beats, and Others*. Garden City, NY: Doubleday Anchor.

Rabinow, Paul. 1977. *Reflections on Fieldwork in Morocco*. Berkeley: University of California Press.

Riemer, Jeffrey W. 1977. "Varieties of Opportunistic Research." *Urban Life* 5 (January):467–77.

Schneebaum, Tobias. 1988. *Where the Spirits Dwell: An Odyssey in the New Guinea Jungle*. New York:Grove Press.

Stewart, George Lee. 1972. "On First Being a John." *Urban Life and Culture* 1 (October):255–74.

Styles, Joseph. 1979. "Outsider/Insider: Researching Gay Baths." *Urban Life* 8 (July):135–52.

Turnbull, Colin M. 1962. *The Forest People: A Study of the Pygmies of the Congo*. New York: Simon & Schuster.

————. 1986. "Sex and Gender: The Role of Subjectivity in Field Research." Pp. 17–27 in *Self, Sex, and Gender in Cross-Cultural Fieldwork*, edited by Tony Larry Whitehead, and Mary Ellen Conaway. Urbana: University of Illinois Press.

Van Lieshout, Maurice. 1995. "Leather Nights in the Woods: Homosexual Encounters in a Highway Rest Area." *Journal of Homosexuality* 29(1):19–39.

Wade, Peter. 1993. "Sexuality and Masculinity in Fieldwork among Colombian Blacks." Pp. 199–214 in *Gendered Fields: Women, Men, and Ethnography*, edited by Diane Bell, Pat Caplan, and Jahan Karim Wazir. London: Routledge.

Wafer, James. 1996. "Out of the Closet and into Print: Sexual Identity in the Textual Field." Pp. 261–73 in *Out in the Field: Reflections of Lesbian and Gay Anthropologists*, edited by Ellen Lewin and William L. Leap. Urbana: University of Illinois Press.

Warren, Carol A. B. 1982. *Court of Last Resort: Mental Illness and the Law*. Chicago: University of Chicago Press.

————. 1988. *Gender Issues in Field Research*. Thousand Oaks, CA:Sage.

Whitehead, Tony Larry and Mary Ellen Conaway, Eds. 1986. *Self, Sex, and Gender in Cross-Cultural Fieldwork*. Urbana: University of Illinois Press.

5. On Having One's Research Seized

David Sonenschein

To my knowledge, Ernest Borneman (1984) is the only one thus far to have made any mention of being arrested in the course of conducting research on children's sexuality or adult-child sexual relationships. Actual arrest of researchers is rare in the history of sexology, although ridicule, harassment, job loss, and violence have been all too common. Some recently documented examples include that of psychologist John Watson, who was purged from Johns Hopkins for his "unorthodox" sex research (Magoun, 1981), and of Max Meyer, whose career at the University of Missouri was ruined by academic officials and inflammatory news reports (Esper, 1967; Magoun).

The difficulties experienced by Kinsey and his associates which were brought on by colleagues, legislators, and the press are well known. I have also learned that in the mid-1950s, the FBI approached Kinsey wanting him to reveal to them his sources of sexually explicit materials. Kinsey and Wardell Pomeroy resisted, and, in turn, pressed the agency to share its holdings with the Institute for research, causing great indignation at the Bureau. Internal memos indicate that the FBI continued to monitor Kinsey's "intrepid band" (as the agency referred to them), particularly because they were afraid the research would lead to an increase in "permissiveness" and "sexual deviancy." Further, the FBI condemned the Rockefeller Foundation's funding of the Institute, feeling that continued research in Kinsey's direction would corrupt and endanger the nation's children. A May 19, 1959, memo says that the foundations have "a stranglehold on the training ground of youth," but goes on to say that "no better instance of a reputable name being lent to enhance an unsavory cause can be found than that offered by the Rockefeller Foundation's support of the Kinsey sex studies." The agency was very upset by Kinsey's "revelation" that sex between adults and children can "contribute favorably to their later sociosexual development."

It appears that 30 years after Kinsey's day, we are again in the midst of a renewed effort to discredit and damage critical sex research. This environment brought Myers (1981) to urge the scientific countering of conservative and religious myths such as those then being promoted through *Medical Aspects of Human Sexuality* and the *Journal of the American Medical Association*. Constantine and Martinson (1981) warned about the risks of research on children's sexuality, incest, and pedophilia. Baker (1984) called attention to the ongoing flow of religious and

Journal of Sex Research, 23, (3), 408–414.

pseudo-scientific nonsense, especially the Vatican's pronouncement that masturbation "is a seriously and intrinsically disordered act."

The histories of sex education testify well to this assault. Even though the punitive intervention of the state into sexual populations or artifacts is consistent and almost predictable (Gilbert & Barkun, 1981), and the increasing "criminalization of sex" (Money, 1985) is an extension of those politics, it has been very easy—even *necessary* from those same political premises—to attack the projects and lives of researchers and educators, especially when they offer newer subject matter, methods, viewpoints, or activism.

At the 1985 Annual Meeting of the Society for the Scientific Study of Sex, Betty Brooks alluded to her 1982 suspension from California State University at Long Beach (CSULB) after being accused of "promoting lesbianism." A more sensational instance at the same time and the same university involved Barry Singer, who was suspended and felt pressed to resign amidst charges by the same conservative and religious groups of "promoting homosexuality," "immoral conduct," and "taunting license" (the latter by George Will, 1982). The police-like seizure by CSULB officials of Singer's instructional materials aroused no such indignation, however, on the part of news commentators. Included in the confiscated material was a videotape of one of his lectures, not on sex at all, but one critical of academia and "higher education." Lastly, Roger Libby was denied tenure at the University of Massachusetts allegedly because of the content of his sexuality courses; Richburg (1985) included relevant comments by John Money, Lynn Atwater, Ira Reiss, and Larry Constantine.

Most vulnerable, however, are nonacademics. The numbers of unaffiliated researchers have grown considerably since the late 1960s, and particularly when combined with progressive elements of gay liberation and feminism, thinking and research on gender and sex has had their most original and important sources beyond university endeavors. Such investigators and writers, on the other hand, lack the insulations of professions and institutions that have traditionally helped define credibility and deflect attack. More importantly, as the professions and popular media continually advertise a monolithic view of child-adult sex, accounts that are carefully edited to hint of the professional controversy, the projects of independent workers threaten to produce data severely qualifying or contradicting official views of desire, relationships, and artifacts.

In this regard, there have been a number of arrests and seizures that are pertinent to the history of sex research and crucial for the issues they raise for all researchers trying to work under erotophobic constraints. In February, 1984, independent researcher Patrick LaFollette was entrapped and arrested by Los Angeles police during the course of his inquiry into child "pornography" and pedophilia. His defense was based on his right to do research and the misdemeanor charge of exchanging "pornography" was dismissed (P. LaFollette, personal communication, 1985; Stewart, 1985). Al Katz, a State University of New York law professor, was similarly arrested in May, 1985, and all of his research materials on child "pornography" have been seized; the case is still in process (A. Katz, personal communication, 1985).

In April, 1985, the personal papers and research files of Gerald Jones were seized by the FBI using an "open warrant," a document of questionable Constitutional validity that allows the seizure of materials deemed seditious or blasphemous by the state without requiring anything other than possession. No charges have been filed against Jones, and as of this writing (mid-1986), his papers are still in the hands of the state. In a total misreading of the situation, Southern California Civil Liberties Counsel Susan McGreivy refused assistance, asserting the Southern California Civil Liberties Union did not "support pedophila" (G. Jones, personal communication, 1985, 1986). Ironically, it was McGreivy who defended Betty Brooks against charges of "advocating homosexuality." An educational psychologist, Jones is known to sex researchers for his background work on pederasty (Jones, 1982); he is also the first to take legal resistance by filing suit against the FBI and others for violation of his Constitutional rights.

In a move with some uncomfortable similarities to the 1933 Nazi raid on Hirschfeld's sexological institute, San Diego police forces seized the entire library of the lay research and educational organization, The Child Sensuality Circle, in June, 1984. It was over half a year before most, though not all, of the nearly 300 books, articles, and other documents on children's liberation were returned. No charges were filed against the group's leader, 84-year-old Valida Davila, a longtime progressive political activist. The news media participated with police in depicting her Reichian-influenced group as a "sex ring," and police fabricated reports of finding "kiddie porn" in the seizures (V. Davila, personal communication, 1984, 1985).

In January, 1986, Terry Morris, a research pyschologist, was arrested and sentenced to 10 years in federal prison for receiving child "pornography" in the mail during the course of his research; the court has also ordered psychiatric counseling. I know of three other cases of arrest and seizure but cannot detail them because the individuals do not care to be publicly identified.

Finally, in September, 1984, my own 4-year accumulation of research on pedophilia and children's sexuality was seized. At this writing, nearly 2 years later, the materials (including illegally seized legal files and personal and political writings) are still held; it was over 7 months before American Civil Liberties Union lawyers and I were able to inventory the documents. The news media again helped directly in promoting the project as a "ring," and I was charged with "sexual performance of [sic] a child" for photocopying photographs from commercial "kiddie porn" magazines for content analysis. I have been fined $5,000 and sentenced to 10 years in prison.

The content analysis was not completed, and the project, an ethnographic study of child-adult sexual relationships, has been destroyed. Fragments will appear if materials are returned; only one historiographic paper has been published (Sonenschein, 1984). Comments by arresting officer Sgt. John Russell may be of interest to other investigators: "Your research is through. Your research is over. I have finished your research for you. You can research anything but this."

These events raise a number of issues in two major areas. One is, of course, the right to do research, to conduct critical inquiry into areas of one's choice, without having that choice defined or restrained by the state. Corollary issues entail having the rights of access to and possession of materials necessary for that research, and the freedom to present publicly documents, findings, and opinions for open consideration. At issue is the right of *any* citizen to inquire into the validity of "expert" claims, to have access to materials and voices supporting or denying any given position, and to speak or write critically of official views without fear of arrest or exploitation and abuse by the news media.

More than half-a-dozen states now have laws against the mere possession of visual representations of children and sex, and a similar federal law is now being considered, one which also recommends the legal age of a child be raised from 18 to 21 for such depictions. Some states do have exemptions for research, but the burden of proof, after arrest and seizure, falls upon the investigator. More crucial are the laws which require the reporting of individuals (both the adults and the minors) known or merely suspected of engaging in adult-child sexual activity. There are not now, nor have there ever been, exemptions for researchers, although the ethical guidelines of the professional organizations call for the confidentiality of study participants. Therefore, because of the risks involved in collecting data and contacting participants, it is imperative that study design in current research on pedophilia, "pornography," and children's sexuality incorporate adequate protections against seizure and destruction of data by the state. Laws passed in the heat of phobic hysteria, whether against anarchists, communists, Jews, nonwhites, homosexuals, or pedophiles, nearly always violate Constitutional protections. Further, these laws tend to stay on the books for use at the state's determination. . . .

The second general area of concern is more serious. It has to do with professional support and participation in increasing the state's powers of surveillance and control over sexual behavior, representations, and thought. In the relative absence of dissenting voices, such behavior has, again, contributed to a historically continuing break-down of professional and scientific integrity. I want to mention briefly three ways in which this has been happening while reserving more detailed discussion and documentation for a later work.

The first is perhaps the most astounding and involves the direct and conscious abandonment of science itself. In an article that helped set sexology back 100 years, David Finkelhor (1979) returns research and analysis to an exclusively ideological basis. By asserting his personal belief that children inherently cannot consent to sex with adults, Finkelhor says he deliberatively "puts the argument on a moral, rather than empirical footing" (1979, p. 695). This opinion is of such a high order that Finkelhor, now a consulting editor for *The Journal of Sex Research*, further insists that any empirical evidence to the contrary is irrelevant and is to be totally discounted.

More incredible that such a statement could appear in a professional publication in the late 20th century is the fact that not only was so little notice taken of it by way of protest, but that it has come to be accepted as a "scientific fact.". . .

A second professional failure is that personal attack has come to replace scientific debate. The idea that evidence contrary to a position must be discounted is extended into the practice of discrediting those who present conflicting data. Fraser (1981) and Russell (1984) indicate that those who do critical research do so because they have "a self-evident interest." Russell, a featured speaker at the 1985 SSSS Annual Meeting, also censures those who contest the image of adult-child sex solely as abuse because she feels the data would "reduce society's inhibitions" against such relationships, a position remarkably similar to that taken by the FBI against Kinsey. Russell, in fact, pejoratively cites Kinsey's term "contact" as opposed to "abuse" as an example (1984, p. 248).

Like Fraser (1981), Russell (1984) suggests that such people—those discovering the varied and complex range of relationships, including positive and productive ones—are nothing more than "would-be participants" (p. 248). These accusations are easily made and accepted now because there is is a triple supportive resonance with popular prejudices, with an earlier rhetoric which included terms like "sympathizer" or "fellow traveler," and with an ongoing institutional inquisition against sexual dissidents by psychiatrists, clinical psychologists, and social workers.

Consequences of this ideological position include not only extensive disfigurement of data but the support of a climate tending to suppress critical views. Martinson's early book (1973) was rejected by 29 publishers because of the topic, its findings, or its "marketability" (F. Martinson, personal communication, 1985). In another example, the editor of the *International Journal of Law and Psychiatry* refused for 4 years to publish a solicited article by Edward Brongersma commenting on the cultural scapegoating of pedophiles. The editor indicated the reason was that Brongersma "needed to be protected from criticism." The paper, well received by the World Congress of Law and Psychiatry in 1981, was published only after a coeditor threatened to resign if the invited paper continued to be suppressed (Brongersma, 1984, personal communication, 1985).

The third area of irresponsibility is especially crucial because it involves the direct collaboration of professionals with the state in justifying and expanding its powers of ideological and behavioral control. There is a clear symbiosis between those who selectively provide theory and data for the administrative apparatus and the latter which, in turn, expands to accommodate and encourage an uncritical intensification and physical enforcement of the current science-*cum*-morality.

Further, there are instances of academics and others who are actively participating with the state in the identification, surveillance, and arrest of pedophiles simply as a *class* of individuals. I have one report of an investigator passing data and identities to the FBI, an organization famous for its criminal activities and punitive erotophobia (cf. Bullough, 1985). As another example, a book by Ann Burgess (1984), promoted as a scientific study of child "pornography" and "sex rings," includes a chapter by an FBI agent and an appendix on "fighting" to eliminate sexually explicit material. The political intent of such work is very clear and overriding of any purported scientific affiliation.

These positions are not without historical precedent, and it has been argued that medicine, psychiatry, and sexology have, in fact, been largely oriented toward the rhetorical and surgical promotion of social control. Be that as it may, the "moral" ideologies mentioned here have supported, if not originated, two major actions which continue to gather strength and efficiency. They run parallel to contemporary purity movements and a resurgent homophobia as well as relating to the ever-popular sentiments of mysogyny and ageism.

One is the most intense antisexual terrorist campaign against children since the professionally managed antimasturbation frenzies of the 19th century; the other is a movement against pedophiles reaching to predatory levels. The former is fairly obvious and easily documented, but the latter is very recent. Now, it is largely out of the hands of researchers and under the guidance of theraputic and legal agents who, like Finkelhor, consider the matter closed empirically and morally. Ideologically oriented researchers and the news media have provided the scientific and popular authorization the state needs to justify its moves toward arrest and detention of individuals on the basis of sexual interest alone. There was in late 1985 and early 1986 similar planning for "irresponsible" gays triggered by the AIDS issues. I have not yet seen the transcripts of the November, 1985 Miami hearings of the Meese Pornography Commission, but reports forwarded to me by observers indicate that it was a strategy session for prosecutors and police rather than fact-finding on pedophilia. The phrase "predisposed to crime"—a delightful essentialist expression—was added to the forensic inventory of what pedophiles are supposed to be like, and one prosecutor claimed to have a list of 5,000 pedophiles, apparently awaiting passage of appropriate laws to begin arrests. Beyond sexual interest, Bullough (1985) has documented the outrageous instance of his being targeted for arrest and detention by the FBI ("in case of national emergency") because he had the double stigma of being a sex researcher and a rights activist for sexual minorities.

At the 1985 Annual Meeting of SSSS, I heard one young professional while speaking of pedophila remark, "It's a shame such populations have to exist." The phrasing of the sentiment is rather striking. Clearly, some are doing what they can to find a solution to "the pedophile question," a solution which also seems to call for the erasure of data and researchers at variance with the state's purposes.

References

Baker, J. (1984). Sexuality, science, and social responsibility: The Georgetown scandal. *The Journal of Sex Research, 20*, 210–212.

Borneman, E. (1984). Progress in empirical research on children's sexuality. In R. Seagraves & E. Haeberle (Eds.), *Emerging dimensions of sexology* (pp. 77–90). New York: Praeger.

Brongersma, E. (1984). Aggression against pedophiles. *International Journal of Law and Psychiatry, 7*, 79–87.

Bullough, V. (1985). Problems of research on a delicate topic: A personal view. *The Journal of Sex Research, 21*, 375–386.

Burgess, A. (1984). *Child pornography and sex rings*. Lexington, MA: Lexington Books.

Constantine, L., & Martinson, F. (Eds.). (1981). *Children and sex: New findings, new perspectives*. Boston, MA: Little, Brown.

Esper, E. (1967). Max Meyer in America. *Journal of the History of the Behavioral Sciences 3*, 107–131.

Finkelhor, D. (1979). What's wrong with sex between adults and children? *American Journal of Orthopsychiatry, 49*, 692–697.

Fraser, M. (1981). The child. In B. Taylor (Ed.), *Perspectives on pedophilia* (pp. 41–58) London: Batsford.

Gilbert, A., & Barkun, M. (1981). Disaster and sexuality. *The Journal of Sex Research 17*, 288–299.

Jones, G. (1982). The social study of pederasty: In search of a literature base. *Journal of Homosexuality, 8*, 61–95.

Magoun, H. (1981). John B. Watson and the study of human sexual behavior. *The Journal of Sex Research, 17*, 368–378.

Martinson, F. (1973). *Infant and child sexuality: A sociological perspective*. St. Peter, MN: Book Mark (Gustavus Adolphus College).

Money, J. (1985). The conceptual neutrality of gender and the criminalization of sex. *Archive of Sexual Behavior, 14*, 279–290.

Myers, L. (1981). Sex researchers and sex myths: A challenge to activism. *The Journal of Sex Research, 17*, 84–89.

Richburg, K. (1985, September 17). Classroom sexology is study in controversy. *Washington Post*, p. A11.

Russell, D. (1984). *Sexual exploitation: Rape, child sexual abuse, and workplace harassment* Beverly Hills, CA: Sage.

Sonenschein, D. (1984). Breaking the taboo of sex and adolescence: Children, sex, and the media. In R. Browne (Ed.), *Taboos and tabooism in culture* (pp. 111–132). Bowling Green, OH: Popular Press.

Sonenschein, David. 1987. "On having one's research seized." *Journal of Sex Research*, 23, (3) 408–414.

Stewart, R. (1985, March 2). Man cleared of child exploitation count. *Los Angeles Times*.

Will, G. (1982, May 27). Sex in Long Beach: Academic extremism invites popular extremism. *Los Angeles Times*, p. II–11.

6. Collecting Sensitive Data:
The Impact on Researchers

Barbara Johnson
Jill Macleod Clarke

The authors undertook an exploratory study to identify issues that arose for researchers while conducting fieldwork. Ten researchers engaged in "sensitive" inquiry were purposefully sampled and encouraged to talk about their experiences during the data collection process. Interviews were transcribed and common themes identified. The findings indicate that these researchers experienced a number of difficulties that centered around issues of lack of training, confidentiality, role conflict, costs to the participants, the desire for reciprocity, and feelings of isolation.

Although it has been argued that any research topic, depending on its context, is potentially sensitive (Lee & Renzetti, 1990), there are perhaps some areas and topics where the process of research is more likely than others to be threatening, or even damaging, to both the researcher and the researched (Gibson, 1996). This includes, for example, exploring deeply held personal experiences, deviance and social control, vested interests of powerful persons, and issues sacred to the individual (Gibson, 1996; Lee & Renzetti, 1993). It would seem, therefore, that defining "sensitive" research is problematic. Indeed, in many instances, the literature fails to offer a definition (Lee, 1993); rather, the words are treated in a "common sense way" (Lee & Renzetti, 1990), thus leaving the term open to interpretation. Meanwhile, Cowles (1988) argued that sensitive topics are those that have the potential to arouse emotional responses. In this context, they can be regarded as "intensely personal experience(s)," and, therefore, as research topics, they will probably be approached with a degree of apprehension (Cowles, 1988). Taking a somewhat broader view, Sieber and Stanley (1988) believe that sensitive research includes those topics where there are implications not only for participants but also for the group of individuals represented by the inquiry. Although there is no indication of what those implications might be, the authors contend that their definition of *sensitive* moves beyond the immediate or more obvious interpretation to include topics in which the outcome can have social implications. These they refer to as "socially sensitive" topics.

Drawing on the earlier definitions, Lee and Renzetti (1993) suggest that a sensitive topic is "one that potentially poses for those involved a substantial threat, the emergence of which renders problematic for the researcher and/or the researched the collection, holding, and/or dissemination of research data" (p. 5). Taking the discussion a step further, Lee (1993) offers a simpler definition, describing it as "research which potentially poses a substantial threat to those who are or have

Qualitative Health Research, Vol. 13 No. 3, March 2003 421–434 been involved in it" (p. 4). In both of these definitions, the cardinal word is *threat*: threat to participants and threat to researchers. Clearly, the implication here is that if the research process incurs costs for either party, then it can justifiably be defined as sensitive.

Some authors are more specific than others are in their definition of sensitive research, in that they refer to the sensitive nature of the particular topic under investigation. These include HIV/AIDS and issues around mental health (Alty & Rodham, 1998), cancer (Davies, Hall, Clarke, Bannon, & Hopkins, 1998; Johnson & Plant, 1996), chronic pain in the elderly (Higgins, 1998), terminal illness (Beaver, Luker, & Woods, 1999), and dying and death (Benoliel, 1980). Such definitions are drawn from personal accounts reported in the literature by researchers working in these particular areas of inquiry. In turn, they have given rise to an increasing concern about the moral and ethical implications of conducting research in sensitive areas, particularly when participants are ill or coping with life-threatening illness (De Raeve, 1994). This is of particular importance given the current emphasis on seeking the patient's perspective when assessing the outcome of medical and nursing interventions (Blaxter, 1995; Department of Health, 1989). However, the process of gathering such information necessarily involves direct contact with vulnerable people, with whom sensitive and difficult topics are often raised and sometimes raised within difficult contexts (Davies et al., 1998; Higgins, 1998; Johnson & Plant, 1996). Thus, accessing patients' views and experiences can present serious difficulties not only for the participant and possibly their carers but also for the researcher (Alty & Rodham, 1998; Davies et al., 1998; Higgins, 1998; Johnson & Plant, 1996).

There are numerous accounts of field researchers' experiences associated with the data collection process (Davies et al., 1998; Edwards, 1993; Finch, 1984; Graham, 1983; Higgins, 1998; James, 1989; Johnson & Plant, 1996; Kellehear, 1994; McRobbie, 1982; Meyer, 1995; Oakley, 1981). In examining such personal accounts, there appear to be some recurring features that include the implications of in-depth interviewing, such as the cost to participants and, in some instances, to the researcher (Beaver et al., 1999; Davies et al., 1998; Johnson & Plant, 1996; Meyer, 1995). Another feature is the researcher's concern regarding coercion. Although researchers aim to avoid this, in-depth interviewing often encourages participants to develop a relationship founded on trust, which invariably involves them in a role relationship beyond that of the more conventional participant and interviewer role. The concern here is that however "sensitive" researchers might be during the negotiation period, participants might still feel obliged to consent to being interviewed (Johnson & Plant, 1996; Smith, 1992; Stacey, 1988). Indeed, taken a step further, there is the argument that by "being friendly" in order to obtain data, researchers risk being exploitative in the field (Beynon, 1983; Stacey, 1988).

Other features include concerns about role-conflict (Buckingham, 1996; Davies et al., 1998; Johnson & Plant, 1996) and the impact of in-depth interviewing on participants' coping strategies (Davies et al., 1998; Johnson & Plant, 1996). Davies and colleagues and Johnson and Plant argue that although the process of being interviewed might appear to be acceptable to participants, researchers need to be constantly aware that participants can find the experience unpleasant and compromising, particularly if the process challenges their adopted coping strategies.

A theme common to most of the personal accounts reviewed is one of unpreparedness for dealing with concerns and issues arising from undertaking sensitive research. Some authors go so far as to question whether neophyte investigators should undertake such research, given that the costs conferred on the participants by the research might be difficult, if not impossible, to establish (Beaver et al., 1999; Smith, 1992). What is not clear is the extent to which researcher concerns are linked directly first to the type and level of their research experience and second to the support available to them during the research process.

In the literature discussed here, the researchers have largely addressed the practical and ethical concerns regarding in-depth interviewing. To date, however, little attention has been directed to the ways in which researchers respond to and cope with research that is personally very demanding and challenging as well as being highly charged emotionally and ethically. Indeed, most of those who have written about their research experience focus on the impact and effects of the research on the researched or else confine themselves to questions of access or technical rigor. Such questions and the lack of any systematic inquiry into the experiences of field workers while collecting sensitive data led to a small exploratory study, the findings of which are reported and discussed below.

Method

Study Aim

Our purpose in this study was to explore the experiences of researchers while collecting sensitive data.

Identifying the Focus of the Study

Cancer, HIV/AIDS, dying, and *death* were chosen as topic areas for the purpose of the inquiry. We deemed them sensitive because they generate ethical and moral issues as well as concerns and problems for the research design. Such areas of inquiry often require examination and approval from ethical bodies attached to hospitals, hospices, health authorities, educational institutions, and funding bodies. Concern arises for both researchers and members of ethics committees, in that there is the potential for such research to cause distress for those who agree to participate. Although the research designers might make every attempt to eliminate the risk of upsetting participants, it has been reported that research in these areas can be very unpredictable (Beaver et al., 1999; Johnson & Plant, 1995; Kleinman & Copp, 1993). A further and hitherto relatively neglected aspect of sensitivity is the extent of "emotional and moral unease" that such inquiry can generate for the researcher (Johnson & Plant, 1996; Kleinman & Copp, 1993). Furthermore, cancer, HIV/AIDS, dying, and death all have significant implications for the researcher's personal life; cancer and HIV/AIDS are diseases commonly feared by the majority of people (Corrado, 1992), whereas dying and death will inevitably affect everyone. . . .

Sample

An opportunistic sample of 10 researchers participated in the study. All were recruited from institutions of higher education in England and Scotland. . . . Their background and previous research experience varied, in that half the sample comprised nurses (all undertaking postgraduate study), three were medical sociologists (one postdoctoral and two in postgraduate study), and two were teachers (one postdoctoral and one in postgraduate study). . . . Just over two thirds of the sample was female (five nurses, one teacher, and one medical sociologist). All participants perceived themselves to be engaged in sensitive research, and at the time of interview, all were, or had recently been, engaged in fieldwork in the areas of cancer, HIV/AIDS, dying, and/or death.

Data Collection and Analysis

Initial contact was made by telephone, followed by an interview at either the researcher's home or the participant's place of work. Participants were interviewed in a place of their choice, five choosing their home and five their place of work. . . . The duration of the interviews was between 1 and 3 hours. Having described the nature of their inquiry, participants were asked to talk about their experiences and any concerns or issues they might have encountered during the research process. The recorded interviews were transcribed, and themes common to all areas of research were identified.

Findings and Discussion

Participants talked freely and generally reported that they had found the data collection process stressful. A number of issues and concerns common to all participants were raised and were categorized as follows: *inexperience and lack of training, confidentiality, role conflict, impact of interviews on participants*, and *feelings of isolation*.

Inexperience and Lack of Training

In describing their preparation for conducting in-depth interviews, some researchers felt the emphasis had been placed too heavily on procedures for accessing participants and data analysis, with little or no orientation to the kinds of difficulties and concerns they might encounter during the research process. Thus, a number of researchers felt they had entered the research field with little or no experience in accessing and interviewing people in depth, particularly in their own home. Issues raised within this theme include (a) contact anxiety, (b) confronting and dealing with anxiety, and (c) working in uncharted territory.

Contact Anxiety.

For some researchers, the difficulty lay in making the first contact with potential participants, and the anxiety experienced in some instances was quite considerable. For example, when talking about accessing participants (who had been diagnosed with cancer) by telephone, one researcher said, "Sometimes I felt physically sick before phoning them...it was like a minefield...I didn't know what to expect...I would put off making the calls and then I would pluck up the courage."

Confronting/Dealing With Resistance.

For some researchers, the real difficulty came when confronting and dealing with resistance on the part of either the participant or their relative/friend. Here, the issue for the researcher was the length to which they should go to secure an interview. This was a particular problem when the relative seemed unhappy about their partner's participation in an interview. For this situation, some researchers felt completely unprepared. As one explained,

> Nobody had warned me that they [relatives] might object [to the study]...I didn't know what to do...she wanted to do the interview...but he was very unhappy about it...he thought it would make her ill again...I felt he really didn't want me in the house.

Working in Uncharted Territory.

Another problem for researchers was the issue of being in "uncharted territory" and, again, feeling unprepared for what might happen. While reflecting on her experiences of interviewing people with cancer, one researcher admitted,

> I felt as though nothing had been thought out in advance . . . and it was a question of feeling your way as you went. . . . I was just not prepared for some of the things that happened even though I thought I would be.

Although such feelings are possibly compounded by the sensitivity of the topic, it is reasonable to assume that a fear of the unknown is a feeling commonly held by field researchers, particularly the neophyte, and not peculiar to those undertaking sensitive inquiry as defined in this paper. Problems associated with gaining access and seeking consent are concerns that many researchers experience irrespective of whether they consider the topic of inquiry to be sensitive (Meyer, 1993; Rogers, 1996; Smith, 1992). Furthermore, it seems reasonable that when having to deal with the unexpected during the research process, feelings of anxiety are generated for the majority of field researchers. However, it could be argued that such feelings are more likely to occur and be experienced at a more intense level if the research topic is highly sensitive.

Concerns About Confidentiality

Maintaining confidentiality when reporting their study findings was a concern expressed by a number of the researchers. This was particularly true where the location of the inquiry could be identified easily by those having access to the research reports. The issues raised and that fall within this theme include (a) fear of participants' being identified and (b) pressure to "report back" to health professionals.

Fear of Being Identified by Others, Such as Family Members.

Some researchers remained very anxious that what some participants disclosed during interview other family members could identify. This was particularly true where the participant's partner or significant others were included in the inquiry:

> I mean . . . in terms of going in and saying "This interview is confidential" . . . people are very vulnerable . . . they don't realize what they're letting themselves in for . . . we could write great chunks of their interviews and things . . . spread across the pages and they recognize themselves or husbands will recognize their wives . . . all those sorts of things.

Pressure to "Report Back" to the Health Professionals.

In one or two instances, there was also concern about maintaining confidentiality when in contact with those involved in the health care of interviewees. One researcher had felt under pressure to report back to the health professional responsible for referring patients to the study.

> The difficulty is when they give you the names and then they say "Let me know if there are any problems" . . . Well that can be a bit difficult because by saying "No . . . unfortunately I'm not able to do that" . . . then they might stop referring so many patients.

The majority of authors describing or discussing the research process refer specifically to issues concerning confidentiality and anonymity. In summarizing the debates surrounding the morals, ethics, and politics in research, Barnes (1979) emphasizes the rights to privacy and protection of those being researched. This view is supported by others (Brink & Wood, 1988; Burns & Grove, 1993), but Sieber and Stanley (1988) take the argument further by urging researchers to weigh the privacy of individual participants against the interest of society. Thus, it can be assumed that the majority of researchers will be acutely aware of the difficulties they might encounter when trying to safeguard the confidentiality and anonymity of their participants. Some field researchers have discussed at length the difficulties they encountered during their data collection and reporting of their study findings.

Finch (1984), in her study of vicars' wives, discusses not only her own concern about who will handle her data but also the fears expressed by her participants of being identified as study participants by other vicars' wives. Some authors engaged in action research have highlighted the difficulty in maintaining confidentiality and anonymity, because the study design requires the researcher to report findings to other participants to decide on any further action that might need to be taken (Lathlean, 1996; Meyer, 1995).

However, what we did not find in the literature is the anxiety expressed by some researchers in this study concerning the request to report to the person referring the participant any concerns or problems the interviewee revealed with respect to their care and health status. This might be peculiar to inquiries where the topic is sensitive and/or where the route of access to participants is via a professional or informal caregiver. An added concern for the researchers was that the refusal to report back might restrict the number of referrals made to their study. However, this latter concern, often referred to as "gate-keeping" (Burgess, 1984), is not uncommon among researchers, particularly those using a qualitative approach, where difficulties vis-à-vis access are inherent in the research design (Ersser, 1996). Nevertheless, although such concerns do not appear to be unique to sensitive research, it is argued that the level of concern is probably linked directly to the level of sensitivity of the topic being investigated.

Role Conflict

Role conflict, including the issue of reciprocity, was mentioned by several researchers as being of major concern, particularly during the data collection process. Issues they raised included (a) researcher versus health care practitioner, (b) friend versus data collector, (c) influencing the course of the interview, and (d) not being able to reciprocate.

Researcher Versus Health Care Practitioner.   An ethical dilemma for the researchers who were also health care professionals was the situation whereby participants were obviously either misinformed or had not understood the information given to them about their condition. Clearly, the conflict here lies in the researcher versus health care practitioner role. It would be impossible for such professionals to shed their previous knowledge and experience and enter the "data field" with blank curricula vitae. It is reasonable to assume that training and experience will provoke within the researcher a need to intervene, a need that is likely to be more problematic when researching sensitive topics.

However, if the participant raised concerns about a lack of information or misunderstanding, the researcher usually had a strategy in place for dealing with them. This included explaining potential sources of help and information, and, in some instances, researchers would arrange for participants to discuss their concerns with an appropriate health care practitioner. However, where a participant did not express concern, the researcher was often left feeling extremely anxious about whether confidentiality should be breached in the interest of the participant's welfare. One researcher remained concerned about such an incident long after the study had been completed.

> I was really concerned about one person . . . in fact it's still unresolved and I don't know what to do . . . she told me she was taking Tamoxifen® . . . and that was OK until later on she talked about starting a family . . . and I just felt she didn't realize that this drug could . . . actually probably would stop her from ovulating. She didn't say she was concerned so it was difficult for me to chip in. But then I came away and felt I should mention it to the breast nurse . . . but how could I? I promised her I wouldn't talk about anything she said to anyone.

Some researchers expressed guilt at not feeling able to "help" participants because this, they believed, would be in direct conflict with their role as data collector. For some, this concern was compounded by previous training and experience, such as in counseling. For example, "It was very difficult not to do anything about some of the things I was hearing . . . and I felt very bad, very guilty and extremely frustrated especially as I had been programmed to try and help people."

Other issues around confidentiality included participants' not complying with treatment regimes and, in one instance, threatening to take his or her life.

Friend Versus Data Collector

Some researchers felt confused about their role as interviewer in that they found themselves acting on their instinct while trying to establish an empathic rapport with participants. One or two talked about the need to behave as a friend and felt that in doing so, they almost lost sight of their professional role. This was particularly the case when accessing participants who were very ill or dying.

> I wasn't sure how I was supposed to be when I went to an interview with these people . . . I just went on my gut reaction—which was this "befriending" thing—but it was always a worry . . . I kept asking myself "Is this research?"

Influencing the Course of the Interview

Taken a step further, one or two participants raised concerns about the way they had "handled" some of their interviews and the impact such handling might have had on the research process. In other words, they were concerned about the way in which they might have influenced the course of the interview. For example, one researcher believed that by exploring people's experiences as a counselor, she was generating data that might not otherwise have been produced, either because it did not exist or because it was not of particular importance/relevance to the participant.

> I was sort of modeling myself on how I felt a counselor would be in that situation . . . so I was thinking "Is this what a researcher should be doing?" . . . and this became a methodological problem for me . . . I found I was exploring ideas with them . . . and I sort of felt I was putting ideas into their heads.

Not Being Able to Reciprocate

Linked with role conflict is the issue of reciprocity. This was mentioned by several participants in that they expressed concern about not being able to repay participants for their time and energy. One or two sought refuge in the knowledge that some participants were "happy to help others who might follow." Thus, the "helper-therapy" principle (Reisman, 1976) was perceived by these researchers to be of benefit to the interviewee. However, in others, the feeling of not being able to reciprocate caused considerable anxiety. For example,

I think it was just hearing their awful stories . . . I felt so helpless . . . you can't offer them anything . . . you can't do anything to help . . . it would have been so much easier if we could have given back something . . . just something . . .

I felt so pathetic . . . all I could give them was a leaflet . . . but I suppose that was something.

Much has been written about the role relationship between field researcher and study participant (Ball, 1990; Cannon, 1989; Hammersley & Atkinson, 1983; Johnson & Plant, 1996; Oakley, 1981). To foster an empathic approach to their data collection, field researchers will endeavor to develop close ties with their participants (Kleinman & Copp, 1993) while maintaining a certain social and intellectual distance (Hammersley & Atkinson, 1983), often referred to as "detached concern." Achieving and sustaining this kind of balance can generate considerable difficulty for the researcher (Buckingham, 1996; Johnson & Plant, 1996).

In this study, we noted with interest that issues around the researcher's role emanated mainly from those who were qualified nurses. Their difficulty lay in the fact that as people trained to relieve suffering, they experienced some instances in which sustaining the impartial data gatherer role seriously challenged the very essence of their professional code of practice. The question raised here is, Do concerns about role stem from the sensitive nature of the inquiry alone, or are these concerns compounded by the knowledge and experience of the researcher undertaking the inquiry? For instance, if the researcher in the first example in this section had not been aware of the physiological effects of Tamoxifen,® would she have experienced the level of anxiety expressed so clearly during the interview? Moreover, there is also the question of how the participant perceives the researcher's role. As May (1997) points out, if the participant is aware that the researcher is a nurse, to whom then does the participant consent to interview—nurse or researcher? If the participant has an expectation that the researcher will enact the role of nurse, this will inevitably put the researcher under considerable pressure to "step out of" the researcher role into the role of nurse and possibly even counselor.

Although there is evidence that field researchers who are not nurses experience role conflict (Ball, 1990; Cannon, 1989; Oakley, 1981), it would seem that nurses working in sensitive areas of inquiry might have greater difficulty in resolving their concerns, such as reciprocity and role conflict, than others working in similar fields of inquiry. Is there a degree of inevitability that nurses, by virtue of their professional background, will, as researchers, experience role conflict? If so, to what extent can they be helped, realistically, to develop strategies for coping with such concerns?

Impact of the Interview on Participants

Here, the main issue was concern about the effect of in-depth interviewing on participants. Although the majority of researchers believed that "telling their story" was probably of some benefit to participants, they expressed concern that they could never be certain some were not harmed by the experience. In comparing the research interview with the counseling interview, some researchers drew a clear distinction between the client who expresses a need to be interviewed and the research participant who is approached and, possibly albeit, unwittingly coerced into being interviewed. The following quotes are examples of the concern researchers felt after reflecting on the impact the interview might have had on their participants:

> I was never sure how they really felt . . . sometimes they said it was the first time they'd been able to talk about it . . . but I'm not sure . . . I mean for some of them . . . the cancer was all behind them and then we come along and open it all up again . . . one or two were really quite upset by the experience . . . it really worries me.
>
>   I do remember going back to do the second interview and then she told me that she had been very upset by the first one even though she had said it was fine at the time . . . so I don't think you ever know what they are really feeling like . . . Funnily enough, I had really impressed upon her to ring me if she had any concerns about the interview—or anything to add.
>
>   And looking back . . . sometimes they found it helpful to talk . . . other times it really distressed them . . . so I don't know . . . I don't know how you can tell what's going to be OK for them . . . it's like a minefield.

Little is known about the impact in-depth interviewing has on study participants, particularly in sensitive areas of inquiry. However, there has been some attempt to follow up on the impact on participants immediately following an interview (Eardley, Cribb, & Pendleton, 1991; Johnson & Plant, 1996), and, although the general opinion is that the benefits outweigh the costs, we found in this study that it continues to be of considerable concern for researchers working in sensitive areas. De Raeve (1996) argues that although researchers frequently suggest that, in general, participants value the opportunity to reflect on their experiences, it is nevertheless not difficult to imagine that reflecting in the face of emotional pain is likely to be a distressing experience. Thus, the implicit assumption that participants might find it beneficial to talk about their experiences, particularly when someone has the time and space to listen to them (Johnson & Plant, 1996), is open to debate.

In this study, the researchers were very aware that the kind of research in which they were engaged conferred both costs and benefits on their participants. However, the issue for them was that they were not always certain about the impact of the interview on participants, and, furthermore, what was of benefit to one participant seemed to be a cost to another. This suggests that it is almost impossible to predict the impact of the research process on participants, which in turn has serious implications for researchers when seeking informed consent. There is no guarantee that prior to interview, participants will be aware of what they will disclose and at what risk such disclosure might be (Raudonis, 1992). Taking the discussion a stage further, there are those who argue that there exist strong moral grounds for objecting to research in sensitive areas, for example, in

palliative care (De Raeve, 1994), unless there is adequate moral scrutiny by research ethics committees of the proposed research process. However, given the
unpredictable impact of in-depth interviewing on participants, the definition of
"adequate moral scrutiny" is contentious and, therefore, might not offer an acceptable solution to the moral dilemma faced by researchers, particularly those
interviewing in-depth people with life-threatening diseases. The question of
whether research should be conducted with such vulnerable groups (Beaver et
al., 1999; De Raeve, 1994) needs to be examined more closely before strategies for
dealing with problematic access to participants can be developed further.

Isolation for the Researcher

At the more personal level, several participants felt very isolated and unsupported during their fieldwork experience. The issues raised here were (a) feeling
isolated and unsupported, (b) needing to separate home and work, and (c) the
need for supervision.

Feeling Isolated and Unsupported. Some researchers commented that
frequently when they needed support, only their partners, family, or friends were
available to help them reflect on their experiences. For example, "Sometimes days
would go by and I wouldn't have anyone to off-load onto . . . anyone who really
understood . . . except my boyfriend when I saw him."

The Need to Separate Home and Work. Feeling isolated and hav-
ing to share their experiences with partners and friends raised other concerns
for researchers. Some felt a strong need to separate work from their personal
life. For example,

> I found I desperately wanted to talk to someone about it . . . but who? I mean I couldn't
> . . . I told Jack my partner about it . . . but he didn't particularly want to hear it . . . I
> mean he doesn't want to have to deal with that pain . . . and I don't want it [the con-
> cern] at home . . . yet I didn't know what to do with this information.

The Need for Supervision. Although participants acknowledged that
some of the isolation they experienced was due to fieldwork undertaken some
distance from the institution supervising the project, some were nonetheless concerned that project team meetings tended to focus only on issues relating to the
research process. This left one or two participants feeling that some of the concerns they had could reflect some kind of "weakness" or "deficit" in themselves
as researchers rather than issues raised by the nature of the research. Thus, they

felt isolated in dealing with their concerns because they found it difficult to discuss such matters with their project directors and/or supervisors. For example,

> I didn't really think I could talk about it [role conflict and reciprocity] to my director. . . . I was afraid I might feel I shouldn't be doing research . . . everyone else seemed to know what they were doing . . . so I just kept it to myself.
>
> It was difficult to talk about some of the problems I was having with the interviews. The meetings [project] seemed to focus on things like how many interviews we'd done . . . the analysis and so on . . . I suppose I felt I shouldn't be feeling the way I did so I couldn't talk about it [in the meetings].

For the majority of people, cancer is the most feared disease, and in this respect, researchers are not exceptions. For some researchers in this study, the data collection process became a life-threatening event, in that the impact of listening to people's stories left them worrying about whether they, too, had cancer. They felt that closer supervision and peer support would have helped them to work through such fears as they arose, thus preventing the cumulative and damaging effect such fears can have.

> It was silly really but I began to think I had cancer of this and that . . . it was awful . . . I think we should have help really with that kind of thing, you know . . . but then again you feel so stupid . . . I do think it would have been better if someone else had been out there with me, you know . . . doing the interviewing.

Although feelings of isolation might be common to the majority of researchers, they perhaps take on greater significance for those working in sensitive areas. There is some evidence that interviewing in such areas can lead to feelings of hopelessness and impotence (Johnson & Plant, 1996) and even insomnia and nightmares (Cowles, 1988). If the process of data collection leaves the researcher vulnerable and traumatized, then feelings of isolation and lack of professional support might intensify such states. Why do researchers feel isolated and unsupported? One possible explanation is that project directors and academic supervisors lack awareness and insight into the kind of issues raised by field researchers. Furthermore, they are not necessarily equipped to provide counseling support to deal with such issues. Finally, they might not be privy to such issues if field researchers are unable, for whatever reason, to raise and discuss them.

Conclusions

The findings from this small exploratory study demonstrate that researchers investigating sensitive areas, such as cancer, HIV/AIDS, dying, and death, do indeed experience a number of difficulties and concerns during the data collection process. These include accessing participants, confidentiality, role conflict, impact of in-depth interviewing on participants, and feelings of isolation. Although it is argued that sensitivity is a prerequisite of any carefully grounded social research (Lee & Renzetti, 1993), it would seem that some topic areas could be identified as more sensitive than others in terms of the nature of the data being accessed. For example, the emotional content, such as human pain and suffering associated with life-threatening illness, are real life experiences with which researchers often can readily identify (Benoliel, 1980; Higgins, 1998; Johnson & Plant, 1996; Kleinman & Copp, 1993).

The findings also strongly suggest that field researchers require skilled preparation and training, particularly with regard to negotiating access, interviewing skills, and their role relationship with participants. This should include helping them to develop strategies for dealing with potential difficulties and concerns that they might encounter during the data collection process. Furthermore, adequate supervision and support for field researchers should be built carefully into any research design, particularly if it is qualitative and exploratory in nature. This should not be left to chance. It is suggested that by providing ongoing training and support, for example, regular personal supervision, group support, and action learning (McGill & Beaty, 1995), field researchers will become better equipped to engage with and resolve difficult issues arising during their fieldwork experience.

In trying to identify and meet the specific educational and training needs of field researchers working in sensitive areas, however, it is important to answer some of the questions raised in this small exploratory study. For example, what impact does the background of the researcher (nurse, counselor, sociologist) have on his or her data collection experience? Does a nurse, for example, trained and experienced in the art of helping and alleviating human suffering, find it more difficult to ignore participants' needs (explicitly or implicitly expressed) than someone who has not had that kind of training? Are there researchers who, by dint of their professional development and depth of experience, are more "sensitized" to the "needs" of participants in health-and-illness and death-and-dying research?

Moreover, it could be argued that the age and life experience of the researcher can have a direct bearing on how he or she will react and respond to issues arising during data collection. Because we did not set out to examine the relationship between maturity and levels of coping, it is not possible to provide a clear answer to this question. However, to answer this and previous questions, a systematic inquiry comparing the experiences of different groups of researchers investigating topics they consider to be sensitive needs to be undertaken.

References

Alty, A., & Rodham, K. (1998). The ouch! factor: Problems in conducting sensitive research. *Qualitative Health Research, 8,* 275–282.

Ball, S. (1990). Self-doubt and soft data: Social and technical trajectories in ethnographic fieldwork. *Qualitative Studies in Education, 3*(2), 157–171.

Barnes, J. (1979). *Who should know what?* Harmondsworth, UK: Penguin.

Beaver, K., Luker, K., & Woods, S. (1999). Conducting research with the terminally ill: Challenges and considerations. *International Journal of Palliative Nursing,* 5(1), 13–18.

Benoliel, J. Q. (1980). Research with dying patients. In A.J. Davis & J. C. Krueger (Eds.), *Patients, nurses, ethics* (pp. 119–128). New York: American Journal of Nursing.

Beynon, J. (1983). Ways-in and staying-in: Fieldwork as problem solving. In M. Hammersley (Ed.), *The ethnography of schooling: Methodological issues.* Driffield, UK: Nafferton.

Blaxter, M. (1995). *Consumers and research in the NHS.* Leeds, UK: Department of Health NHS Executive.

Brink, P. J., & Wood, M.J. (1988). *Basic steps in planning nursing research: From question to proposal* (3rd ed.). Boston: Jones & Bartlett.

Buckingham, S. (1996). "Watching me watching you": Dilemmas in pain assessment of children. In L. De Raeve (Ed.), *Nursing research: An ethical and legal appraisal* (pp. 57–70). London: Bailliere Tindall.

Burgess, R. G. (1984). *In the field.* London: Allen and Unwin.

Burns, N., & Grove, S. K. (1993). *The practice of nursing research: Conduct, critique and utilization.* Philadelphia: Saunders.

Cannon, S. (1989). Social research in stressful settings: Difficulties for the sociologist studying the treatment of breast cancer. *Sociology of Health and Illness,* 11(1), 66–77.

Corrado, M. (1992). *Report—The social impact of cancer.* London: MORI.

Cowles, K. V. (1988). Issues in qualitative research on sensitive topics. *Western Journal of Nursing Research,* 10, 163–179.

Davies, E. A., Hall, S. M., Clarke, C. R. A., Bannon, M. P., & Hopkins, A. P. (1998). Do research interviews cause distress or interfere in management? *Journal of the Royal College of Physicians,* 32(5), 406–411.

De Raeve, L., Ed. (1996). *Nursing research: An ethical and legal appraisal.* London: Bailliere Tindall.

De Raeve, L. (1994). Ethical issues in palliative care research. *Palliative Medicine,* 8(4), 298–305.

Department of Health. (1989). *Working for patients.* London: Her Majesty's Stationery Office.

Eardley, A., Cribb, A., & Pendleton, L. (1991). Ethical issues in psychosocial research among patients with cancer: A review. *European Journal of Cancer,* 27(2), 166–169.

Edwards, R. (1993). An education in interviewing: Placing the researcher and the research. In C. Renzetti & M. Lee (Eds.), *Researching sensitive topics*. Newbury Park, CA: Sage.

Ersser, S. (1996). Ethnography in clinical situations: An ethical appraisal. In L. De Raeve (Ed.), *Nursing research: An ethical and legal appraisal* (pp. 42–56). London: Bailliere Tindall.

Finch, J. (1984). "It's great to have someone to talk to": The ethics and politics of interviewing women. In C. Bell & H. Roberts (Eds.), *Social researching: Politics, problems, practice*. London: Routledge Kegan Paul.

Gibson, V. (1996). The problems of researching sensitive topics in health care. *Nurse Researcher, 4*(2), 65–74.

Graham, H. (1983). Do her answers fit his questions? Women and the survey method. In E. Gamarnikow, D. Morgan, J. Purvis, & D. Taylorson (Eds.), *The public and the private* (pp. 132–146). London: Heinemann.

Hammersley, M., & Atkinson, P. (1983). *Ethnography: Principles in practice*. New York: Tavistock.

Higgins, I. (1998). Reflections on conducting qualitative research with elderly people. *Qualitative Health Research, 8*(6), 858–866.

James, N. (1989). Emotional labor, skills and work in the social regulation of feeling. *Sociological Review, 37*(1), 15–24.

Johnson, Barbara and Jill Macleod Clarke. Collecting sensitive data: The impact on researchers. *Qualitative Health Research, 13,*(3), 421–434.

Johnson, B. M., & Plant, H. (1996). Collecting data from people with cancer and their families: What are the implications? In L. De Raeve (Ed.), *Nursing research: An ethical and legal appraisal* (pp. 85–100). London: Bailliere Tindall.

Kellehear, A. (1990). *Dying of cancer: The final year of life*. New York: Harwood Academic.

Kleinman, C., & Copp, M. A. (1993). *Emotions and fieldwork*. Newbury Park, CA: Sage.

Lathlean, J. (1996). Ethical dilemmas in action research in L. De Raeve (Ed.), *Nursing research: An ethical and legal appraisal* (pp. 32–41). London: Bailliere Tindall.

Lee, R. M. (1993). *Doing research on sensitive topics*. Newbury Park, CA: Sage.

Lee, R. M., & Renzetti, C. M. (1990). The problems of researching sensitive topics: An overview and introduction. *American Behavioural Scientist, 33*, 510–528.

Lee, R. M., & Renzetti, C. M. (1993). The problems of researching sensitive topics: An overview and introduction. In C. M. Renzetti & R. M. Lee (Eds.), *Researching sensitive topics* (pp. 3–12). Newbury Park, CA: Sage.

May, K. A. (1997). The nurse as a researcher: Impediment to informed consent? *Nursing Outlook, 27*(1), 36–39.

McGill, L, & Beaty, L. (1995). *Action learning* (2nd ed.). London: Kogan Page.

McRobbie, A. (1982). The politics of feminist research: Between talks, text and action. *Feminist Review, 12,* 46–48.

Meyer, J. E. (1993). New paradigm research in practice: The trials and tribulations of action research. *Journal of Advanced Nursing, 18*(7), 1066–1072.

Meyer, J. E. (1995). *Lay participation in care in a hospital setting: An action research study.* Unpublished doctoral dissertation, University of London, UK.

Oakley, A. (1981). Interviewing women: A contradiction in terms. In H. Roberts (Ed.), *Doing feminist research* (pp. 30–61). London: Routledge Kegan Paul.

Raudonis, B. M. (1992). Ethical considerations in qualitative research with hospice patients. *Qualitative Health Research, 2,* 238–249.

Reisman, F. (1976). How does self-help work? *Social Policy, 7*(2), 41–45.

Rogers, J. (1996). Ethical issues in survey research In L. De Raeve (Ed.), *Nursing research: An ethical and legal appraisal* (pp. 18–31). London: Bailliere Tindall.

Sieber, J. E., & Stanley, B. (1988). Ethical and professional dimensions of socially sensitive research. *American Psychologist, 43,* 49–55.

Smith, L. (1992) Ethical issues in interviewing. *Journal of Advanced Nursing, 17,* 98–103.

Stacey, J. (1988) Can there be a feminist ethnography? *Women's Studies International Forum, 11*(1), 21–27.